This book belongs to

Appointment with Nature

For the Birds
An Uncommon  *Guide*

Laura Erickson

Illustrations by Jeff Sonstegard

Pfeifer-Hamilton
Duluth, Minnesota

Pfeifer-Hamilton
210 West Michigan
Duluth MN 55802-1908
218-727-0500

Appointment with Nature series

For the Birds: An Uncommon Guide

Printed in the United States of America

10   9   8   7   6   5   4   3   2

Editorial Director: Susan Gustafson
Manuscript Editor: Patrick Gross
Art Director: Joy Morgan Dey

The illustration for April 1 comes from *The New Who's Who on Sesame Street.* © 1989, 1977 Children's Televsion Workshop/Jim Henson Productions, Inc. Illustration by Joe Mathieu. Reprinted by permission of the Children's Television Workshop.

Library of Congress Catalog Card Number: 93-85419

ISBN 0-938586-91-2

For Russell,
Who gave me my first cloudless days,
balmy nights, books, babies, and birds.

Introduction

What would the world be like without birds? If just one species—say, Blue Jays—were missing, North American forests would have a different character: as glaciers retreated, acorns planted by mobile Blue Jays won the germination race against wind-borne seeds, and oaks became the dominant forest pioneers. Without Blue Jays, other creatures would lose their noisiest and most reliable sentinels, making them more vulnerable to predators. American folklore would be devoid of tales of jays carrying sticks to the devil, and Mark Twain's jolliest story, "Baker's Blue-Jay Yarn," wouldn't exist. How could we jaywalk or strut around naked as a jaybird? And without Blue Jays the Braves and the Phillies would have won the 1992 and '93 World Series.

No creatures in the world give us as much as birds do. Bird song awakens us in the morning, and birds' down cushions our heads as we go to sleep at night. Birds bring to our human world nourishment, warmth, inspiration, beauty, and enjoyment—and all that before we look through our first pair of binoculars.

We arrive on this planet unaware of everything except our physical comfort. As our eyes clear, eventually we notice a bird. In my case that took longer than for most, but perhaps living twenty-three years without once seeing a chickadee made me appreciate the vision all the more when my eyes finally focussed.

It is possible, I suppose, to learn about birds in isolation, though Audubon himself carefully studied the writings and drawings of other early American ornithologists. My journey has hardly been a lonely one. Ellwood and Helen Erickson gave me my first binoculars and field guide—my passport. Joseph Hickey's *Guide to Bird Watching* was my road map. My ornithology professors at the Kellogg Biological Station and Michigan State University, William L. Thompson and Donald Beaver, gave me plenty of driving skills. They and Bob Mainone at the biological station also gave me the inspiration to make my journey meaningful. Janet Green, Fran Hamerstrom, Peggy and

Joe Hickey, Robert Nero, Sam Robbins, Chandler Robbins, and Harrison Tordoff became my secret heroes as I tried to emulate their birding skills, exacting scientific standards, and generous spirits. Birding buddies in East Lansing and Madison, Wisconsin, made my journey jolly fun. I mastered peeps and hawk identification thanks to Kim Eckert and Molly Evans. I learned rehab skills and stole my funniest bird jokes from Koni Sundquist.

I have from the first been an incurable lister, but as my interest grew to encompass other aspects of ornithology, people were there to guide and encourage me. Stephanie Hemphill and Paul Schmitz at KUMD gave me a voice and the opportunity to use it. Larry Anderson helped when my injured birds needed real veterinary care. My mother-in-law Helen Erickson cared for my birds whenever I took off on a vacation. When birds migrating along the Hawk Ridge flyway were in imminent danger, Charles Batemen gave me the legal clout to protect them. Professional ornithologists inspired me, and their research gave me fodder for radio programs. Mary Clench, Jack Kirkley, Judith McIntyre, and a lot of other scientists took this stay-at-home mother seriously at professional meetings and made me feel welcome. When my questions about nighthawk physiology exceeded the answers in the literature, Gary Duke accepted me as a Ph.D. candidate to find out for myself. Each of these people has been as necessary and irreplaceable in my life as Blue Jays themselves, and my journey has been richer and finer because of them.

For the Birds is a loose account of my journey toward awareness of birds. Whether your bird interests include quiet breakfasts enjoying backyard feeder birds, freezing drives through the countryside searching for Northern Hawk Owls, or lazy afternoons stretched out next to a pair of plastic lawn flamingos, I hope you'll join me a ways. *For the Birds* won't be complete until you've written in your own account of the journey.

January

January

This is the perfect day to start a "year list"—a list of all the birds seen during the calendar year. Starting afresh on January first, you'll find even the most ordinary starlings and sparrows new and exciting, at least for a moment. In northern places, a year list won't grow rapidly until April or May, but winter birds are like diamonds—all the more precious for their rarity.

1 The New Year's baby, clad in nothing more than diaper and banner, has no mother to change it or feed it or rock it to sleep. It doesn't even have a propped-up bottle to stave off hunger.

Perhaps we would have been wiser, and kinder, to choose a different symbol for the coming year. The chickadee shows the exuberance and spirit of the jolliest baby, and has more probability of surviving the winter on its own. Chickadees face the New Year with optimism grounded in reality, enthusiastic even as they brave the fiercest blizzards. Chickadees wear even less clothing than the New Year's baby, but scales and special circulatory adaptations protect their feet from frostbite, and their birthday suit of thick down insulates them against bitterest cold. They eat frozen dinners of seeds, suet, and insect pupae and larvae and sip from dripping icicles, yet maintain their body temperatures at 104 degrees, with heat enough to spare to warm our hearts. Our hopes and dreams for the coming year make a heavy burden for a half-naked orphan babe; let them take wing in the form of a chickadee.

Notes

2 In fall, Black-capped Chickadees form flocks. The year's young separate from their siblings and join different groups; this prevents them from choosing a closely related mate when the time comes. Flocks are more efficient at finding food and spotting predators than individual birds would be.

Nuthatches and Downy Woodpeckers associate with these flocks in winter. Like mail carriers, they move through woods and backyards and feeding stations on a fairly regular route, and neither rain nor snow nor sleet nor hail will keep them from their appointed rounds. Unlike mail carriers, they aren't rooted to the ground lugging letters and packages, and they lightly flit from place to place. One moment the feeder is empty. Next moment, there they are—chickadees clinging to a suet bag and darting in and out of the sunflower feeder, a Downy Woodpecker stolidly hammering at the old apple tree, two nuthatches bickering over a peanut. A Blue Jay hears the commotion and flies in to investigate. The feeder bustles for ten minutes or so before the flock moves on, but it'll be back. You can depend on it.

The best feeder fare is sunflower seed, for both its nutritional value and its appeal to a wide variety of birds. Suet is an excellent supplement for insect-eating birds. Peanut butter attracts many species, including Boreal Chickadees. Cracked corn spread on the ground or in a low tray is a good choice for juncoes, Mourning Doves, and sometimes grouse. Blue Jays and squirrels are especially fond of peanuts.

Notes

January

Bald Eagles winter as far north as Alaska, gathering in large numbers along open water, especially near dams. They're attracted to roadkills, occasionally catch mice and rats, and aren't above raiding bait pots or grabbing a slow-witted duck from the water. One winter a Bald Eagle visited a bird feeder near Lake Superior every morning to eat a hard-boiled egg. It made for an enviable entry on a bird feeder list, and scared away squirrels to boot.

Notes

3 Bald Eagles are earthbound in winter more than in other seasons. Magnificently graceful in the sky, they have an awkward bulkiness on the ground that makes one wonder whether perhaps Ben Franklin wasn't right.

Eagles can't spend their hours leisurely angling for fish above sun-dappled waters when an eight-inch slab of ice blocks the way, so they gather at dams, eagle-styled fish-monger shops where they pick up dinner already filleted and chopped into bite-sized pieces. Some eagles with a fondness for fresher fare have figured out a more intriguing angle. They search above frozen water for little huts, each conveniently set alongside a hole in the ice. When an eagle spots one of these setups, it perches in a tree and bides its time. Eventually a human comes out of the hut, pulls a fish out of the water, and sets it on the ice. This person, who is clearly not interested in eating the fish, quickly disappears back into the hut leaving the fish just ripe for the taking, there for all to see. Sometimes the eagle carries the whole thing off, but sometimes it just picks at it a bit, leaving the bones and head as a gratuity for fine service and an excellent meal.

4 Uncontrollable shivering is evidence of hypothermia in humans, but it's a worthless indicator of discomfort or danger in birds. Northern Cardinals and Blue Jays begin shivering when the temperature drops below 65 degrees, and smaller birds like nuthatches and chickadees shiver when it's even warmer.

A bird is like a well-insulated cabin, but instead of burning wood or oil, it metabolizes food and harnesses the heat by shivering. Small songbirds maintain a body temperature of about 104 degrees, which requires a lot of shivering, which, in turn, burns a lot of fuel. In extremely cold weather, some birds feed continuously from dawn until dusk. Fortunately, many birds can turn down their thermostats to conserve fuel during long, hungry nights. The Black-capped Chickadee may drop its temperature over 12 degrees at nighttime.

For added insulation to conserve heat produced by shivering, birds grow a large number of extra feathers in early winter. White-throated Sparrows average about 1,525 feathers in October, and well over 2,500 in February. "Feather light" isn't an exaggeration. This huge number of body feathers makes up less than 10 percent of the white-throat's total one ounce weight.

Notes

January

Suet is popular with woodpeckers, jays, chickadees, and nuthatches. When a warbler spends the winter in the northern United States, it's usually found at a suet feeder. Birds eat suet as is, but some people prefer to melt it and skim the purified white fat that floats to the top. Other ingredients are often added to this "rendered" suet—cornmeal, peanuts, and peanut butter are especially good choices.

5 Fat and cholesterol are fearsome entities to humans, especially after the holiday season, but fat keeps birds alive during the winter. In autumn, birds pig out, building up fat reserves against hard times ahead. Long-distance migrants can actually double their weight with fat deposits. Winter birds don't lug around that much extra bulk, but when food is adequate they do maintain about 10 percent of their weight in fat. Fat deposits form under the skin, in the muscles, and in the peritoneal cavity. Excess fat can be a nuisance in day-to-day living, but seldom threatens a bird's health. Unlike humans, birds accumulate virtually no fat in their heart muscle, even when obese.

Birds convert fat to energy twice as efficiently as they convert carbohydrate or protein. That's why black-oil sunflower seed makes a better choice than the less-fatty striped variety, especially during the worst of winter.

Suet, 100 percent saturated animal fat and fatty vegetable oils, are transformed into fluff and fire in a chickadee and jaunty impertinence in a Blue Jay—magical stuff, indeed.

Notes

6 The stark blacks and whites of a winter landscape have no finer contrast than the pink glow of an adult male Pine Grosbeak. The plumage of females and young males, gray accented with russet or yellow, is more subtly beautiful. Pine Grosbeaks have daintier beaks than other grosbeaks, and their smaller heads aptly give them a gentler appearance.

Pine Grosbeak plumage is thicker and softer than the finest velvet, as they sometimes give us opportunity to discover firsthand. Many birds of the Far North are unafraid of humans, but the Pine Grosbeak is uniquely tame when approached. The first one I ever saw caught my attention by whistling from a bare elm in a Madison, Wisconsin, park. I whistled back, and it hopped to a lower, closer branch. We whistled back and forth for a while, the bird steadily coming closer. I reached out, and it suddenly hopped onto my finger. We studied each other for twenty seconds or so, and then it hopped leisurely onto a nearby branch and resumed whistling. The bird's claws were cold and sharp, but something in its eyes penetrated deep into my spirit; the memory warms me even today.

Pine Grosbeaks usually appear in northern forests in early winter, but are nomadic like other northern finches. They're shy and unobtrusive at feeders, taking little but sunflower and vanishing the moment more feisty Evening Grosbeaks appear. Pine Grosbeaks also dine on mountain ash berries and crab apples, and take salt and grit on roadsides. They sometimes associate with winter robins; the two species are similar in size and shape, tricky to separate by silhouette in flight.

Notes

January

Nighthawks, like all native American birds, are protected by law and cannot be kept as pets. Only licensed rehabilitators can legally care for injured or orphaned birds, and then only temporarily. To become rehabilitators, people must apply with their state department of natural resources and the U.S. Fish and Wildlife Service and must demonstrate proficiency at the necessary skills. Only researchers and educational institutions can be licensed to keep birds permanently.

7 A nighthawk is as out of place in Minnesota in January as a fish in the Sahara. Many nighthawks leave the North Country in August, and virtually all are gone by September's end. They winter in South America, and sensible ones don't return until late May.

But convalescent nighthawks sometimes spend the season in my living room. On sunny days, these left-behind birds gather in the warm patch of sunshine on the carpet, and, like wind-up sundials, move with the sun throughout the day. When I hold one up to the window to see snow, something most nighthawks never hope to see, he placidly gazes at it the same way that he studies TV or watches my cat across the room.

The Common Nighthawk has a huge mouth, but its beak is tiny and fragile and its vestigial tongue worthless for manipulating food; this relative of the Whip-poor-will can eat nothing on its own except flying insects.

I hand-feed my January birds mealworms, crickets, and a mixture of dry dog food and other ingredients. They accept their captivity with equanimity, but sometimes I sense an almost palpable yearning for a Brazilian sunset. How I wish I could oblige them.

Notes

8 The Blue Jay inspires bitter hatred or devoted love—as with a cat, no one is apathetic about a Blue Jay. This curious, opportunistic omnivore eats plenty of insects and plant material, but in spring and summer it fuels human hatred by stealing eggs and baby birds of other species, mainly to feed its own hungry brood. It also acts as a raucous alarm clock that simply cannot be turned off.

But what else in the universe combines brains, beauty, and a perky little crest in an elegant three-ounce package? Blue Jays are related to crows, ravens, and magpies; many people consider these corvids to be the most intelligent of all birds. And the world is a finer place because of jays. They plant more acorns than they eat, reforesting for future generations. They do steal eggs and baby birds, but in turn perform an invaluable service by alerting other birds of even more dangerous predators. Jays valiantly protect their mates and young, and many mate for life. A group of jays was once recorded feeding and guarding an old, partially blind jay, and even protectively leading it to water.

The word jay probably comes from the Roman name Gaius. Blue Jay calls are described as "jay, jay," but the name originated in Europe, where jays don't say "jay." The word is also slang for a simpleton or rustic. That derogatory meaning was augmented with the unpopular first chief justice, John Jay. The silliest jay expression is "naked as a jaybird." Jays wear no fewer clothes than any other bird except Donald Duck.

Notes

January

In caring for injured waxwings, I've found that mountain ash berries, which are hard, pass through the digestive system unchanged unless I roll them between two fingers first to soften them. It appears that the waxwing's convivial dining habits serve both a social function, cementing the bonds among the flock, and a physiological one, making food more digestible.

9 Bohemian Waxwings, plump and amiable as members of Dickens's Pickwick Club, gather for congenial dining and conversation in mountain ashes and crab apples and along salted and gravelled roads. Their jaunty crests give them a slightly eccentric look even as their sleek, elegant plumage seems to come from the closet of an English gentleman. This is the only waxwing found in England, where it is simply called the Waxwing.

Waxwing meals are jovial gatherings. Both Bohemian and Cedar Waxwings pass berries back and forth to one another, seemingly enjoying the sharing as much as the eating. Because of the high water content of this diet, every day waxwings devour three times their weight in berries, which are quickly digested; the snow beneath is often spattered bright orange. Many times a waxwing gets so caught up in the conviviality that it eats to excess. Sometimes when the flock flies off to a new gathering spot, a bird is left behind, its wings unable to support the added weight of the enormous meal. After it spends some time in solitary digestion, it's off to join the others—perhaps to regale them with Dickensian tales of its misadventures.

Notes

10 The most distinctive characteristics of Blue Jays, waxwings, and Pileated Woodpeckers are their crests. A Blue Jay erects its crest to show aggression, displaying it most conspicuously when fighting over territory or a mate or when mobbing an owl or other predator. When courting and feeding young, a jay flattens the crest tightly against the head. The crest is also lowered during foraging and preening. The skin beneath the crest raises and lowers it in the same way that our skin raises goose bumps.

No other North American corvids have crests, but many unrelated birds do, from ducks to cardinals. Ornithologists have yet to figure out why some birds have crests and others don't. The Blue Jay's closest relative, Steller's Jay of western North America, uses its crest for essentially the same displays. But some crests serve different purposes than do jays'. For example, waxwings don't defend a territory or show much aggression toward anything; their distinctive crested silhouettes may simply help them locate one another. However, not one bird in the world has developed a use for one crest: Crest Toothpaste.

Wood Ducks, Tufted Ducks, and mergansers have shaggier crests than the Blue Jay—the Red-breasted Merganser's crest makes it look as if it had stayed under the hair dryer too long. The Belted Kingfisher also has a shaggy crest. The California Quail's teardrop-shaped topknot arches forward over its head; this and its habit of running about in flocks in single file make the species a favorite in Disney cartoons.

Notes

January

When I sat in seat 24-F of a DC-9 jet, I could see the wing flaps going up and down, attached by rivets to the wing. The entire wing shuddered ominously whenever we passed through a turbulent spot. Birds protect themselves from turbulence with tiny feathers growing from a small bony projection called an alula, attached to the thumb bone at the farthest bend in the wing.

11 When I first flew in an airplane, from Duluth to Dallas, I imagined I was a bird in flight. It was hardly the same—I was cocooned within tons of steel. Birds have nothing but feathers to protect them, and no chewing gum to keep their ears from popping. Come to think of it, they don't carry airsickness bags, either.

As I looked down on the sun-splashed earth, not for one second did we pass a stretch without highway incisions and rectangular and square patches of farms and developments. Nature uses sweeping lines and irregular shapes, but even rivers were straightened. As we descended upon Dallas, hundreds of blue dots gleamed below—I suddenly realized they were swimming pools. Egrets, herons, and other water and wetland birds have been decimated as their homes are drained, and small farmers of South Texas struggle to bleed out of their parched land a paltry $2500 a year, but the affluent squander that precious liquid in swimming pools.

Flying through the skies, I yearned to glimpse the handiwork of God. All I could find was the work of people.

Notes

12

Every winter, birders gather in northern Minnesota to add the Northern Hawk Owl to their lists. Even the most acquisitive lister cannot check it off and just leave—this is an owl to whom attention must be paid. It has finely etched horizontal barring on the underside, delicate spots above, and the arresting eyes characteristic of owls, but its unique allure comes from something intangible.

Whenever I chance upon a Great Horned Owl perched alone and silent, I feel like an intruder who mustn't linger, betraying it to a passing crow. Great Gray and Snowy Owls stare past or through me as if I didn't exist. Saw-whet and Boreal Owls endure observation out of innate politeness, or possibly because they have trouble seeing in daylight. But every hawk owl I've found has seemed genuinely pleased, even eager, to see me, as if it expected me to pull a gerbil out of my pocket to share for lunch. Of course, that's exactly what some birders do to lure hawk owls closer, but I'd hate to think that mine are merely acting out a conditioned response to food. Isn't it possible that this one wild little creature simply likes me?

The Northern Hawk Owl was never common—Audubon didn't see one in all the years he spent in the American wilderness. He painted the hawk owl from stuffed specimens sent to him by Thomas MacCulloch of Nova Scotia. Hawk owls are seen regularly in all the Canadian provinces and Alaska, but in only eight other states are they reported even irregularly. Northern Minnesota is the most reliable place to see one south of Canada.

Notes

January

Of the Gray Jay, Arthur Cleveland Bent wrote: "This much-maligned bird has its redeeming traits; it greets the camper, when he first pitches camp, with demonstrations of welcome, and shares his meals with him; it follows the trapper on his long trails through the dark and lonesome woods, where any companionship must be welcome; it may be a thief, and at times a nuisance, but its jovial company is worth more than the price of its board."

13 The winter woods are more pleasant when a whiskey jack flies in on ghostlike wings. The Gray Jay doesn't resemble its perky blue relative so much as it does a chickadee on steroids. Gray Jays' diet gives new meaning to the word *omnivorous*—they've been reported eating moccasins, fur caps, matches, soap, and plug tobacco. They audaciously followed the sleds of early trappers, sometimes lighting right beside a trapper and poking holes in his pelts. Gray Jays enter tents to carry off anything remotely edible, including candles.

Although Gray Jays live in the North Woods year-round, some winters they appear in huge numbers. The all-time record on a Christmas bird count was set in 1987, when 177 were seen at a wildlife reserve in Alberta. The previous record was set the year before, with 154 counted in Isabella, Minnesota. Just one or two Gray Jays at a feeder is plenty—at mine, they empty out the suet first thing every morning, carrying off big chunks of fat to hide in tree crevices, abandoned squirrel nests, and my neighbor's gutter. They vanish by March, long before spring rains make a mess of the rain spout. Bob will never know what hit him.

Notes

14 The Red-breasted Nuthatch is a dapper but undersized, somehow comical little gent—an avian Charlie Chaplin. It spends its life in topsy-turvy fashion, winding about tree trunks and clinging to the tips of pine and spruce cones, probing with its sharp, forcepslike beak for the seeds within. This quarter-ounce bird, common in the northern coniferous forest, usually stays high up in the trees, but its "ank, ank, ank" call, described as a tiny tin horn, reveals its presence.

Although Red-breasted Nuthatches are forest birds, they visit cities and towns where conifers are abundant. At feeders they favor suet, sunflower seeds, and peanuts, though even in a backyard they eat mostly natural food. Like chickadees, Red-breasted Nuthatches carry away a single seed at a time to eat in the shelter of a tree. Nuthatches don't hold the seed in their feet—they wedge it into a crevice in the bark or between branches and hack away, breaking off bite-sized pieces of the sunflower heart. Although most nuthatches spend their lives in North Country, in years of food shortages they move south in great numbers.

Red-breasted Nuthatches sometimes chip tiny pieces of mortar from brick buildings—as with Northern Finches and other seed-eating birds, their diet may possibly be deficient in some minerals. Some nuthatches spend a great deal of time on chimneys during extremely cold days—they work at the mortar part of the time, but mostly they just warm their little fannies.

Notes

January

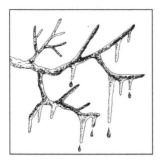

At least once every January I pull out my bird recordings. There's nothing like a Prothonotary Warbler's "sweet, sweet, sweet" to conjure up a steamy hot southeastern swamp in June. But then I notice that my feeders are empty. The blast of cold air when I go out to fill them blows illusory southern swamps away. The days get longer, but we can't escape the fact that January is the coldest month of the year.

15 By mid-January, day length surpasses November levels, and on mild, sunny days birds take momentary breaks from feeding. Chickadees whistle their sweet "fee-bee" song, a Ruffed Grouse drums once or twice, ravens croak overhead, Pine Siskins twitter in spruces and sing their zippy little tune. I listen for a downy to drum, but he isn't as quick to forget that it's still winter.

Icicles drip under the January sun and chickadees hover, taking a quick sip. Evening Grosbeaks find some melted ice on the road; they drink and pick up grit and road salt the way they do everything else, as a group. The mailman comments about spruce cones dropping on his head throughout the neighborhood—letter carriers are often the first to notice White-winged Crossbills.

I get a phone call about a robin in a Cloquet mountain ash. The caller is surprised that one would come back so early, and shocked when I tell him that this one must be spending the winter up here. Most robins avoid the northern winter, but a few endure the worst of it—and get the best territories come spring. Clinging to hopes of the future is what January is all about.

Notes

16 Something about walking—the repetitiveness of movement, the mesmerizing trees, the clouds keeping their distance no matter how long and far we walk toward them—cleanses the soul. Trivial worries are out of place in the woods; the most nagging thoughts retreat, leaving us alone and free. I set out in Port Wing with three intentions: to find the Pileated Woodpecker that's been working a dead cottonwood, to check how Hairy Woodpeckers are doing this year, and to see what unusual birds are lurking about. I've hardly gone a quarter mile before I've slipped free of even that modest purposefulness.

I'm not quite sure what I've been thinking about when a Gray Jay swoops in on silent wings and lands in an aspen just ahead of me. I say "Hey!" companionably, but my voice jars the stillness and he moves on. I keep walking. A Great Horned Owl, eyes half-closed, watches from a spruce; I almost miss it. Any owl is a magical gift. A raven flies over, and in another half mile a Pileated Woodpecker flies by. It's too far away for me to tell whether it's male or female, but I don't mind. I'm too far into the woods to mind anything at all.

It is not sensible to walk in the frozen winter woods. We see more birds sitting home watching the feeder, but sometimes we need something wilder. It takes a drive through the countryside to get rare owls or Spruce Grouse for a year list, but sometimes we need something slower. We cover more ground on cross-country skis, but sometimes we need something quieter. At times like these, a walk in the woods is simply necessary.

Notes

January

In the spring of 1850, Nicolas Pike, director of the Brooklyn Institute, released eight pairs of House Sparrows in Greenwood Cemetery, Brooklyn. Although this was the first documented introduction of the species in America, many more releases took place during the late 1800s throughout the United States and Canada, especially by immigrants who missed the familiar cheep-cheeping. Within forty years House Sparrows inhabited the entire continent.

17 House Sparrow urchins have many strategies for surviving on the street. When we get a really cold spell—when the mercury refuses to budge above twenty below—my sparrows become carjackers. When any car stops on Peabody Street, the gang descends upon it en masse. Before the driver even gets out they've darted under the hood to bask near the hot motor. They fly out when the engine cools down, and hurry to the bushes on the south side of my house to wait for the next car.

Before people on Peabody Street started making their old houses more energy-efficient, we had more sparrows. At night, they'd gather in arbor vitae bushes close to heat-leaking houses. One or two still winter in the streetlight on the corner, and a few hide out in a neighbor's garage, but most are gone; and in some more modern neighborhoods, they're completely absent. They concentrate downtown, where streetlights and electric store signs heat their roosts. House Sparrows probably originated in Africa, and the Northland in winter is about as far from Africa as you can get. But wherever little pockets of human heat remain, sparrows are sure to be.

Notes

18 When it's thirty below, a bunch of common city pigeons wheeling and soaring with abandon in the frozen blue sky is a fine sight. Pigeons fly with power and gusto, clapping their wings together on both the upstrokes and downstrokes when taking off, and rocking from side to side with wings raised in a deep V once aloft. It's hard to believe that they fly with pleasure when it's so cold—wouldn't they be more comfortable huddled on the ground, out of the biting wind? When it's warm, pigeons maintain an internal body core temperature of 107.9 degrees, and even in the cold their blood runs hotter than most songbirds'. Flying burns calories and generates heat—the activity keeps them warmer than they would be if they just sat around complaining.

Pigeons are not native to America. Europeans brought them along on countless occasions, to use for food and sport. Captive birds that escaped or got lost in homing races became feral. Most varieties of domestic pigeons were originally bred from wild Rock Doves native to Eurasia, and pigeons have been used for transporting human messages since the days of the ancient Egyptians.

Some city pigeons are descendants of heroes from world wars. During World War II, the British Services used about 200,000 pigeons, and the U.S. Army Signal Corps about 50,000. Nearly 17,000 pigeons were parachuted to supporters of the Resistance in German-occupied Europe, 2,000 returning safely. A pigeon named Cher Ami saved an entire American battalion behind enemy lines, losing an eye and leg in the effort. After the war, she was fitted with a tiny wooden leg.

Notes

January

Although just about everyone in America dislikes starlings, in New Zealand some people actually set out nest boxes to attract them. Starlings are fond of fruits and berries, but they also eat grubs and agricultural pests, and few seeds, so where grain is the only crop, they sometimes benefit economic interests.

19 Three of the most abundant bird species in America today, the Rock Dove, the starling, and the House Sparrow, were unheard of when native people were the only Americans.

Rock Doves weren't actually introduced—some just slipped the surly bonds of domestication. In mountainous areas of the West, some have reverted to a genuinely wild state, living as their Mediterranean ancestors once did, but most concentrate in cities. These pigeons may be a nuisance, and their droppings may cause property damage, but at least they don't compete with native species for food and nesting sites.

European Starlings and House Sparrows, both intentionally introduced in the 1800s, live in rural and agricultural settings as well as urban ones; starlings can even be found in some wilderness areas. House Sparrows eat grain, and so are considered agricultural pests. Both species cause immeasurable ecological harm by stealing nest cavities of native birds like bluebirds, flickers, and Great Crested Flycatchers.

Notes

20 Birding in solitude has a quiet magic, but at times we need a birding buddy. This frozen morning I meet Billie at five-fifteen—her eyes are still sleepy. I drive twenty miles to Two Harbors, then head up Highway 2 straight toward Spruce Grouse country.

The sky is cloudy and black. The sun won't rise until almost eight and there won't be much of a dawn. That's good—grouse gather on the road early but head into the woods at first light. The wind roars—that's not good.

The drive is silent and lonely when I'm alone. It's quiet with Billie, too—we're too sleepy to talk—but it isn't lonely. The grouse area begins forty-five miles up the road. We start feeling hopeful, and our stomachs start growling. Hot tea stops my teeth from chattering; we eat muffins and talk about Spruce Grouse and about the hawk owl we saw last time. Shouldn't a Boreal Owl turn up one of these days? A logging truck thunders by, then another. We cruise the Spruce Grouse area twice but no luck, and suddenly it's light. We're quiet on the drive back home, discouraged, but already calculating how soon we can try again.

Audubon wrote of Spruce Grouse in Maine: "Every person to whom I spoke about it, assured me that it was rather abundant during the whole year . . . but no one told me of the difficulties I should have to encounter in watching its habits." Hunters find them more easily—the Minnesota Department of Natural Resources reported a harvest figure of 31,000 for 1991. Once found, Spruce Grouse are fairly tame, earning their nickname, "fool hen."

Notes

January

Great Horned Owls from the Far North are almost as white as Snowy Owls, but are forest birds and usually perch in trees unless they catch something too heavy to lug through the air. Snowy Owls, from the tundra, stay in more open areas, perching in the snow or on flat structures. Occasionally snowies alighting on chimneys drop right through. They apparently don't spend those long arctic summer days talking to Santa Claus.

Notes

21 A phone ringing at night summons with urgency. It's a girl with a small voice, maybe twelve or thirteen. Someone from the DNR told her to call me.

"There's an owl in my yard. He must be hurt. People come real close to him and he doesn't fly away. Maybe he was hit by a car."

"What kind of owl?" I ask.

"I don't know—big and white. He's been here over an hour now. I know you can't come when it's so late, but can you tell me how to help him?"

She's home alone; I'll have to go. I need to know what I'll be dealing with. "Can you see if it has feathers sticking up on top of its head like horns?"

"Okay." She has a cordless phone. I hear her put on boots and open the door.

"He's gone!" she whispers. The dry snow crunches under her feet. "There's feather prints in the snow." She sounds both relieved and forlorn. Suddenly she cries, "Oh, no! There's blood in the snow! And there's pieces of something—" I can hear her voice harden as her allegiance is transferred from the owl to something else. "There's a foot—and an ear—it was a bunny rabbit!"

22 Many birds suffer dietary deficiencies in winter. A good feeding station provides minerals that the frozen natural world lacks. Cuttlefish bone and pieces of eggshell replenish calcium. Fireplace ashes are rich in a variety of minerals, though ashes from newspapers are also laced with toxic chemicals.

Seed-eating birds need grit (to help them digest their food) as well as minerals. When snow covers the ground, northern finches congregate on roads to take salt and sand. Cars kill crossbills and grosbeaks in large numbers every year because of this need. A children's sandbox kept clear of snow is a safer gathering place for them. Grit can also be spread in a feeder. The kinds packaged for pet birds are especially valuable.

In the rare event that a robin, mockingbird, or oriole visits in winter, dried fruit is a perfect offering; raisins are especially appreciated. Orioles drink plain sugar water, but orange juice is even better—set it out each morning and bring it in when it freezes.

Even birds that leave the Northland in fall sometimes change their diets for the duration. Eastern Kingbirds that ate bumblebees, moths, and other flying insects all summer are now dining on fruit in the tropics. A balanced diet for them isn't a daily but an annual regimen.

Notes

January

Bird baths aren't practical during a northern winter. Electric heaters may keep them thawed, but in extreme cold, when the water steams too much for drinking anyway, they waste energy. Freezing water expands, damaging many bird baths, and the slab of ice is a nuisance to remove. It's simpler to set out plastic cereal bowls of water on a feeding tray, deck rail, or porch, and bring them in when ice forms.

23 Snow and ice have sparkle, charm, and utility, but they simply don't quench thirst. Yet when the water supply freezes up for the season, birds usually have no choice but to eat snow to replenish fluids.

In arid climates, small seed-eating birds must drink at least 10 percent of their total body weight in fresh water every day. Our winter birds conserve body water and survive with much less. Birds don't sweat, and they reabsorb some respired moisture before they exhale, but they still lose moisture through their skin by evaporation. To compensate, they recycle water from their excretory and digestive systems, making their winter droppings concentrated and dry. In winter, some finches can survive for weeks with no water at all.

Even though winter birds can survive long periods without drinking, we help them by setting out water whenever the temperature is above 10 degrees or so. When it's much colder, freezing water steams, which could coat feathers with ice. But on pleasant days, birds will appreciate a bowl of water more than the finest birdseed.

Notes

24 Red-tailed Hawks are scarce in North Country in winter. An average of 4,907 are counted migrating over Hawk Ridge in Duluth every fall, most headed for an area between the south central states and Nicaragua. But some adult redtails do winter up here, and a few of these hardy souls are already gathering sticks for nests. They won't lay eggs until March or April, but it takes time to build a perfect baby cradle.

The Red-tailed Hawk is one of the best known and most common of North American hawks, able to survive in an enormous variety of habitats, from deserts and forests to farms and major metropolitan areas. This huge bird, with a four-foot to almost-five-foot wingspan, takes prey ranging in size from grasshoppers and mice to rabbits, skunks, and porcupines. Its hunting ferocity compensates for the lightness of its hollow bones—the largest females weigh only about three-and-a-half pounds.

In winter, we usually see redtails sitting on fences and telephone poles along roads. Urban ones sit atop buildings in harbors and railroad yards, benevolent guards protecting the city against rats and pigeons.

Female raptors are larger than males. Female Red-tailed Hawks and Snowy Owls weigh about 30 percent more than males. Female Sharp-shinned Hawks are almost twice as big as males. Mated pairs of different sizes may be able to hunt a wider variety of prey successfully, and larger females may prevent males from injuring them during mating.

Notes

January

Sometimes a bird objects to being reduced to supper. If its attacker is a hawk or owl, which uses talons for attack and transport, the prey may struggle but usually can't reach the predator's face to inflict serious damage. The shrike has no talons—its heavy, hooked beak must do most of its dirty work. A shrike must be quick and fierce or it will soon be dead.

25 The January feeding station bustles with activity—Evening Grosbeaks pigging out at feeding trays, redpolls and siskins perched on the niger seed feeder and swarming over the ground beneath, chickadees darting to and fro. Suddenly they all vanish. One lone bird remains—a robin-sized gray songbird perched atop a spruce. As long as that Northern Shrike sticks around, the feeder will stay empty.

The Northern Shrike, called the Great Grey Shrike in Britain, is a two-and-a-half-ounce killing machine. It summers in the Far North, where it eats insects, birds, and its preferred food—mice and voles. In winter, when cold-blooded food is unavailable and mice tunnel beneath the snow, it concentrates on birds—mostly small ones, though it can manage even Blue Jays. A hungry shrike will eat its prey on the spot, but sometimes it carries a bird off and impales it on a buckthorn or piece of barbed wire for storage—a grotesque practice that led to its nickname, the butcher bird. Food is scarce in winter—to survive, it must strike whenever it can. It'll return to its meat locker when the hunting isn't so good.

Notes

26 An odd chickadee appears at the feeder. It's drab, with brown back and cap, rusty flanks, and a short tail. It eats frozen peanut butter for about a minute, then flies into a spruce. This Boreal Chickadee returns twice that afternoon, and falls into a routine of coming three or four times each day. It takes nothing but peanut butter. Within a few days, it calls and flies up companionably when anybody fills the feeder.

The Boreal Chickadee lives in the northern coniferous forest, visiting only the luckiest feeders. It eats insects along with the seeds of balsam fir, spruce, and birch, usually working the highest branches of the tallest trees. It's a quiet bird, deliberate and cautious, with a wheezy "chick-a-dee" call that sounds like a blackcap with a terminal disease. Its subtle attractiveness and shy but friendly manner make it a comfortable and most welcome guest. Out-of-town birders check the Boreal Chickadee off on their lists and hurry on to more glamorous owls and grouse. But every moment in the company of this pleasant visitor is a moment well spent.

Boreal Chickadees are often seen with Black-capped Chickadee flocks, though the browncaps aren't tightly bound to the group. Because of their more selective diet, boreals often stay in conifers while the rest of the flock moves on to feeders and hardwoods. In spring and fall, boreals are more likely to associate with Golden-crowned Kinglets than with Black-capped Chickadees. In some winters, large numbers of Boreal Chickadees migrate south.

Notes

January

Ravens, with blatant disregard for all human laws, violate *Allen's Rule*. In bird species with a wide range, those individuals living in colder areas usually have smaller bills, to reduce heat loss. But ravens from the Far North or the Himalayas have huge beaks, the most enormous on ravens from Greenland. Ravens in cold climates kill more live food than ravens elsewhere—apparently the advantages of a more lethal weapon offset the added loss of heat.

27 The hoarse, resonant croak of the raven exemplifies the wild beauty of the northern forest, but ravens do not limit their range to the Far North. Over the world the raven wanders, and over the world people take notice. Our forest sentinel is the same raven that rejected the role of Noah's messenger in Genesis; the raven of Nordic sagas, Indian legends, Middle Eastern folklore, Eskimo tales; the raven of Edgar Allan Poe's most famous poem.

This largest of all songbirds seems also the most human of birds—in intelligence, devotion to family, complex social structure. Its diet is human enough that it might have sustained the Old Testament prophet Elijah. Ravens sometimes bring so much food to their young that a bit of surplus drops to the ground. Biblical scholars with an ornithological bent suggest that ravens didn't actually bring food to Elijah—he just chanced upon provender dropping from a nest above. Ravens eat some items that not even a starving Elijah would have considered—in addition to fresh meat and carrion, they follow sled dogs to pick up their droppings, and visit rotting carcasses to feast on blowfly maggots.

Notes

28 Driving along country roads one frozen dawn, Billie and I discover a running river. Wisps of rising steam cloud our view, but we spy ghostly shapes in the water. Twelve Common Goldeneyes swim about, more alive than anything we've seen so far today. One male scoots about the water and snaps his head back like a bizarre wind-up toy, revving up for mating season. It's ten below—cold enough to fog our binoculars—but the ducks seem comfortable enough, perhaps because the water is over forty-two degrees warmer than the air.

The goldeneye, a dapper little fellow, is found throughout the northern hemisphere, wintering on both fresh water and oceans. In flight, its wings make a vibrant whistling sound, recognizable long before it comes into view. On the water, the male appears black and white with a round white patch in front of and below his gold eye. Females are recognized by the company they keep. Billie and I watch this little group swim along the winding stream until they turn a bend and are gone. We've already added goldeneyes to our year lists, but this little flock on this frozen morning is a gift of beauty and warmth.

Canada Geese and many kinds of ducks can be seen during the worst of a Northland winter, especially in harbors and near power plants where warm inflows keep the water open. The ducks most often seen include the American Black Duck, Mallard, Greater Scaup, Oldsquaw, Common Goldeneye, Bufflehead, and Common and Red-breasted Mergansers.

Notes

January

Eighty percent of all down used in sleeping bags, quilts, pillows, and jackets in the United States is imported, from thirty different countries. The main source is China, but Germany and France are also major suppliers. The down feathers are a by-product of their goose- and duck-meat industries.

29 Ounce for ounce, down is the finest insulating material known. And the finest down in the world comes from a northern sea duck, the Common Eider, which readily survives temperatures colder than fifty below zero. Female eiders line their nests with this down, insulating their eggs from the permafrost inches below.

Eiders were extirpated from much of their range during the 1800s due to eiderdown collectors' destruction of nests. They stripped the down from each nest every few days, forcing the mother to tear more feathers from her breast to refurbish it. After she had ripped away her best down, she pulled out inferior feathers in desperation, leaving both her babies and herself vulnerable to cold.

Now the eiderdown industry is heavily regulated in Greenland, Iceland, and Canada. A female eider produces enough down for about one and a half nests, so collectors can take a bit of down from a nest without harm, but it takes the down from thirty-five to forty nests to make just one pound of eider down. In 1986, only thirty-six pounds of eiderdown were brought into the United States, valued at four hundred dollars per pound.

Notes

30 The snowplow's been busy, along with a dump truck trailing sand and salt. I look out onto Peabody Street this morning to thirty birds, most of them bright pink, gathered in a sandy brown spot in the middle of the road—White-winged Crossbills. I scan the neighborhood spruces with my binoculars. Every cone-laden tree top has several crossbills attacking the seeds. They mouth the cones steadily, never flitting about, but their work dislodges fresh snow from the treetops. They'd be hard to notice up there except for their "chip chip" calls and an occasional cone dropping to the ground.

The bizarre feature that gives the crossbill its name is an adaptation for tearing off the sheaths of pine and spruce cones. The bird then uses its long, muscular tongue to extract the seeds. I've occasionally had Red Crossbills take sunflower seeds, but I've never had whitewings visit any of my feeders. They do spend time in my children's sandbox, eating grit and perching on a little yellow dump truck. The best way to attract White-winged Crossbills to a North Country yard is to plant some spruce trees and wait. And wait.

The male White-winged Crossbill is dark pink, with two wide white bars on dark wings; the male Red Crossbill is dull brick red with solid dark wings. Females of both species are greenish yellow with the same wing patterns as their mates. Red Crossbills associate with pines, and were more common when giant white pines dominated the forest. Whitewings associate with spruces, and are now relatively more common than reds.

Notes

January

A Downy Woodpecker's beak packs a painful wallop against a predator, or even against a rehabilitator trying to rescue it. Downies are intelligent, and quickly adapt to temporary captivity, sometimes gently probing into a rehabber's clenched fist to take hidden mealworms inside. They can live surprisingly long—one downy banded in St. Paul was caught and released when ten years, five months old.

31 Charlie Brown sometimes beats his head against a tree, especially after an unpleasant encounter with Lucy van Pelt. Beating a head against a tree or brick wall, metaphorically or not, is a desperate and futile act—unless you happen to be a woodpecker.

Downy Woodpeckers spend their lives beating their heads into trees, and profit from the experience. Tap, tap, tap, then probe with a long, barbed tongue, and voila! A tasty wood-boring beetle larva squirms in a hungry tummy. Tap, tap, tap with patience and skill, and a rotted tree snag is transformed into a snug shelter. Tap, tap, tap with testosterone-fueled longing, and an attractive female with an interest in romance appears.

The skull bones of a downy are ossified, almost as hard as concrete—a handy adaptation for a tree-beating lifestyle. A three-quarter-ounce male, light enough to be mailed with a single stamp, has striking black and white plumage, with a splash of red on the back of the head to proclaim his masculinity. Downy Woodpeckers may be hardheaded, but they're also engaging and placid, almost like Charlie Brown himself.

Notes

February

February

The lengthening days of February stir avian hormones, and many birds begin choosing mates. One year three Boreal Chickadees stayed in a tight flock in my neighborhood until February. When two paired off, the remaining bird tried to tag along like always, but the two no longer tolerated their former companion. After a couple of weeks, the lone bird moved on. Sometimes love is as cold and unyielding as February itself.

1 February is relentlessly hard on the wild birds of the North Country. The few seeds clinging to trees and shrubs in January have been picked over by February, and snow still lies too deep to expose seeds fallen to the ground. Mice hide securely in their tunnels; hawks, owls, and shrikes become thinner and more desperate. If our end of Lake Superior hasn't frozen over already, the February ice closes in with a finality that makes talk of groundhogs ring hollow. With every snowstorm, animals succumb. Owls from the Far North appear, and some drop dead in the snow. When we pick them up we are astonished by their weightlessness—feathers and hollow skeletons and nothing more. Surely the spirits that rose from their defeated bodies weighed more.

February is unyielding and cruel, yet hope is astir in the land. Ruffed Grouse and Downy Woodpeckers drum. Chickadees sing their "fee-bee" song in earnest. Crows return. One morning we hear them cawing, and see one optimistically carrying sticks. It doesn't shake our certainty that spring is a long time away, but it does chip away at our despair, opening cracks where the bright sun and crisp blue February sky may shine in.

Notes

2 February is the shortest month on the calendar, but it's the longest month by any other measure. Right when we need a fairy godmother or two to keep us going, a flock of redpolls appears. These tiny northern finches visit feeders earlier in the season, but when we need them most, they descend upon us in earnest.

The Common Redpoll, a half-ounce sprite with ruby forehead and delicate pink breast, is exceptionally hardy, able to survive colder temperatures better than any other songbird—it can last three hours in a chamber set at almost 60 degrees below zero. Chickadees survive the night protected from the wind inside tree cavities. Redpolls sleep on conifer branches more exposed to the elements. They survive in part because they pig out just before bedtime, stuffing special pouches in their esophagus. Then, as they sleep, they can stoke their metabolic furnace without even getting out of bed.

If the redpoll's hardiness amazes us, its friendly manner cheers us. Redpolls are among the easiest birds to hand-tame, and their colors brighten the February landscape. Who could ask for a finer fairy godmother?

Redpolls visit sunflower and niger seed feeders. In the wild they eat seeds of birch, alder, willow, pine, and many weeds. As the snow piles up and food sources are depleted or covered, redpolls turn more and more to bird feeders for sustenance. They twitter constantly, and also make an ascending note like a goldfinch's or a pet canary's—they often respond to imitations of this call.

Notes

February

Gyrfalcons have wintered in the Duluth harbor many years since 1979. In 1984-85, as many as four different individuals were present; in 1991–92 two were occasionally seen. These wanderers from the Arctic may turn up anywhere in the northern half of the United States, but seldom remain in a single spot for longer than a day or two. The Duluth harbor is one of the most likely and accessible places for seeing them in winter.

3 Out-of-town birders meet me in the harbor in search of Snowy Owls and a Gyrfalcon. The snow is sooty, the buildings gray, machinery and boxcars old, even the sky is leaden. But we focus beyond the dinginess—we're searching for avian fragments of sparkling tundra.

The Gyrfalcon might suddenly cruise overhead on powerful wings, chasing pigeons. It might be perched on a sign. Every redtail stops our breath. Today's gyr sits atop the Cargill grain elevator. It's dull gray, not white, and we need a scope to see it, but it satisfies any birder filling the gaping hole between Peregrine and Prairie Falcon on a life list.

Visitors should see Snowy Owls before they get to Duluth—a hundred and fifty miles of possibility lie between the Minneapolis airport and here. The Snowy Owls in our harbor are research subjects, each one marked with a paint spot askew on its head like a New Year's party hat. These birds are perfectly adequate lifers, but nothing in the world beats a Snowy Owl sitting on a snow pile on a windswept field, its yellow eyes benign yet wild and mysterious.

Notes

4 I meet Jim, Verna, and Dick in a motel lobby at 5:30 A.M. They need Spruce Grouse, Boreal Chickadee, and Northern Hawk Owl. I guarantee the owl, but warn that the other two are iffy.

We've never met before, but share a history—Elf Owls at Madera Canyon, Mexican Crows at the Brownsville dump. There's plenty to talk about along Highway 2. Two grouse appear and pose twenty miles before we plan to start searching for them. The hawk owl isn't at the first regular place but a Great Gray Owl is—we'll see hawk owls elsewhere. We head for Stoney Point along Lake Superior for a long-shot Boreal Chickadee. It comes immediately. I head complacently for a guaranteed hawk owl spot, then another. No bird shows. We cruise roads through the lunch hour, my growing anxiety overpowering hunger. In desperation we check an Eagle Lake feeder—we won't find an owl, but we'll at least get redpolls. As we pull in the drive, a long-tailed shadow wings into the woods. We concede the loss and head for home, on a hunch taking a different road. There, perched in a spruce in full view, is our hawk owl. It just didn't want to be taken for granted.

Birders planning to visit a new area can read about the best birding spots in regional and state bird guides, some available locally and all available by mail from the American Birding Association. The A.B.A. also publishes a directory of bird hotlines and a list of members who enjoy guiding birders from other places. The A.B.A.'s address is P.O. Box 6599, Colorado Springs, CO 80934-6599.

Notes

February

Hairy and Downy Woodpeckers have almost identical plumage, but the downy is actually more closely related to the Ladderbacked Woodpecker of the Southwest. Until a birder recognizes the two Northland woodpeckers by call and size, the best field mark to clinch an identification is the tail. Both have white outer tail feathers, but the hairy's are pure white, while the downy's have several black dots.

5 Urban birdwatchers who don't get many woodpeckers at their feeders often struggle to master the differences between Hairy and Downy Woodpeckers. Town and country people recognize the more wary and wild Hairy Woodpecker by its bigger body and longer, stronger bill. It tends to select living trees for its nest holes, requiring a more effective chisel than does the downy, which often chooses dead, rotting wood.

The Hairy Woodpecker is sedentary and solitary, but by February pairs often reunite, the female lured in by the male's drumming. Females have black-and-white heads, while adult males and most immatures have a red mark above the nape. Oddly, many woodpecker babies look more like their fathers than their mothers. Immature flickers have a mustache mark like adult males. When one scientist marked a mustache on a female flicker, her mate attacked her and wouldn't allow her on the territory until the scientist removed the mustache, when he accepted her again. The scientist didn't record whether the female reaccepted her mate, and probably never even wondered whether or not she should have.

Notes

6 Kathy and Judy have a Brown Creeper visiting their Eagle Lake cabin. I sit at their window drinking cocoa and watching it spiral up the cedar and mountain ash. It occasionally takes suet, but not while I look. Creepers are rare here in winter—watching one from a cozy cabin is a good way to spend a frozen afternoon.

Brown Creepers are usually seen in vertical pose, creeping steadily up the trunk of one tree, then flying down to the bottom of another and repeating the action. They're more at home in a vertical world than a horizontal one—they even build their crescent-shaped nest against a tree trunk, supporting it with a piece of loosely attached bark or lichen. Against a tree we see the creeper's brown plumage delicately etched with white, its handsome white eye line, and the curved beak—a precision instrument for probing into tiny crevices. In the hand, the creeper has a snow white underside and an intelligent aspect. Its forward-facing, close-set eyes provide binocular vision for inspecting tree bark for insects. Creepers allow us to come quite close as they feed. They aren't tame—they just can't see the people for the trees.

When a creeper crashed into a school where I once taught, it recuperated in my classroom. The sixth graders brought it mealworms and fresh branches. It had an endearing habit of creeping up our pants legs during science. When we released it, it flew to nearby pines, where we watched it for many minutes before we reluctantly said good-bye. For homework that night the children looked up the definition of the word ambivalence.

Notes

February

House cats should always be kept indoors, at least during daytime, because they kill so many birds, especially redpolls, siskins, juncoes, and other ground species. Dr. Stanley Temple and John Coleman of the University of Wisconsin estimate that rural cats kill 20 million to 150 million songbirds annually in Wisconsin alone. And this doesn't even count the damage done by urban cats.

7 Winter is the slow season for rehabilitators. Most of the birds I receive in winter have flown into windows. Dr. Daniel Klem of Southern Illinois University estimates that 95 million to 950 million birds are killed annually by striking windows. The Cornell Laboratory of Ornithology's Project Feeder Watch calculates that 100 million feeder birds die annually at windows. Stunned birds may recover, but sometimes they have internal or brain injuries, and die later.

Closing the draperies seldom prevents the problem, because glass can reflect sky and trees with or without the curtains open. Taping hawk silhouettes to the windows helps in some cases, mainly by helping birds to notice the glass. Some people affix all manner of things, from flapping strips of aluminum foil to soft screening, to the outsides of their windows, sometimes destroying the whole purpose of having a window in the first place. It is often just as effective to build a feeding tray directly on the outer window sill, or to attach acrylic feeders with suction cups to the pane. Birds at these feeders quickly notice the glass.

Notes

8 Several rules for bird rehabilitation are not covered in any of the standard references.

1. Never turn on a light at night if there are free-flying warblers about—every time, they'll fly up and crash into it.

2. Nighthawks on a bed, especially on a spouse's pillow, cause both extra laundry and marital disharmony.

3. It is never wise to allow a free-flying bird in a room with a decorated Christmas tree.

4. Nighthawks like to watch television. They don't care what's on.

5. If you are missing the last puzzle piece and you have a crow about, check all your houseplant pots.

6. Never sit directly beneath a perched crow.

7. If you have a scaup in your bathtub, inform your mother-in-law before she goes to the bathroom.

Most injured birds must not be kept in regular bird cages, even just to transport them to a licensed rehabber. When a bird beats against the cage or perches on the side bars, its tail and wing feathers become frayed against the metal, impairing flight until the next molt. If a wooden cage with dowels or plastic window screening isn't available, an injured bird should be temporarily housed in a cardboard box.

Notes

February

Once I showed a bright orange bell—the kind rung by pushing a button on top—to a baby Blue Jay named Ludwig. He was fascinated, but whenever he pushed the button, his breast dampened the sound. Hours later, the bell rang once. Then again. And suddenly it was ringing and ringing. I ran in to see little Ludwig hovering above the bell, beating his wings furiously and dinging with all his might.

9 Caring for Blue Jays involves special rules.

1. Never clean a crystal chandelier in front of a free-flying Blue Jay. If you do, from that day on, every time you wash dishes the jay will pull off crystals and plop them in the dish water.

2. Never leave the cupboard with the Froot Loops open.

3. If children's Legos are lying about, expect to find them wedged into furniture and the folds of draperies. A corollary: Every time you open or close the drapes, expect Legos to fall on your head.

4. Never leave a couple of baby Blue Jays alone with your dog. With most dog breeds, something bad might happen to the birds. With a meek dog like my golden retriever Bunter, it will go bad for the dog. Once I walked into a room where I had left Bunter alone with Sneakers and Jake, two baby jays. Jake was hammering on Bunter's back like a woodpecker. Sneakers was perched on Bunter's snout, leaning over and probing with her beak into the poor dog's nostrils. Bunter had the golden's typical guilty expression. She was innocent as could be, but clearly had been thinking about what she'd like to be doing to those birds.

Notes

10 On a morning's cross-country ski, a flock of Snow Buntings offers a pleasant sight. They allow even me, a clumsy beginner, to approach fairly close before they take off, whirling about in the air with big white wing patches sparkling against the blue sky.

The Snow Bunting nests as far as the northern boundary of Ellesmere Island, retreating to our latitude in winter. It can't be found in the woods—the "snowflake" is a bird of the tundra, and here it prefers open country and agricultural areas. It eats weed and grass seeds from the exposed tips of plants on windswept fields, and picks at manure spread on snow-covered pastures or at debris along lake and stream shores, often associating with Lapland Longspurs and Horned Larks. My birding buddy Billie has a way with Snow Buntings—if she dreams about them, one will soon appear.

In the late 1800s, John Burroughs wrote of the snowflake: "Its twittering call and chirrup coming out of the white obscurity is the sweetest and happiest of all winter bird sounds. It is like the laughter of children . . . ever a voice of good cheer and contentment."

Snow Buntings can readily survive temperatures of 40 degrees below zero. One ornithologist found that when the temperature plunges to 58 below, the Snow Bunting's body temperature falls rapidly. To protect themselves from the coldest weather, these birds burrow under snow. When frightened, they also dive under snow for cover.

Notes

February

Eskimos called the Boreal Owl "the blind one," believing only blindness could make it so amazingly tame. Linnaeus assigned it the scientific name *Aegolius funereus* for its mournful cry, like the "slow tolling of a soft but high-pitched bell." Actually the call of the Boreal Owl is a sharp and chipper "hoo-hoo-hoo-hoo-hoo-HOO!" in the same rhythm and pace as a winnowing snipe—Linnaeus may have been influenced more by folklore than careful observation.

11 Kim Eckert phones one morning. A friend has discovered a Boreal Owl not far from town, and he knows I need it for my life list. A *lifer!* I grab my jacket and binoculars and rush to the car, boots still unlaced.

Five birders are gathered on Vada's driveway. One does a little dance—the bird is still there. Boreal Owls are tiny, shorter than loose-leaf paper and lighter than a quarter-pound burger with cheese. Guys who normally cultivate a serious, unemotional image are calling it "cute" with exclamation points in their voices.

Swearing chickadees first located the owl. Vada, walking her dog, investigated the ruckus. Though they most often eat mice, Boreal Owls do occasionally take small birds, and when a chickadee flock spots one, they do their best to drive it away before its evening mealtime. The little owls accept the harassment with equanimity—this one even allows a birder to touch its tail. We are mightily grateful. Our life lists have grown, but our elation comes from something bigger. This tiny owl with enormous spirit has graced us with a visit, enriching our hearts forever.

Notes

12 Abraham Lincoln apparently had no penchant for ornithology, but one unrelated Lincoln, Thomas, who lived at the same time, was an excellent bird spotter who accompanied John James Audubon on a trip to the coast of Labrador in 1833, where he discovered a pretty little sparrow. Audubon wrote, "Chance placed my young companion, Thomas Lincoln, in a situation where he saw it alight within shot, and with his usual unerring aim, he cut short its career. On seizing it, I found it to be a species which I had not previously seen; I named it 'Tom's Finch,' in honor of our friend Lincoln, who was a great favorite among us."

Lincoln's Sparrow is closely related to the Song Sparrow. Both have streaked breasts, but the Song Sparrow's streaks look as if they were painted on with a coarse brush. The streaks on Lincoln's Sparrow are delicate, as if drawn with a fine-point pen. Lincoln's Sparrows are unobtrusive during migration and on their northern breeding grounds. They winter in Mexico, Guatemala, and the extreme southern United States, where they are tame and inquisitive. The Great Emancipator missed out on a good thing.

Thomas Jefferson, an accomplished naturalist, commissioned Lewis and Clark to study and collect birds on their expedition. Theodore Roosevelt, who studied birds throughout his life, may have been the last person to see a living Passenger Pigeon in the wild, at Pine Knot, Maryland, in 1907. Franklin Roosevelt was a lifelong member of the American Ornithologists' Union—he sometimes escaped his wartime cares at the White House to watch birds.

Notes

February

Some species, like bluebirds and starlings, which actively defend a personal space all day, lose this inhibition against touching one another at dusk when they enter a flock's roosting cavity. One by one they enter the dark space, and end up snuggled and sometimes piled inside. Chickadees prefer sleeping alone. They often have bent tail feathers in winter from squeezing into tiny cavities.

13 People like to think of birds as supremely friendly creatures, cozying up side by side as in Disney cartoons. A few birds are almost that amiable—waxwings and Pine Grosbeaks defend virtually no territory against their own kind during the breeding season, and in winter most defend virtually no personal space, bumping up against one another without getting the least bit testy.

But most birds get as hostile as a New York subway rider when another violates their personal space. Siskins, redpolls, and Evening Grosbeaks crowd onto feeders, but each one stays at beak's length from the others or risks attack. Chickadees defend larger personal spaces. If a chickadee gets too close to one higher ranked within the flock, the offended party gargles, which, translated into English, might mean, "Get your tail off my turf!" Chickadees carry off seeds partly to reach shelter, and partly to distance themselves from feeder traffic. In spring, it takes elaborate courtship songs, displays, and rituals for one bird to momentarily trespass into another's space in order to do what birds and bees and educated fleas do best.

Notes

14 The avian heart is one of the most powerful pumps known. Like mammals, birds have a four-chambered heart, but a mammal heart is puny and weak compared to the heart of a similarly sized bird. A robin's heart beats 570 times every minute, a Blue-winged Teal's 1,000. An active Blue-throated Hummingbird's heart beats 1,260 times per minute. Our own rubythroat is too tiny to measure while active, but its heart races at 614 beats per minute while resting in a dark chamber—and probably more than doubles that when awake.

Birds also have high blood pressure. The systolic pressure for a starling is 180 mm, and for a canary is 220—a healthy human's systolic pressure should be much less. Blood rushes through a bird's body fast—it takes only about eleven seconds for it to make a complete circuit through the body of an adult turkey. High blood pressure pushes a bird's heart to the limits of mechanical safety. A cardinal that died after a territorial squabble was autopsied—it had no surface wounds at all, but did have a seven-millimeter hole in the ventricle, probably caused by the intense pressure built up during the excitement.

Hearts and birds go together. The poet Robinson Jeffers said to give your heart to hawks. Bill Cosby preferred a chicken heart. Othello wore his heart on his sleeve for daws to peck at—referring to European jackdaws, relatives of our crows. Edgar Allan Poe begged his raven to "take thy beak from out my heart." Christina Rosetti was definitely having a better day when she said that her heart was like a singing bird.

Notes

February

A Great Gray Owl's incredibly soft feathers not only allow it to sneak up on its prey unheard, they also allow it to listen to the mouse's every move as it flies in. Flapping with the noisy feathers of other birds would be as bothersome to a great gray as walking in corduroy pants with metal binoculars clunking against a zipper would be to a birder.

15 A Great Gray Owl perches at the very top of a spruce, its white bow tie catching my eye from a long distance. The spire doesn't bend or even sway under its weight, which is perplexing for a moment—this is, after all, the largest owl in the world. But despite its immense size and enormous presence, the great gray is a featherweight—literally. Adult females average a bare three pounds, males little more than two. Some emaciated birds in winter wither to three-quarters of a pound. The tremendous bulk comes from thick feathers, which insulate the owl from cold and protect it from shards of ice as it plunges through the snow's crust to grasp tunneling mice.

Great grays have relatively smaller eyes than most owls. They sacrifice a little visual acuity in exchange for enormous facial discs, which gather enough sound to pinpoint a mouse under eighteen inches of snow. When we find the characteristic imprint of wing feathers in the snow, we know exactly where a Great Gray Owl has found a sustaining morsel. The owl may have vanished, but it has left behind the finest snow angel on earth.

Notes

16 In the winter of 1992, during a Snowy Owl invasion, my father-in-law's life ebbs away. He is something of an owl himself, inscrutable, given to long silences, a Blue Jay magnet. Like an owl, he hates jays, and is equally ineffective at keeping them at bay. Perhaps it is his owlishness that I love so.

My husband, Russ, and I drive to Port Wing every other day to see him, and everywhere we see the owls—atop signs and rooftops in the city, along the winding country highway leading to his house. Some of these owls may die soon, too—they left their tundra home in starving desperation as the lemming population crashed. Owls are not savvy in the ways of man—some will be hit by cars, some electrocuted, some shot. Some may starve. Yet, even with death closing in, I thrill at these ghostly specters. Their tenacious hold on life led them to us, and will carry many home to the Arctic to recreate new life come spring. Coming home from the funeral, we pass an owl. Our eyes meet, we fellow travelers on this little planet. We wish her well as we, too, move on toward the rest of our lives.

Ancient Greeks loved the owl—their goddess Athena took an owl's form. But owls have portended death and misery in folklore spanning centuries and cultures. In 1894, W. J. Broderip explained, "Their retired habits, the desolate places that are their favorite haunts, their hollow hootings, fearful shrieks, serpent-like hissings and coffin-maker snappings, have helped to give them a bad eminence."

Notes

February

The chickadee's tiny heart, pumping 522 times a minute while sound asleep, over 1,000 times a minute when flitting about, will give out years before cholesterol has a chance to clog its threadlike blood vessels. Most chickadees die before their first birthday, and the oldest one on record lived only twelve years. That is no cause for sorrow—a chickadee lives so intensely that even the shortest life is a victory.

17 Winter in the North Woods is hard in the way that a raw diamond is hard. It takes a trained eye to see into the brilliant beauty within. The twinkling black eyes of a chickadee have this skill. Is the temperature forty below? A chickadee celebrates its amazing luck at being equipped with built-in down underwear. After weeks without fresh water, is a chickadee's throat dry? It splashes about in a trickle of melted snow on a rooftop and drinks it like champagne in a World Series victory locker room.

A chickadee seems to find good fortune in the very act of looking, perhaps knowing that a cheerful eye sees more clearly than one clouded with despair. A few frozen insects wedged in the crevices of tree bark constitute a Thanksgiving feast. Sunflower seed tables and suet bags provide dining fit for a king. Every minute it sucks in more than sixty-five breaths of fresh air and blinks over forty times. A chickadee weighs a mere ten grams—you could mail three of them with a single postage stamp—but the energy and enthusiasm within its tiny frame would dwarf Santa Claus.

Notes

18 With a February thaw, receding snow exposes a huge pink bird—at least three feet tall—with a long neck and heavy, down-curved bill. It never moves about, but stands firm on wiry legs. Its feathers must provide fine insulation—an old snow pile still sits atop its head. I don't need a field guide to know I am in the presence of the Plastic Lawn Flamingo, known to scientists everywhere as *Flamingo tackyvulgaris*.

The Plastic Lawn Flamingo was first documented in 1957 by inventor Don Featherstone at a Union Products plant in Massachusetts. Earlier sightings of enamel-painted plywood specimens have also been recorded. It's hard to predict where and when one will turn up, but its preferred habitat seems to be lawns and gardens. Unlike other flamingos, the plastic lawn species stays pink without shrimp or other crustaceans in its diet—as a matter of fact, ornithologists have yet to record it feeding at all. They've also never recorded it nesting or breeding. They don't understand everything about this enigmatic species, but have every confidence that, not even barring all-out nuclear war, the Plastic Lawn Flamingo is one bird that is definitely here to stay.

The Greater Flamingo, which optimistic birders search for in Florida, is actually a Caribbean species that appears in the United States only accidentally. Virtually all Greater Flamingos spotted in Florida each year have escaped from zoos and parks. John James Audubon saw several flocks of flamingos in the Keys in 1832, but couldn't get a shot at any. The one he painted in his *Birds of America* was collected in Cuba in 1838.

Notes

February

The Boreal Owl is high on the "most wanted" list of the American Birding Association. Kim Eckert and Terry Savaloja discovered the first nest reported in the lower forty-eight states in Cook County, Minnesota, in 1978. We know that boreals nest in northern Minnesota regularly, but most are seen in winter during *invasion* years. Many of these are starving. Some birders bring them mice, which the owls appreciate. No one asks the mouse's opinion.

Notes

19 A woman brings me a dead Boreal Owl she found on her porch. She has never seen a living one, and is heartbroken holding this one in her hand, wondering how it came to her home to die. I freeze it to send to wildlife biologist Steve Wilson, keeper of the official death toll—160 this season. To learn why the owls are dying, he sends many to the Raptor Center in St. Paul for autopsies. The answer is tragically simple—they're starving. Mouse populations are low, and two-foot snow depths may keep the few mice there are out of reach. A Great Gray Owl can plunge into deep snow to grasp mice, but the tiny boreal is simply not built for that.

If we hypothesize why the owls are dying, we still don't understand why they die on people's porches, and in basement window wells and garages. Ninety-four percent are found within seventy yards of a building, these secretive birds of remote forests. In 1906, A. W. Anthony wrote of Boreal Owls taking up quarters in abandoned igloos in Alaska. William Brewster wrote in 1925 of them wintering in barns at Lake Umbagog in Maine. Do these birds of wilderness see windows, doors, and igloo entrances simply as oversized tree cavities?

20 It is dusk. We were supposed to leave Grandma's house in Port Wing a half hour ago, but I've been stalling, hoping to see the Ruffed Grouse evening show. My delay tactics are rewarded—suddenly, five grouse skulk in from the dark woods, their necks outstretched as they scurry to the feeding station. Partridge are supposedly solitary birds, but this winter group comes en masse almost daily. As I call my children to the window, we flicker the drapes slightly, and the wary grouse retreat to the woods.

We wait—in less than a minute they return. One flaps hard and lurches to a platform feeder, but the rest remain on the ground. They scarf down sunflower seeds for five full minutes, and then one male puffs out his feathers, erects his ruff, and fans his tail. He struts for more than a minute, walking around and between the females on the ground, but they ignore him, apparently finding food more exciting. He does inspire the other male to fly down from the feeder and get into the same mode. Suddenly two deer walk tentatively toward the corn feeder, and the grouse disappear as silently and warily as they came.

In winter, Ruffed Grouse grow projections on their toes. These probably serve less as snowshoes than as grippers for hanging onto icy branches and slippery terrain. Their summer diet—insects, berries, fruits, nuts, and mushrooms—changes in winter to male aspen flower buds. To adapt, their digestive system also changes, as intestines and two intestinal branches called caeca grow measurably. Bacteria in the caeca produce enzymes that break down cellulose in the woody food.

Notes

February

Henry David Thoreau wrote of the crow in his 1856 journal, "This bird sees the white man come and the Indian withdraw, but it withdraws not. Its untamed voice is still heard above the tinkling of the forge . . . It remains to remind us of aboriginal nature."

21 Suddenly crows appear everywhere, cawing and flying about. A few always winter on Peabody Street, but this sudden rush of migrants provides definite proof that spring will arrive soon—well, certainly within the next two or three months.

During most of the year, people associate crows with evil, or hate them for eating baby robins, or shoot them for stealing corn, but today just about everyone welcomes them, North Country's true harbingers of spring. I often wonder why people hate crows so. True, their "caw caw" hardly qualifies as an ethereal song, especially at six in the morning, their plumage could use a bit more color, and they eat baby birds, but if that's sufficient explanation, why do we like bears? Of course, if bears were as abundant as crows, they would be equally hated, but I suspect that our problem with crows is more deep-rooted. These sly, adventurous, opportunistic, greedy, intelligent, sociable creatures are attracted to glitter, devoted to friends and family, and suspicious of strangers. When we humans look at a crow, perhaps our discomfort stems from a feeling that we are looking through a mirror into the human soul.

Notes

22 What's so stupid about a bird brain? Ornithologists and psychologists constantly devise elaborate experiments to test just how intelligent birds are. In one experiment, a jackdaw (a European relative of crows and ravens) was trained to open the lids of little boxes to retrieve treats. From a selection of eight boxes, the jackdaw was supposed to open lids until it had exactly five treats and then return to its cage. In one trial, all the treats were placed in the first five boxes in the order 1,2,1,0,1. The jackdaw raised the lids of the first three boxes, received four treats, and returned to its cage. The investigator was about to record a failure, since it had taken fewer than five, when the bird suddenly returned to the boxes. It stopped at the first and bowed once, at the second and bowed twice, and at the third it bowed once again. Then it checked the fourth box, which had no treat, went to the fifth box, took the fifth treat, and returned to its cage for good. The bird's bowing movements were likened to a child's moving lips while counting.

Tests to measure intelligence in nonhumans are difficult to interpret. For example, one pigeon maintained a pecking response for food even though it was rewarded only once every 875 pecks. B. F. Skinner thought this was remarkable evidence of the pigeon's superior memory and intelligence, but as good an argument could be made that any bird that pecks 875 times for a single piece of food is pretty stupid, or woefully hungry.

Notes

February

Birds have immunity to many human diseases. Thrush, a fungus disease of the mouth that human babies get, is not found in real thrushes. Pigeons are supposed to have pigeon toes. Airsickness and seasickness are not bird problems. Birds have no appendix to develop appendicitis, no teeth to decay, no nose to run. And no bird has ever developed tennis elbow, writer's cramp, or jock itch.

23 Influenza arrives on Peabody Street. I'm too sick even to read—all I can muster the strength to do is curl up on the sofa and watch old movies. My favorite actor, "Jimmy the Raven" (who is actually a crow), performs in Frank Capra films—he plays Uncle Billy's pet in *It's a Wonderful Life*, and is practically a member of the family in *You Can't Take It with You*. I hope Jimmy the Raven isn't the crow that sits atop Norman Bates's mantle, stuffed, in *Psycho*.

I watch Hitchcock's *The Birds*. He uses a few crow actors, but the crows flying up in attack are fakes, flapping way too fast for any aerodynamically sound corvid and making calls recorded in a tropical aviary. Hitchcock uses stuffed crows as well as live actors in the most ominous scene of all, where they gather in silent vigil on the schoolhouse stairs. I think I recognize Norman Bates's stuffed bird among them. Real actors play in the gull attack scenes, but it's easy to picture some guy behind the camera tossing French fries to them. Small wonder *The Birds* gets a "two beaks down" rating from movie reviewers Siskin and Abert.

Notes

24 As I recover from the flu, I consider the many diseases birds get. Pneumonia and bronchitis are usually side effects of a fungus disease called aspergillosis. Mold spores lodge in the bird's lungs and air sacs, slowly killing it. At least forty-eight species, from Bald Eagles to songbirds, are vulnerable. The birds gasp and wheeze but don't lose their appetites, so they spread the disease at feeding stations before they die. Once aspergillosis attacks, there's no cure. To prevent it, set out only clean seed. If it gets moldy, burn or dispose of it where no birds can find it. And keep feeders clean. Infected birds spread the disease through their droppings.

Perhaps the worst bacterial disease birds get is botulism. In one Oregon lake in 1925, botulism killed a million birds, mostly waterfowl. Botulism occasionally kills feeder birds, but the bacterium is mainly found in soil and water. Parrot fever, also known as psittacosis or chlamydiosis, can be transmitted from birds to humans, but it's more often found in captive than wild birds.

Birdsongs betray the fact that "Little House on the Prairie" was filmed in California. Northwestern Crows and a sapsucker calling in the background during the climactic chase scene in *Stakeout* give a touch of authenticity to the film. The movie *Far North* was panned by most critics, but birders were pleased by the authentic bird calls, provided by the Cornell Laboratory of Ornithology's Library of Sounds.

Notes

February

We don't often see sick birds at a feeder, but if one shows up, it is always best to stop feeding immediately. The more birds gather together, the more likely the disease will spread.

25 Viruses treat birds as cruelly as they do humans. Encephalitis, quail bronchitis, and duck plague are all horrible avian diseases. Newcastle disease has rare outbreaks—in the summer of 1992, it killed hundreds of pelicans and cormorants in Minnesota and Wisconsin. Birds get bird pox, but apparently not chicken pox.

Birds also suffer from internal parasites. Those birds eating fish, snails, or earthworms get the widest variety of worms, but even birds with extremely limited diets, like nighthawks, can host tapeworms.

Birds develop cancer, heart disease, and other afflictions that also plague humans. Avian metabolism is so rapid that sick birds usually die quickly, and those weakened by disease or parasites are often caught and eaten by predators before the disease progresses far. That may partly explain why the life expectancy of an American Robin is only a year and two months, while the life expectancy of an American human is a good seventy years. Whatever it is that gives chicken soup its curative powers must be a lot more beneficial to humans than it is to chickens.

Notes

26 Ornithologists once believed that Neotropical migrants maintained territories only during the breeding season; they thought that birds floated about their tropical wintering grounds as free as well, as free as birds. But it turns out that it's a jungle out there. The only way many of our Northland birds have any chance of surviving the season, strangers in a strange land, is to defend a territory just as aggressively as they did up here. A good winter territory provides an abundance of riches—food and water, of course, but also a piece of real estate that the bird knows intimately. Knowing every nook and cranny to slip into when a hawk cruises over is mighty useful.

Birds defend their breeding territory in pairs. In the tropics in winter, they own and defend property as individuals. Studies on thrushes indicate that individuals with winter territories are much more likely to survive than those without. As deforestation continues inexorably, our birds compete for ever-shrinking tracts of ever more degraded habitat. Small wonder that, come spring, many never return.

Most people feel helpless to change the course of rain forest destruction. Organizations at the forefront of tropical conservation help make our voices heard, purchase critical habitat, and work with landowners and governments to find practical alternatives to habitat destruction. These organizations include the International Council for Bird Preservation, the Smithsonian Migratory Bird Center, The Nature Conservancy, and the Environmental Defense Fund.

Notes

February

Fred arrived at my house in June 1991, after crashing into a telephone wire. His wing was shattered at the bend. Because adult nighthawks require frequent hand feeding every day in captivity, those with bad injuries are routinely euthanized at most rehab centers. Caring for them isn't easy, but their gentle, subtly affectionate ways and comical habits as they waddle about like Charlie Chaplin more than repay the effort.

Notes

27 Fred the Nighthawk attends a Cub Scout pack meeting. The school gymnasium echoes with noisy children, but he's used to it. He gives me his cocker spaniel look—he's expressive for a nighthawk—and I pop him a thawed cricket. After the flag ceremony and awards, boys crowd the floor near my table. They're supposed to sit in chairs, but they're drawn like magnets to this handsome, unfamiliar bird.

Fred is named after television's Mr. Rogers because of his shy, gentle nature and slow, deliberate ways. I know he's an adult male because of his white throat patch and tail markings. His nocturnal eyes are huge. I pass around a nighthawk skull—the enormous eye sockets leave little room for brain. When I offer Fred a cricket, his capacious mouth amazes the boys. I know he flew to Brazil and back at least once before being injured because that's where nighthawks winter.

The boys line up to pet him. They stroke gently, avoiding his eyes, but Fred wearies after twenty or so strangers have touched him. He waddles around, turning his back on them. The boys continue petting as he looks at me, patiently suffering the touch of forty-five boys and their parents. He's earned extra crickets tonight.

28 A February thaw breezes in, long enough to confuse American Robins. Most migrate along the 38-degree isotherm—the line along which day-night temperatures average 38 degrees—but a few move when it's even colder, and these first-runners suddenly appear on lawns and in cattail marshes. Assuming they survive, they'll get first choice of prime real estate come spring. In years when thaws are followed by mild conditions, the earliest migrants raise extra babies, maximizing reproduction; in years when early migrants succumb, the robins predisposed to migrate later have the advantage; and in the long run, both groups keep their genes alive. Many robins are flexible enough to turn around and head south if bad weather returns.

People phone me, concerned about these new arrivals. Robins survive long periods eating nothing but berries—these first birds invariably show up near mountain ashes or crab apples, and usually don't need dietary supplements. Considering how close to people robins live, they're surprisingly wary, but some condescend to visit feeders for jelly, raisins, cranberries and other fruits, and even mealworms.

Brief mild spells are great for finches and chickadees. They often disappear from feeders for a time, exploring other food sources. They get a sudden supply of fresh drinking water, and, since they're not burning as many calories as when it's colder, they replenish fat reserves against the April Fools' blizzard yet to come.

Notes

March

New birds seen beginning today are officially spring migrants, according to the editors of *American Birds.* Equinox watchers wait three weeks before they announce the season. Dandelions, understanding the true meaning of spring better than ornithologists or astronomers, hold off until April or even May. We bide our time, eager for the return of warblers and hummingbirds, but dreading the farewell to winter owls and finches.

1 Seven snowbirds gather beneath my feeder, scratching out a meager meal of spilled seed as snow swirls about. These juncoes, described by Thoreau as "leaden skies above, snow below," are more pleasing than a March lion, a March lamb, or even a March hare. Their call notes brighten the snowy hush as gaily as jingle bells.

When I bring out a bucket of sunflower seeds, they fly into the lilac bushes, all but one flashing white tail streamers. This one has lost its tail—to a cat? a shrike? the Peabody Street Merlin? As the days go by, I'll watch new feathers grow in. One researcher measured the rate of a Dark-eyed Junco's tail growth as 1.1 millimeters per day. I can't verify the statistic, but any new life in March is welcome, even new feather life. The juncoes watch me fill the feeders, the wind ruffling their feathers as they sit in the bare bushes. They don't come near—no self-respecting junco would ever alight on a human—but they zip in and resume feeding before I reach the porch, and I feel important and useful. It's almost as if they needed me as much as I need them.

2 When I was in high school, I found a tiny dead bird on a bustling Chicago Loop sidewalk. It was exquisite, with a lovely soft brown back, a snow white breast dotted black, an orange crown with black border, and a perfect circle of tiny white feathers around each eye. I shrouded it in napkins from a nearby McDonald's and placed it in a wastebasket, wondering what it was and how on earth it came to be in downtown Chicago.

Several years later, when my mother-in-law asked my husband for gift ideas for me, he remembered me talking of my grandpa's pet canaries, and suggested binoculars and a field guide. When I opened my first Peterson guide that Christmas morning, the first page I turned to showed the Ovenbird. That's what that bird must have been! And it was possible to see one alive! The book showed hundreds of birds I had never imagined—anhingas and gallinules and kinglets. Apparently it was also possible to see exotic "zoo" birds in the wild—pelicans and eagles and owls! I couldn't explain why, but suddenly I needed to see every single bird in that book. My course was set.

Ovenbirds and other warblers often crash into tall buildings. These tiny nocturnal migrants, which use star patterns to guide them through the darkness, are attracted like moths to bright lights, especially on foggy nights. The little Ovenbird lying in downtown Chicago was probably migrating along the Lake Michigan shoreline when the city lights and skyscrapers disoriented it, luring it to its death.

Notes

March

Recordings help beginners learn bird sounds, but the vast array of songs and calls on most recordings is overwhelming in long listening sessions. It's best to buy a record or compact disc, and then tape onto a cassette five or ten songs you're most interested in, putting easily confused ones beside each other. After you master these, tape a new batch.

3 When I decided to learn birds, I knew robins, cardinals, sparrows, and nothing else. I devoured the Peterson guide, Golden guide, and *A Guide to Bird Watching* by Joseph Hickey. I bought a field notebook, and finally, on March 2, 1975, set out to be a birdwatcher.

I walked every trail of Michigan State University's Baker Woodlot, watching and listening as hard as I could, but for over an hour I couldn't perceive a thing. Finally, a little bird flitted in and allowed me to study it from beak to tail. I rifled through my Golden guide from page one until I came to some likely suspects on page 214. I held the page with my finger and continued to the end, just in case, and then went back. I found two identical possibilities. I wasn't sure where southern Michigan was on the range maps, but the book said you could tell the two apart by voice. I listened hard to this amiable and cooperative creature, then hurried to the university library to consult recordings. Eureka—an exact match! The number one bird on my life list—the Black-capped Chickadee.

Notes

4 One morning as I fill the feeders, little pieces of fluff float through the air. At first I think my aspen is flowering, but it's way too early for that. I trace the fluff to its source—there atop the dead balsam fir in the back of the yard, a Merlin is eating a redpoll, and the light wind carries soft gray insulating feathers through the air.

This Merlin spent the winter in our neighborhood. In January and February it visited my yard every five or six days, sometimes nabbing a bird at one of my feeders, but more often missing. Now it comes first thing every morning, and it has developed a strategy that vastly improves its success—it sneaks up Peabody Street from the west, staying hidden from view until it suddenly rips at top speed around the corner of the house into the east yard, where redpolls and siskins collect. They never know what hit them. The Merlin cuts a dashing figure as it bullets past, and watching it eat so hungrily, I'm glad it found breakfast. But sometimes I wish that old adage were true—if you really are what you eat, redpoll-eating Merlins would quickly become vegetarians.

The origin of the Merlin's name is unrelated to King Arthur's wizard. It comes from the Old French *esmerillon*, referring to a female bird in falconry. Merlins are found in forests throughout northern Europe and Asia as well as America.

Notes

March

Woodpeckers are courting now. Something in the March breeze sets their hearts a-thumping and their beaks a-tapping, and they slowly overcome their inhibitions in order to reproduce. These birds are so solitary and staid that I can't help but wonder how baby woodpeckers ever got started in the first place—in the same way, I sometimes wonder where baby Norwegians come from.

5 Thick ice still covers Lake Superior, but cawing crows and trilling juncoes guarantee that spring is near. My pair of White-breasted Nuthatches spent the winter studiedly avoiding each other. They'd come to the feeders at the same times each day, but could hardly be said to be hanging out together—they reminded me of high school kids with a crush on each other, too shy to be caught looking in the other's direction. Now they're at the first-date stage—they sometimes sit on the feeder at the same time, but the moment one looks up and sees the other looking back, it flies off in a hurry.

Red-breasted Nuthatches are carrying off tiny chunks of suet into the spruce trees, wedging them in the bark. My friend Koni tells of some redbreasts she once had that stuffed a birdhouse half-full of suet.

The Peabody Street Merlin rips across the yard every morning. Once it grabs a redpoll and eats it in the box elder as Sneakers, a too-tame Blue Jay, watches out the window in horror. From that day forward she refuses to go outside ever again.

Notes

6 I was hungry for new birds. In tropical Minneapolis, redwings have already been sighted, but Lake Superior, the world's largest air conditioner, slows migration. Hoping for something new along the shore, I wandered, like Wordsworth, lonely as a cloud that floats on high o'er vales and woes, when all at once I saw a crowd, a host of cold and daffy crows, beside the lake, beneath the trees, fluttering and cawing in the breeze.

Yes, the only migrants I could find were crows. Some were in flight, but most gathered on a slab of decaying ice, picking up bits of dead fish and other aquatic debris. They were quiet, but the lake creaked and groaned, huge ice floes smashing and grinding one another in mutual destruction, geysers of sparkling water spurting up occasionally between fault lines. An eagle fed alongside the crows, where the ice was safe. Crows and an eagle are hardly robins, but they do hold the promise of warmer days ahead. So oft, when on my couch I lie in vacant or in pensive mood, they flash upon that inward eye, which is the bliss of solitude. And then my heart with pleasure fills—these crows are harbingers of daffodils.

Although not many southern migrants are back, hundreds of Common Redpolls, and one or two Hoary Redpolls, gather at feeders, many on their way back to the Far North from southern Minnesota and Iowa. They are spring's advance agents, preparing the way for the big show to come.

Notes

March

Owls breed late in winter, and to protect eggs from freezing, the female begins incubation as soon as she lays the first egg. Most birds don't incubate until their clutch is complete—their babies develop together and appear to be the same age. But owlets develop and hatch at different times, so a family ranges from small to large, like Russian nesting dolls. When food is scarce, only the biggest survive.

7 Few new birds are around yet, so on March evenings when the wind is still, we listen for owls. They'll call more often in April, but now is when we need them.

The Great Horned Owl has soft, mellow hootings, often accented on the third "hoo." This huge owl and the smaller Long-eared Owl are the only ones in North Country with tufts of feathers on their heads. The Great Horned Owl has a catlike silhouette, and even its fiercely yellow eyes are catlike. We usually find it by listening—at night for hoots, during daytime for cursing crows.

Barred Owls have a higher-pitched, strident hoot that follows the rhythm pattern, "Who cooks for you? Who cooks for you-all?" The barred is a bit smaller than the horned, with solid brown eyes and a round head.

If we're in the right place at exactly the right time, we may hear the deep, resonant hoots of a Great Gray Owl, given in steady rhythm—a simple but evocative "Hoo, hoo, hoo, hoo, hoo." These wondrous birds breed in bogs, nesting in abandoned hawk, raven, or crow nests and sometimes on platforms provided by humans. Hearing one even from afar infuses us with a feeling of joy and beauty.

Notes

8 The Pileated Woodpecker, which inspired the creation of Woody, is the most impressive woodpecker remaining in North America. Few people forget the first time they see this enormous bird, with its pterodactylean aspect and striking black, white, and red plumage.

Although the logcock is associated with wilderness and mature forests, it appears regularly in residential areas, often feasting on the bugs that are in turn feasting on diseased elms. As aspen forests are managed for shorter and shorter rotations, pileateds sometimes search for the aging trees they need in towns. Banded pileateds in New York have survived nine and ten years; one in Minneapolis lived to be thirteen.

These shy, wary birds were hunted for market in the eighteenth and nineteenth centuries despite their formic acid flavor. John James Audubon, who sampled most of the birds that he painted, labeled their meat tough and "extremely unpalatable," apparently from the pileated's fondness for bitter-tasting carpenter ants. Pileateds sometimes eat so many of these ants that stricken trees actually recover.

The word *pileated* comes from the Latin *pileus*, for a round, brimless skullcap worn by ancient Romans. If you pronounce the word "pill-le-a-ted," don't look it up in the *American Heritage Dictionary*—it isn't there. *Webster's New World Dictionary* equivocates, listing "pie-le-a-ted" first but also giving "pill-le-a-ted" as an acceptable alternative. Say it either way to the bird and it will fly away.

Notes

March

9 Spring and birds are on everyone's mind. We're invited to a first-grade classroom to talk.

We ask the children what makes a bird, and the first guess is wings. Insects and bats have wings, too, so we ask for something unique to birds. Eggs? No—insects, fish, amphibians, most reptiles, and even duck-billed platypuses lay eggs. But bird eggs do have a different kind of shell—calcified and brittle. One child shyly suggests feathers. For their size and weight, feathers are the strongest material known. Every bird has feathers, and no other creatures in the universe, except perhaps angels, have these wonderful and specialized outgrowths of skin.

I show them a nighthawk skeleton, featherlight itself, with hollow bones strengthened with internal struts, reduced tail bones, and elegantly long, flat, thin, jointed ribs, each reinforcing its neighbor. Even the paper-thin skull bones are reinforced. Children see beauty in such functional form—the beauty that inspired early American ornithologist Elliot Coues to call the avian skull a "poem in bone."

Notes

10 Bohemian Waxwings are heading north again, and I'll miss them mightily. A waxwing once lived with me for three weeks. It had been picked up, drunk and injured, by a boy in a shopping mall parking lot.

Waxwings need other waxwings as surely as the sky needs stars. This one took raisins and bits of apple from my hand and often perched on my shoulder, gently preening my hair, but as its foot healed it spent hours gazing out the window, making soft little call notes, like E.T. yearning for home. One warmish morning, I took off the paper wrap protecting its tail feathers, and two-year-old Tommy and I brought it outside.

Early spring music—the zip of Pine Siskins and the trickling gurgle of melting snow—filled the air. It perched on my finger for a minute, then flew to a maple, where it preened wings and tail, perhaps cleaning off the taint of captivity. We watched it for a time, then went inside, Tommy wistfully saying, "Bye-bye, Waxwing." In an hour it was gone. That afternoon a small flock appeared in the yard, and one peeked in the window at Tommy and me. We waved at it and smiled.

On March 10, 1972, crows, ravens, owls, and hawks came under the protection of the Migratory Bird Treaty Act. It is now illegal to possess any wild bird eggs or feathers, or to keep any wild bird—even an injured or orphaned crow—without a permit. Sometimes that seems cruel or unfair, but without training, people do more harm than good handling wild creatures. Our declining songbirds would be even worse off without this law.

Notes

March

Falconers note that peregrines and Merlins single out white pigeons in a flock—they're probably easier to follow on high-speed chases. Also, pigments give feathers structural strength—pure white feathers are often brittle and subject to fraying. Albino eyes usually see poorly, especially in bright light. Albinos are often harassed by their own kind, and may not be accepted as mates because of their odd color patterns. No wonder few albinos reach adulthood.

11 A partial albino Common Redpoll appears at my feeder—a beautiful little bird, with white wing patches, whitish head and sides, snow white rump, and all-white breast and back tinted with a faint wash of pink. Its crown is ruby red, and the few streaks it has are medium colored—too dark to make it a Hoary Redpoll.

Albinism appears to be caused in most cases by a recessive gene that causes a shortage of the enzyme tyrosinase. The rarest result of this is total albinism, with absolutely no pigment in eyes, skin, or feathers. Partial albinism is more common—some patches are white or pale, but other areas are colored normally. The white patches can be symmetric, as in my redpoll, or asymmetric.

As of April 1965, albinism had been documented in 304 species of North American birds, from every taxonomic order. The most frequent reports were in the robin and House Sparrow, but even in these, albinos are rare. Ornithologists who banded thirty thousand birds in a ten-year period found only seventeen albinos among them—that's only a fiftieth of one percent of these lovely jewels.

Notes

12 One morning in 1986, I spied an oddity among the scores of Evening Grosbeaks at my feeder. I almost rubbed my binoculars in disbelief when I realized I was looking at a *gynandromorph*—a bird half male and half female. The left side appeared to be in perfect female plumage, the right almost perfectly male, though the tail was pale and the forehead wasn't as black as on other males. I studied it for five minutes, but then the flock flew off in a flurry of wings and I lost it. The male wing was probably longer than the female wing—I wish I'd seen how it flew, but the bird never appeared again. There's a gynandromorph Evening Grosbeak at the Bell Museum in Minneapolis, but it no longer flies.

Unlike mammals, female birds have one X and one O chromosome, while males have two Xs. Gynandromorphs probably develop as the fertilized egg first divides, if one side somehow loses its X chromosome. Avian sex characteristics are genetic, not affected by hormones in the blood—gynandromorphism could never occur in humans. It may be possible for gynandromorphs to self-fertilize their own eggs, but unless one sticks around for more than five minutes, I'll never know.

Evening Grosbeak bills are green now, somehow triggering mutual feeding between mates. After nesting, when grosbeak families visit feeders in large flocks, the young seem to know that any bird with a green beak will feed them. I've watched a single hungry youngster beg from and be fed by four different adult males and two females, all with green beaks, while it ignored immatures, fully grown but with dull chalky beaks.

Notes

March

13 On March 13, 1904, a storm hit Minnesota and Iowa. Thomas Sadler Roberts recorded the destruction:

> The night was very dark but not cold, and a heavy, wet snow was falling with but little wind stirring. Migrating Longspurs came from the Iowa prairies in a vast horde, and from about 11 P.M. until near morning incredible numbers met their deaths in and about villages by flying against buildings, electric light poles and wires, and by dashing forcibly onto the frozen ground and ice, as in their wet, snow-laden, and bewildered condition they whirled and circled about in aimless flight . . . On two small lakes, with an aggregate area of about two square miles, the ice was still intact and nearly bare from the melting snow. This exposed surface was thickly and evenly strewn with dead Longspurs . . . A conservative calculation showed that there were at least 750,000 dead Longspurs lying on these two lakes alone! The adjoining uplands, the streets of the town, and the roofs of the buildings were strewn with bodies in equal numbers. And this was only one locality in the extensive area throughout which the birds were killed.

T. S. Roberts, shocked by the deaths of millions of Lapland Longspurs in a storm, wrote in *The Birds of Minnesota*, "One hundred of the bodies were . . . dissected . . . All had died by violence, chiefly crushed skulls, broken necks, and internal hemorrhages . . . The stomachs of all were entirely empty, though the bodies were fat and in good general condition. This lack of food may have been a contributing factor in the destruction of the birds."

Notes

14 "The prettiest and jauntiest of our Hawks, and yet no prig" is how early American ornithologist Elliot Coues described the American Kestrel. William Brewster, another nineteenth-century scientist, called it "most light-hearted and frolicsome." Kestrels return to the North Country in March after wintering in the southern states and Mexico. Driving to Port Wing, we usually count at least a dozen, and even children caught up in the escapades of Mario Brothers look up. Kestrels hunt in open country, perching on dead trees, utility wires, and fences in the characteristic pose of falcons, "hunched up and frowning," showing their rufous tails. In flight they often hover, beating wings furiously to remain in one spot while studying the ground below.

Grasshoppers make up the bulk of the kestrel's summer diet, but in winter it takes mostly mice and birds. As with all birds of prey, the female is larger and more aggressive than the male, but even she weighs little more than four ounces. Kestrels usually nest in old flicker holes, but sometimes accept nest boxes. A pair of these lovely little falcons is as welcome at a farm or country home as spring itself.

Early settlers called the American Kestrel the sparrow hawk, after a common backyard hawk of England, but the two are actually in different families. The word *kestrel* probably comes from a French word referring to a leper's clicket—a clapper used for warning people of a passing leper. The name was originally given to the European Kestrel for its noisy call.

Notes

March

Disney birds somehow take wing even though violating every aerodynamic law. And most Disney songbirds have zygodactylous feet, with two toes facing forward and two behind like cuckoos, owls, woodpeckers, and parrots, rather than the normal anisodactyl songbird conformation of three toes in front and one behind. Biochemical studies of mitochondrial DNA would elucidate the taxonomy of these interesting creatures—if only we could capture a specimen for analysis.

Notes

15 The crows of March turn my thoughts to Disney. Snow White's wicked stepmother has a crow with a red bill. A yellow-billed raven perches on Maleficent's shoulder in *Sleeping Beauty.* Dumbo gets off the ground with the help of kindly yellow-billed crows and their magic feather. American crows and ravens have black bills, yet Disney corvids are recognizable despite these bold colors. I once developed a theory that the artists were influenced by the Yellow-billed Magpie, which is found in California, and wrote to the Disney archives to learn the truth about this important taxonomic issue.

Ward Kimball, who gave life to Dumbo's avian friends and directed the Oscar-winning Disney film *It's Tough to Be a Bird,* answered that, to his knowledge, none of the animators had ever heard of a Yellow-billed Magpie. He said, "We exercise artistic license, and yellow looks very good with black. We're not ornithologists, and we go with whatever looks good and reads best against our backgrounds." Mr. Kimball said black bills get lost in shadows, and commented that nobody ever asked this question before. Taxonomists must not be doing their jobs.

16 Eugene Schieffelen, a New York drug manufacturer in the late 1800s, thought America's bird life needed a bit of high culture, and so he organized a club with the aim of importing to America every bird mentioned by William Shakespeare. Most of the introductions didn't take. Robin redbreasts don't migrate and couldn't survive the New York winter. Other birds couldn't compete with native birds or the House Sparrows that already had been imported to hundreds of cities.

But on March 16, 1890, a day that will go down in infamy, Schieffelen's club released sixty European Starlings in Central Park. Within weeks a pair was nesting under the eaves of the American Museum of Natural History. The next spring, the club released another forty starlings as a backup.

Descendants of the original two New York flocks reached Michigan and Wisconsin in the early 1920s, and Minnesota in 1929. From that odd Elizabethan-inspired beginning over one hundred years ago, starlings have become one of the most abundant species on the continent, numbering in the hundreds of millions.

"I'll have a starling shall be taught to speak nothing but 'Mortimer,'" spoken by Hotspur in *Henry IV: Part I*, is the only starling reference ever made by Shakespeare, who apparently confused it with its close relative the mynah. Starlings can learn to speak, but not to repeat one word over and over. We probably wouldn't have even heard of the starling today if only Shakespeare had developed better bird identification skills.

Notes

March

Some people close down their feeding stations when the weather gets nice. Warm weather—anything above freezing—allows microbes to multiply, and fungus on sunflower seeds can cause aspergillosis. Raking up seed shell piles beneath feeders is important when sparrows and other ground feeders are returning. Keeping feeders going in spring helps birds stressed by migration, and gives us wonderful opportunities to watch them.

17 It's time to set out birdhouses before migrants arrive. One or two Purple Martins may scout out conditions, and if they don't find suitable accommodations, they'll go elsewhere. Martins and other swallows are becoming alarmingly rare—they're losing the competition against starlings and House Sparrows, wetlands are disappearing at a horrifying rate, and mosquito abatement programs may both poison them and deplete their food sources. Setting out birdhouses is a small gesture, but at least it's something.

Bluebirds were decimated in the 1950s and 1960s by pesticides, farmers switching to metal fence posts instead of wood, competition from starlings for nest cavities, and small farms with orchards and plenty of edge giving way to huge monocultures. Bluebird trails solved the nest cavity crisis, and DDT was banned in 1972, so bluebirds are returning once again. We set out their houses in twos, ten or twenty feet apart, in open areas. Tree Swallows usually take one box, but are territorial enough to chase other swallows from the second box. Bluebirds don't compete for flying insects, and the swallows leave them alone.

Notes

18 Perhaps to lighten their burden as they fly, birds never carry watches or calendars. Instead, they've developed an internal timepiece, which may not be accurate to the exact second but is guaranteed to last a lifetime—unless an ornithologist tinkers with it.

Scientists kept European birds called Chaffinches in enclosures, keeping track of their activities. When light and temperature were the same as outdoors, the birds were active by day. When the chambers were kept light all the time and maintained at a constant temperature, the birds' schedule hardly changed, even after months. Their clocks ran a little fast—they became active a bit earlier and went to sleep earlier each day—but the daily rhythm was strikingly accurate.

When ornithologists surgically remove the pineal gland from a House Sparrow's forebrain, its activity rhythm is abolished, but returns if another sparrow's pineal gland is transplanted, even into the anterior chamber of the eye instead of where it belongs. The sparrow now lives in its donor's time zone, and the poor donor is dispatched to never-never land.

Ornithologists presume that melatonin, a hormone produced by the pineal gland, is the essential substance that drives a bird's internal clock. When starlings are kept in continuous dim light after their pineal glands are removed, they can be synchronized to a normal pattern if they receive daily injections of melatonin.

Notes

March

Cliff Swallows traditionally return to San Juan Capistrano today. Depending on weather, they may arrive at the mission a week before St. Joseph's feast day, but Californians dutifully direct their eyes downward until March nineteenth. The swallows are said to have taken residence at the mission in 1776. Aristotle's one swallow that "maketh not a summer" was probably the same species as our Barn Swallow, found throughout Europe and Asia as well as America.

Notes

19 The pulse of life in the bird world is driven by the rhythms of the sun. Birds away from the equator experience changing day lengths as the year progresses. As days grow longer in North Country, birds awaken earlier each morning, and have more hours to fill with activities other than feeding. Although day length triggers annual rhythmic behaviors like mating, nesting, and migrating, some species also have an internal calendar. Starlings kept in constant day length indoors for three and a half years still molted and bred in the proper season, without even marking the passing days on the walls of their prison to keep track—their internal calendar kept them on schedule. At least fifteen species have an internal *circannual rhythm*, but many others do not.

To fuel long-distance flights, migratory birds deposit layers of fat with a precise annual rhythm. But the timing of actual flights is affected by weather and may vary by weeks. Males usually migrate before females. The earliest males get the best territories, while the females get a later, safer passage.

20 Tension mounts in the Northland as winter and spring duke it out in the boxing match of the year. Winter takes the opening rounds, out-slugging the more tentative spring, but winter always shows its strength too early in the match. Spring conserves its energy until the final rounds, when it simply melts the opposition. The decisive blow won't come until April, or even May, but come it will.

The tension of the match is too much for many people, who light out for Florida or Texas. But redpolls that made it through the worst of winter on their own now crowd feeders like spectators in an arena. Every day the sun's rays grow stronger, luring more avian cheerleaders in for the final rounds. In plains and pastures, the sweet tinkling of Horned Larks is heard over the roar of the north wind. Snow Buntings gather on farm fields. Eagles fish in patches of open water. Barred Owls are cookin' up a storm. At the start of each day, chickadees cheer spring on and Downy Woodpeckers drum out the score. So far winter's ahead, but spring will soon triumph. I'm betting on it.

Pine Siskins seem lost in their own little world right now, like Rick and Ilsa as Paris surrenders. As the tiny finches pair up, they feed each other with the tender awkwardness of high school kids just learning how to kiss. The fundamental things apply, so here's looking at you, kids.

Notes

March

One or two robins appear on exposed brown patches of lawn where the snow has melted. They run on quick legs and cock their heads, studying the ground for clues about the pulsing subterranean world of earthworms. Even underground the word spreads—spring is coming!

21 In March or April, as the ice sheet on Lake Superior decays, the match between spring and winter can be watched directly from shore. When the wind blows from the south, the mass of ice piles up in Duluth, creaking and thundering, and gulls and crows gather to feast on odd bits of fish and other debris that the lake spews up between cracks. One clear, magical day, the ice sheet disappears. The restless blue water churns up our hopes, but before the referee can count to ten, the wind pushes the gray mass back our way. Even as it sloshes back and forth between shores for weeks, grinding shoreline rocks and our dreams of Floridian days ahead, the ice mass shrinks. One morning soon, Tree Swallows will swoop in on a southern breeze. The comb-scraping trills of chorus frogs will be heard in country puddles of an evening. Dots of dandelions will be as welcome as crocuses, for a time. Buds will grow fat on trees, and burst open just as spring lets loose with its knockout punch. Instead of seeing stars, winter's eyes will spin with the reeling flights of swifts, warblers, and orioles. The winner, and still champion—spring!

Notes

22 Spring is a time of regeneration, and no bird takes part in this annual ritual as lustily as the Mallard. Somewhere south of here right now, a duck is trying to get away from a pack of bachelor drakes. Her mate may fend them off, but chances are he's too busy chasing another female to even notice her predicament. According to a 1987 study, 48 percent of Mallard broods in a wild population were fathered by more than one male. Ducklings all in a row are as likely to be half-sisters and half-brothers as full-blooded siblings.

In captivity, drake Mallards have bred with every duck species, even those in different genera and subfamilies. There are countless cases of wild duck hybrids looking like patchwork quilts. The only other birds with such frequent hybridizations are hummingbirds and birds-of-paradise. In all three families, males are gaudily colored and don't necessarily recognize females of their own species, so mate selection is the responsibility of females. None of these males take part in nest building or caring for the young—they leave child rearing to the Murphy Browns of the bird world.

Mallards range naturally throughout much of the northern hemisphere, and have been introduced to most of the rest of the world. They take their name from the Old French word for male or masculinity and the often pejorative "-ard" suffix as in drunkard or sluggard. Etymologically, Mallards epitomize the worst of masculinity, but anything that starts out as a baby duck can't be all bad.

Notes

March

One of the cheeriest sounds of the early spring woods is so quiet and high-pitched that most people never notice it. The grace note of the Golden-crowned Kinglet sounds a bit like the high-pitched "tsleep" flight note of chickadees, but the kinglet's note is invariably given in couplets or triplets. Kinglets are easy to attract with pishing sounds, but you must look quick to see these hyperactive sprites.

23 Peeking out the kitchen window, I spy a little flock of Golden-crowned Kinglets—the fairy sprites of the North Woods. They sometimes winter in northernmost Minnesota, and virtually never retreat beyond central Texas, so we see them early each spring. Their gold-and-crimson crowns are as exotic as hummingbirds' ruby throats. They're almost as tiny as hummingbirds, too—barely over three inches long; and their weight during fall migration, when they're as fat as they get, is a mere fifth of an ounce. When Tommy was two, he could have balanced 2,720 of them on a scale.

Like a two-year-old, a kinglet never seems to stop moving. Even during momentary rest periods it flicks its wings constantly. Its bright eyes, restless energy, and insatiable curiosity are toddler qualities, and, like a toddler, it has an inner sunshine that brightens even a dismal day. Over my years of birding, I've had two heart-stopping moments when goldencrowns have alighted on my finger. The magic of a wild kinglet trustingly perched in my hand is as close as I've come outdoors to the magic of lullaby time, Tommy clutching my finger as he drifted into sleep.

Notes

24 The Eastern Bluebird was a symbol of happiness for people living in America long before Europeans arrived, but, oddly, grasshoppers, katydids, crickets, beetles, and other insects have always considered it a vicious serial killer. Point of view is important in the natural world.

When we hear the rich warbling of bluebirds in early spring, our spirits soar. But as happy as we feel in the company of these first arrivals, we worry about them and the weather they will face in the next two months. A May snowfall is hardly unknown in North Country, and one year our end of Lake Superior stayed frozen until after Memorial Day. One might think that the bluebird's inner warmth and sunshine would be able to sustain it in the worst weather, but too often we peek into a nest box in April or May to find dead bluebirds—they survived the harsh winter and all the dangers of migration only to succumb when they finally came home to us in spring. When we see a bluebird, we whisper a prayer that these gentle spirits may long survive within their lovely feathered frames.

John Burroughs, nature writer in the 1800s, wrote, "The first Bluebird in the spring is as welcome as the blue sky itself. The season seems softened and tempered as soon as we hear his note and see his warm breast and azure wing. His gentle manners, his soft, appealing voice, not less than his pleasing hues, seem born of the bright and genial skies. He is the spirit of April days incarnated in a bird."

Notes

March

The expression *round robin* was used even before the sailing ship *Catherine* left Gibraltar in 1612. The discontented crew drew up a petition against the captain, realizing he could legally hang the chief dissenter—whatever signature appeared first probably doomed the signer. To avoid this, they signed their names in a circle. A statuette of a robin on a circular base was at hand, and they used it to trace the circle on which to form their signatures.

Notes

_____

_____

_____

_____

_____

_____

25

Red-red-robins are bob-bob-bobbin' along now. The state bird of Wisconsin, Michigan, and Connecticut was named by English immigrants, who missed their little robin redbreast so much that when they came here they named just about every bird with even a tinge of red or russet a robin. At one time or another they've called our Eastern Bluebird the blue robin, our Rufous-sided Towhee the ground robin, our oriole the golden robin, and our Cedar Waxwing the Canadian robin. They called two reddish sandpipers, the dowitcher and the Red Knot, robin snipes, and the Red-breasted Merganser the sea robin. Dozens of other unrelated birds throughout the world are all called robins.

Oddly, the bird most closely related to our robin in England is what they call a blackbird. The nursery rhyme about blackbirds baked in a pie originated during the 1500s. Robin pie was popular in America even after it became illegal to kill songbirds in 1918, when President Wilson signed the original Migratory Bird Treaty Act. Fully fattened in fall, a robin weighs less than three ounces, so it took several to make a meal.

26 In spring and summer, Purple Finches seem like avian kamikaze pilots whenever they come to a picture window. The number of birds that die at windows every year is unquantifiable, but surely staggering, and Purple Finches are especially vulnerable—their short wings can keep their heavy bodies aloft only in rapid flight, so when they hit a window, they hit it hard.

As long as they avoid windows, male Purple Finches spend much of their time singing a long jumble of sweet notes with a rich, liquid quality. The call note, given by both sexes, is a distinctive dry "tick," often heard as they fly overhead.

Like other finches, Purple Finches stay in flocks even during the breeding season. Oddly, just around the time football season arrives, most males abandon the females and young to join predominantly adult male flocks until sometime after the Super Bowl. Although there are no records of Purple Finches actually purchasing Viking season tickets, the timing of these macho gatherings of birds flaunting their team colors can hardly be considered coincidental.

Purple Finches were not named by a color-blind ornithologist, though males are rosy crimson without a speck of what we call purple today. The Latin *purpureus* was derived from the Greek *porphura*, for a shellfish, from which Tyrean purple dye was obtained. This imperial purple of the ancient Romans was quite similar to the color of a Purple Finch.

Notes

March

Birds sing for two main purposes—to proclaim and defend a territory and to attract a mate. In most species, only the male sings. Most baby birds have an inborn song template, but unless a baby hears its father's or another male's songs during a critical learning stage, its songs may never be recognizable. High levels of male hormones can induce singing in females of many species.

27 Bird sounds pierce the awareness of even the most unornithological as spring progresses. In open country, we hear the Eastern Meadowlark's simple, easily imitated whistle that follows the rhythm "Call my mom . . . Spring is here." Western Meadowlarks have a rich, bubbly whistle that mere humans can't produce.

A junco's trilling is short and variable. Song Sparrows begin their song with two or three identical notes and break into a jumble—I learned that one as "Peace, peace, peace, all my little children peace." Savannah Sparrows have a quiet snore often heard on TV commercials. Ruffed Grouse drum, the air under their wings making a deep, resonant sound like a bowling ball dropping and bouncing faster and faster. Snipe will soon be winnowing—the strong "hoo-hoo-hoo-hoo-hoo-HOO!" is produced by two vibrating tail feathers. This bird with the singing tail is closely related to the woodcock, the bird with the singing wings.

Above all, we hear the robins, their long sentences of three-syllable words marked with "cheerily, cheerily" and "Spring is here."

Notes

28 The Mourning Dove's plaintive "hooooo, hoo-hoo" is often mistaken for an owl's hoot. The dove is the only game bird in the United States that nests in all forty-eight lower states, but it is protected in Minnesota, Wisconsin, Michigan, Iowa, Ohio, New York, New Jersey, and most of New England. Mourning Doves are not much smaller than Cornish hens, and falcons and human hunters agree that their flavor is superb.

Despite their song, Mourning Doves are not songbirds. Pigeons and doves form their own taxonomic order, which included the Dodo, because of several characteristics that songbirds lack, like fleshy feet and a soft, waxy cere with slitlike nostrils at the base of the upper beak. Pigeons and doves suck water like a horse—most other birds take water in their bills and then tip their heads to allow it to dribble down their throats. Feathers of pigeons and doves are very loosely attached—possibly to allow these tasty birds to flee predators. And both male and female pigeons and doves produce a unique milk in their crops to feed their young— flamingos and penguins have also mastered this mammalian trick of milk production.

Although a few Mourning Doves remain in winter as far north as Thunder Bay, most retreat south. Their fleshy feet, too small to fit in pack boots, are susceptible to frostbite. On Peabody Street on freezing days, they pig out morning and evening, and spend the rest of the day digesting food in their crops while sitting on sunny branches, their tummies warming their toes.

Notes

March

A female kinglet holds still for longer periods than the male as she incubates their seven to nine eggs. The nest, made of lichens and spider silk, is so tiny that the eggs must be set in two layers. Fortunately, the nest is elastic enough to accommodate growing kinglets—at least for a time. The babies leave the nest when about twelve days old.

29 Ruby-crowned Kinglets, half the weight of chickadees, are among the first migrants to visit Peabody Street. What they lack in size they make up for in liveliness. The only time a male kinglet holds still for more than a second or two is when he bursts into song. As if to compensate for his dinky size, his song is among the richest of all bird songs. He begins with two or three extremely high-pitched notes, and then bursts into a jumble of warbling notes that a patriotic ornithologist once transcribed as "liberty, liberty, liberty."

Kinglets belong to the Old World warbler family, which was named for the rich warbling songs of its colorful European members. Our little rubycrown wears more modest attire than most of its relatives. Both sexes have olive gray plumage adorned with white wing bars and eye rings that make them appear cross-eyed if viewed straight on. Only the adult male has a ruby crown, and he keeps it hidden under gray head feathers unless he's displaying or agitated. You must patiently keep a singing kinglet in view for a few minutes in order to see him show off that glittering jewel.

Notes

30 "Birds of a feather flock together" is true of many birds during migration, but the saying usually makes us think of geese. Canada Goose flocks are often composed of relatives. They even choose "kissin' cousins" as mates—this inbreeding has produced many races, from the enormous Giant Canada Goose to the diminutive Cackling Goose.

The conspicuous line, or V, of geese is energy efficient—the lead bird slices through the air like a motorboat, trailing an invisible wake of waves. The others follow exactly within that wake—not only is turbulence minimized, but they're also drawn forward like bicycle racers drafting. The bird out front works hard, but migrating geese are not competing—they take turns serving as leader. Keep a flock within view as it crosses the sky and you're sure to see the leader change at least once. Cranes, cormorants, some shorebirds, and even gulls adopt a V formation during migration flights, but they haven't the power of honking geese to draw our eyes skyward. As we watch, our hearts rise above earthbound cares, and for a moment we, too, take wing with the geese.

Canada Geese overwinter in several places in Minnesota and Wisconsin, and the first migrants may appear in the Northland in February. Heaviest migration here occurs between the end of March and the middle of April.

Notes

March

We help returning doves, juncoes, and sparrows during storms by scattering millet and other small seeds under spruce trees. Even chickadees, which stay close to the ground and out of the wind during bad weather, will appreciate taking their seeds from more sheltered areas during storms.

31 March and April bring spring storms that pelt birds with ice and wet snow. An ice storm in 1991 claimed many of my Peabody Street chickadees, who were probably entrapped in their roost holes by the thick ice and died of starvation or suffocation. There are records of birds as big as Barred Owls entombed in nest holes during ice storms. Birds survive a January blizzard and thirty-below temperatures more easily than they survive sleet, even when it's thirty above.

By winter's end, birds' fat reserves have virtually disappeared, and before trees leaf out and new insects emerge, food supplies dip to their lowest. Birds are inconspicuous in death—it's usually impossible to quantify how many die in storms. Keeping our feeders cleared of snow and ice and filled with food helps at least some to survive. The first sign that a spring storm has ended isn't the return of TV and radio stations to the airwaves—it's the return of chickadees to feeders. Despite their fragility and their difficult lives, birds brought the first music to this earth, and bird song brings us hope and cheer when the worst is over.

Notes

April

Determining Big Bird's taxonomy poses difficulties because avian relationships are often determined by a close examination of the skeleton, and Big Bird's is still in use. Morphologically, he seems allied with ostriches, but mitochondrial DNA analysis may indicate an ancient hybridization with Wilson's Warbler. Because of the necessary size of the egg, we trust the warbler was the male in that pairing.

1 The rarest bird in the United States—only one individual remains in the whole world—is Big Bird, the only flightless bird endemic to North America. His pink eyelids and unique markings have no known function. The orange and purple banding on his tibia and femur may be adaptations to the New York City habitat, perhaps distracting predators or attracting taxis.

Because Big Bird is the last of his kind, his songs cannot fulfill the purpose of birdsong, to attract a mate and defend his territory against other Big Birds. But despite his tragic predicament, his songs have a cheerful exuberance unique in ornithology.

Big Bird's range is deep within New York City, but because he's endangered, few ornithologists know the precise location. I asked the U.S. Fish and Wildlife Service if they could tell me how to get to Sesame Street, but they refused to divulge the information. Fortunately, we do have excellent film footage—I once saw a sequence in which he manipulated a basketball. This demonstrated a relationship with, or convergent evolution with, another rare species, the Larry Bird.

Notes

2 April is the month of contradiction in the North-land. Some of us are foolishly optimistic about spring's imminence—I once bought a bicycle in April and couldn't ride it until the snow melted in May. That kind of blind hope also drives Horned Larks and Mourning Doves, which often begin nesting this far north in a month when bad weather and taxes provide the only certainties. The nests often fail, but the birds just start over again. Most Tree Swallows and Eastern Bluebirds return in April, and some succumb to icy temperatures. Orioles and warblers wait until May, but even then cold snaps can take a toll on fragile birds requiring insects for survival.

Adult male robins migrate along the 38-degree isotherm. In pleasant weather, they sing out their territorial proclamations, but when we get a surprise blizzard, they skulk in marshes and hide in crab apple trees. Crows seem to take pleasure in late winter weather, like people who buy skis on sale in March and then are gleeful when given an opportunity to use them.

Early spring turns the thoughts of many to romance, and chickadees are no exception. Dapper males sing their pretty "fee-bee-bee" whistle more and more insistently. Chickadee couples leave their flocks on pleasant days, but rejoin the group if the weather takes a nasty turn. They accept the vagaries of April with jolly exuberance, flicking the snow off their wings with grace and good humor.

Notes

April

Conservative estimates indicate that cats kill more than 4.4 million songbirds every day in the United States. In some places, it's been established that cats taking mice and other small mammals sometimes deplete the prey base for hawks and owls. Cats are far more abundant than natural predators and are kept in prime hunting condition by their owners, so they have a greater impact on birds than wild predators. Responsible cat owners keep them indoors.

Notes

3 A stray white cat with an appetite for redpolls lurks under my feeder. Whenever I notice, I send the dog after her. I'm not supposed to touch her—I'm nursing Tommy, and cats who toy with birds are likely to carry toxoplasmosis, dangerous for tiny babies. A visit to the animal shelter is in order, but I put it off.

I catch four-year-old Joey pulling two-year-old Katie in the sled with the cat on her lap. Katie grasps its fur in her fist as the cat purrs and rubs against her. I shoo it away and tell them we absolutely cannot have a cat. That night she's back. Bunter chases her away, but later I find them snuggled, asleep, on the porch.

So we have a cat. After weeks of sleeping and eating cat chow, Sasha sneaks out and nabs a chickadee, presenting it to me like a fine gift. She looks shocked and disturbed that I don't accept it in the spirit in which it was given, but adapts to my strange ways. When she gets desperate for adventure, I let her out, but only after dark, while birds sleep. She takes an occasional mouse or shrew, but the Peabody Street birds are safe once again.

4 One of the tiniest, drabbest of all songbirds, the Winter Wren, has one of the most beautiful of all songs. It spends its summer in deep, dark spruce forests, fragrant with decay, where moss covers standing trees and the spongy soil is littered with soft, rotting wood. The Winter Wren's diet is almost 100 percent insect, although some ornithologists have seen it eat cedar berries. It's hard to see—tiny, brown, and secretive, and so its habits are not well known. Even its scientific name, *Troglodytes troglodytes* reflects its dark, secretive nature—a troglodyte is a reclusive cave dweller.

The Winter Wren looks like the more familiar House Wren, with barring across its underside, a slender, slightly down-curved bill, and a habit of cocking its tail straight up. But the Winter Wren is almost a full inch shorter than the House Wren, and most of the difference is in the tail—the Winter Wren's is just a tiny stump. Many individuals remain in the northern United States, and even Canada, for the whole winter, though if the weather is severe, many die.

Scientists believe that the wren family originated in the New World. The Winter Wren is the only species in the family found outside the Americas—long ago it made its way across the Bering Strait, through Siberia, to Europe, and from there to northern Africa. Folk tales and poems from Europe mentioning "Jenny Wren" or simply "the Wren" refer to this species.

Notes

April

Killdeer pull their crippled act only for perceived predators—if the intruder is a cow, bison, or other herbivore, the Killdeer seems to understand that its babies are in less danger of being eaten than trampled, and may plant itself directly in front of the eggs, squawking and fluttering its wings in the face of the heavy-hoofed marauder. There are records of bison herds parted down the middle by a lone Killdeer defending its eggs.

5 Killdeer are back, running on quick legs over marshes, pastures, and church lawns. Killdeer return early each spring, rushing in with the first flights of robins and bluebirds. It's hard to understand how they survive the inevitable April Fools' blizzard when 98 percent of their diet consists of insects, worms, and other cold-blooded invertebrates. During the worst days, Killdeer often move closer to lakes and streams where the ground is thawed, but as soon as the temperature reaches the thirties again, they return to pastures and lawns.

The Killdeer is one of the most familiar of shorebirds because of its fondness for softball fields and picnic areas. It's famous for its crippled-bird act. If a potential predator approaches a Killdeer nest, whichever parent is on guard duty drops down, invariably on the side away from the eggs, and keels over on its side, crying piteously. It drags its wing on the ground and moves exactly slowly enough to lure the intruder away without being caught. Once the enemy is a safe distance from the eggs or babies, the parent rights itself and flies off, good as new.

Notes

6 The Eastern Phoebe has a dull brownish olive back and dull white underside, with no wing bars or markings, yet what it lacks in color it makes up for in grace and style. It's light and easy on the wing, making swift twists and turns and sudden tumblings as it catches flying insects, reminding some of the graceful, silent dodging of a butterfly. It also scoops up aquatic insects and small fishes from streams. Even when it alights on a branch or wire, it gracefully wags its tail up and down like a restless ballerina. Country people love the phoebe for its tame, gentle manner and its diet of mosquitoes.

Phoebes build their nests from mud and moss, usually near water. In early times phoebes plastered nests in recesses of rock ledges or in caves, but since colonial days they've nested extensively on less natural structures. Their favorite sites seem to be under bridges or trestles over water. The Eastern Phoebe was the first American bird ever to be banded, when John James Audubon tied tiny lengths of colored thread on phoebe legs to prove that the same individuals return to their nest sites year after year.

In Greek mythology, Phoebe was the goddess of the moon and the hunt, daughter of Gaea and twin sister of Apollo. Many Greek gods and goddesses went by two names—Phoebe was also known as Artemis. Phoebe is a name for Earth's moon, and also for the ninth moon of Saturn. But the origin of the avian phoebe's name is less poetic—the bird named itself simply by saying "phoebe" over and over and over.

Notes

April

When suet glistens and peanut butter gets soft, it's time to bring them in for the year. We crumble egg shells and add them to sunflower seed to help female birds build up their calcium reserves.

7 In spring, many people take down bird feeders for the year. Some people don't want wild birds depending on humans. Others worry that diseases will spread rapidly in warm weather where high concentrations of birds gather. Others don't mind the expense of feeding in winter when birds really need it, but figure it's not worth the cost when natural food is available.

I don't mind helping birds through the stresses of migration. I keep my feeding station raked, and get rid of wet seed before it molds, so disease isn't a big concern. I do worry that by subsidizing grackles, cowbirds, and even my favorites, Blue Jays, I'm indirectly hurting small birds. Jays feed their young eggs and baby birds. Grackles destroy eggs and small birds, often without even eating them. And cowbirds are a major cause of the decline of many small birds. I don't like to judge any species, but we humans have already tipped the balance well in favor of predators and parasites at the expense of other birds. So I've trained my dog Bunter to chase blackbirds out of the yard—it's one golden retriever's little way of trying to restore the balance of nature.

Notes

8 One of the first things I learned in ornithology class was that no bird has a sense of smell except the Turkey Vulture, which smells out decaying carrion, and some seabirds, which use smell to detect their own nest among thousands in a colony. I learned that shorebirds don't smell sewage, and that, mercifully, a Great Horned Owl can't smell a skunky dinner.

Birds do lack a specialized nose, and olfactory centers in a bird brain are smaller than corresponding centers in most mammal brains, but a songbird's olfactory centers are comparably proportioned to humans'. We can't smell as well as dogs, and most of our noses are smaller than casaba melons, but we identify a wide range of odors, and apparently birds can, too. European pigeons use olfaction for homing information, and new experiments indicate that Cedar Waxwings have a fairly good sense of smell, possibly to help them select fresh berries. Tree Swallows don't have time to sniff insects before they swoop in and swallow them—their sense of smell is measurably poorer than a waxwing's, but still exists. Birds don't usually stink, but they apparently do smell.

To test the avian sense of smell, an ornithologist placed birds in an enclosure where a fan periodically blew in either ordinary air or small amounts of cyclohexanone. Ten seconds after cyclohexanone was blown in, the bird received an electrical shock. If it detected the odor, its heart rate soon increased the moment the chemical entered, but if it couldn't smell it, it never responded until the actual shock. Being an experimental bird stinks.

Notes

April

Although Great Blue Herons' throats are amazingly elastic, they sometimes catch fish bigger than they can manage. One choked to death on a two-foot shad, and several have been suffocated by suckers. Human anglers don't always appreciate sharing fish with herons—one summer a heron fished alongside humans on the Lester River in Duluth for weeks until it was clubbed to death. Several distraught fishermen called me about it, but the culprit escaped.

9 Walking along Indian Point on the St. Louis River one frosty, fog-hung morning, I spied a prehistoric apparition—four enormous, ghostly shapes winging through the mist. I ran to the crest of the hill in time to see four Great Blue Herons alight in the bare branches of a big oak, as silvery gray as the mist itself. They stood there, gangling and awkward, for a few minutes, and then their spindly legs pushed them aloft. Their labored wingbeats pulled them upwards in ever-widening circles as they gained altitude and disappeared into the mist.

The Great Blue Heron returns while ice still covers many marshes and shallow bodies of water, so it flies hither and yon in search of open water. When it discovers a likely fishing hole, it bides its time, the most patient of nature's creatures, waiting for fish to come. It strikes with lightning speed, its lower beak piercing the fish as the upper snaps upon it. Then it juggles the fish a bit to orient it and swallows it head first. For their huge size, full-grown great blues weigh only five to eight pounds—the same as a newborn human baby. I'd much rather deliver a baby.

Notes

10 April dusk means frogs and timberdoodles. We stand in a woodcock display area—just about any place in open country where the soil is moist and woods and field meet. At the very moment that evening swallows up the trees, when it's barely too dark for an owl to make out a woodcock's squatting silhouette, one begins to call. Soon another joins in, and then another, bobbing their heads with each buzzy "peent."

As evening grows darker, suddenly the light level is exactly right, and a woodcock begins his skydance. A couple of wing feathers whistle in a lovely chittering sound as he spirals up and up. He seems to fly right into the clouds, but that's really just the darkness. When he's high enough—usually about three hundred feet up—wings still a-chittering, he bursts into a liquid warbling song as he circles high overhead. Suddenly he zigzags down like a stalling kite, still singing. Listening hard we hear the "whoosh" of his descent. Once he alights, he "peents" again. He'll continue until it's quite dark, sometimes calling through the night when the moon is bright. Listening here under the stars is a satisfying end to an April day.

If most birds held their beak open to grasp an earthworm under three inches of soil, they'd get a mouthful of mud. If they held it shut, they couldn't open it against compacted soil to grab the worm. The woodcock's three-inch bill has a muscular, uniquely flexible tip loaded with nerve endings. With this exquisite organ it can feel and grasp worms enough to keep its plump figure well filled.

Notes

April

At night we hear migrants coursing through the skies. Their seeping notes and piping calls probably have the same purpose as automobile headlights. Although migrants are all flying in pretty much the same direction, the constant calling helps them stay a safe distance apart, avoiding midair collisions.

11 Since ancient times people have wondered about the mystery of migration. Before people traveled to or communicated with distant lands, they didn't realize that birds went from one place to another. Ancient Greeks believed that some birds spent their winters on the moon and that swallows bided their time in winter buried in the mud. Sure enough, when spring came, the swallows always showed up near muddy ponds first, never appearing over larger lakes until the ice was gone. What more proof could you ask for?

The first breakthrough in human understanding of migration came as European explorers noticed familiar birds in Africa and the Middle East—slowly the idea dawned on them that birds might actually be more experienced travelers than they. The main focus of early migration studies was to determine the breeding and wintering ranges of species. As we learned more and more about the incredible distances some birds travel, and how in many species adults migrate first, leaving the young to figure out travel routes on their own, our questions mounted, and migration seemed more mysterious and wonderful than ever.

Notes

12 An important breakthrough in migration studies came in the 1960s, when William Keeton hypothesized that birds have a sixth sense to feel the magnetic pull of the earth. He tested his hypothesis by fitting little metal bars on the backs of homing pigeons. Half were magnetic, and half were of the same size and weight but made of nonmagnetic brass. When he released the birds away from the home loft on overcast days, five out of seven birds with brass bars oriented correctly and returned to the loft, but those with magnetic bars scattered randomly. On sunny days, they all oriented correctly. Pigeons must normally get their bearings from the sun's location in the sky, using magnetic clues as a backup system. Particles of magnetite have been discovered in the brains of several species.

We also know that night migrants use stars to navigate. In planetariums, songbirds concentrate at the side where projected stars point north, even if that's not true north. Geese use landmarks. Hummingbirds somehow cross the Gulf of Mexico with no land clues at all for most of the flight. The more mysteries we clear up, the more we appreciate the miracle of migration.

Almost all small songbirds migrate by night. This allows them to spend their days fueling up, and makes them less vulnerable to day-flying hawks. The smaller a bird is, the more rapidly its wings must flap to keep it aloft—flying during the cool of the night may help prevent heat exhaustion.

Notes

April

Red-winged Blackbirds perch on old cattail stalks between us and the swans. They're fluffed against the biting wind, showing only the yellow margins of their epaulets, but occasionally something triggers a territorial urge, and one squeaks out an "okalee," exposing his brilliant red shoulders for all the world to see. The vivid red of blackbirds and the soft white of swans against the soft gray overcast are the most welcome colors of spring.

13 The swans are back. As soon as word reaches us, Billie and I race out to the St. Louis River. Tundra Swans are a fine sight, whether winging overhead, swimming gracefully, or dabbling like awkward, ungainly ducks, their big feet struggling to stay on the surface so their buoyant heads and necks can stay under long enough to get a mouthful of aquatic plants. This is the first time Billie's ever seen wild swans, and her eyes shine.

The first swans I ever saw were in flight. Their whistling called my attention to them from far off, and I watched them draw closer, come low over my head, and move on toward the northern horizon in two separate lines, of four and seventeen. Long after they disappeared, I stood rooted to the ground, awestruck with this unexpected apparition, wondering how such beauty could have existed on the earth without noticing it for twenty-four years.

Billie sees more today than I did that April morning of 1976—at least two hundred still swim in the river after twenty-seven take off, flying in wider and wider circles as they gain altitude, then winging on toward their Arctic home, our souls flying along with them.

Notes

14 Every year at tax time I consider the economic systems of birds. Birds have no interest in money—they're into real estate. In summer and winter both, a good piece of land represents security in the form of food, water, and shelter. If property values are high, determined by abundance of natural food, each bird can afford to defend only a small piece of the action. As land value drops, each bird holds onto a bigger plot. Songbirds seldom fight over food, but territory is another matter, though once in a while they negotiate easements. The robins nesting in my back spruce one year spent hours each day chasing the next-door robins from the bird bath. This wasted energy, especially once their eggs hatched, so they worked out an uneasy truce. The neighbors were granted water rights, but could not veer even inches from a precise path between the fence and the birdbath or my robins attacked them vigorously.

As birds develop their property, they invest more in its defense. For many species, development is limited to nest building, but jays and crows add eating establishments. The more food they hide, the more aggressively they defend the land itself.

Except for crows and ravens picking up a shiny coin here and there, birds never have enough money to buy land or to fund research to help them survive. So it's up to us humans to give them a hand. Funding nongame wildlife through a "chickadee check-off" on state income tax forms allows us to help ensure that birds will be around forever, enriching our lives in ways money can't buy.

Notes

April

Trickle-down, supply-side economics should work for birds, if we assume that by maintaining property for the rarest, most elite birds, like Spotted Owls and Red-cockaded Wood-peckers, we also help other, less elite species that also require mature forests. Humans in power often reject plans to set aside real estate for wild crea-tures, apparently believing that environmental ethics are strictly for the birds.

15 In hard times, some birds flock together. They benefit from added eyes in their search for food and predators, but there's a trade-off—these socialists must be nomadic in order to find food enough for all. Some birds are capitalists in winter, preferring the benefits of private property. They study their land holdings intimately to capitalize on every amenity.

Bird feeders represent the welfare state. Some welfare offices are more restrictive than others, requiring recipients to prove their need by being cute or little. Blue Jays and squirrels often experience rejection at these establish-ments. Some welfare offices provide benefits only for red-blooded American birds, turning away starlings and House Sparrows as illegal aliens.

Hairy and Downy Woodpeckers spend their days with socialist chickadee flocks, and even stop by the welfare office for handouts. But at nighttime they retreat to private condos, which they refuse to share with the less fortunate. Perhaps woodpeckers inspired the term "stingy old bird," but at least they donate used cavities to other birds when done with them.

Notes

16 So far the only orioles we've seen this spring have been on the airwaves, usually in flocks of nine birds at a time. These Baltimore Orioles are remarkable in that every specimen ornithologists have found has been male, and all the displays, rituals, and vocalizations ever recorded have been directed at other males. How they reproduce is a great ornithological mystery. This phenomenon has also been noted in two similar species, Toronto Blue Jays and St. Louis Cardinals.

As with many gulls and shorebirds, the habitat of baseball birds is short-grass fields, which attract large numbers of bats, too. There are many fowl balls, and sometimes a batter tries bunting. Flycatchers are popular, unlike fielders who duck. Often runners try to teal a base. If it's a close call, bleacher bums may grouse or snipe or even shout, "Killdeer ump!" These boobirds are all stork raven mad.

Now if you can swallow all this pheasant banter, you're probably veery gullible. So all you baseball plovers out there, just remember, it's one, two, three shrikes you're out at the old ball game.

Birds have fairly good odds of winning the World Series. Baltimore Orioles did it in 1966, 1970, and 1983. Crested birds have an even better chance—Cardinals took the Series nine times between 1926 and 1982. Blue Jays started playing in the American League in 1976, and took their first title in 1992. From an ornithological viewpoint, the perfect World Series would pit Jays against Cardinals, and the game would end with a good flycatcher.

Notes

April

American Tree Sparrows are Arctic birds who use ptarmigan feathers and lemming fur to line their nests. Arctic summer days are long, but the season is short, and these rugged creatures are perfectly adapted to its harsh reality—the young leave the nest in only nine days. Their simple, sweet song is an ephemeral gift of early spring—a lesson to us to enjoy each day as it comes rather than mope around waiting for summer.

17 When sweet songs are added to the icy tinkling call-notes of the American Tree Sparrow, just before it leaves for the Far North, we know that spring is here. This lovely sparrow joins junco congregations on roadsides and beneath feeders, though it seldom alights on the feeders themselves, this bird of solid ground. It's the most poorly-named of birds, christened by nostalgic early settlers who saw in it a superficial resemblance to the Eurasian Tree Sparrow. Our American species, which isn't even in the same family, nests on the ground, under a tussock among dwarf willows and shrubs of the tundra. It often keeps its feet on the ground even as its ethereal song floats skyward.

Our tree sparrow is closely related to the Chipping Sparrow. Both have rusty caps, but the tree sparrow is bigger and browner, with a rusty eye line on its gray cheek. Chippies are daintier, with a black eye line contrasting boldly with a white eyebrow. Tree sparrows have a unique tie tack—a black dot in the center of the plain breast. We seldom see chippies and tree sparrows together—most tree sparrows have left for the Arctic by the time most chippies arrive in mid-May.

Notes

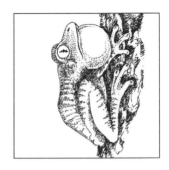

18 When I started learning birds, I was completely on my own, knowing no other birders to consult. My normal technique was to spend five or six hours a day at a campus woodlot and nearby field. If I heard the slightest sound, I searched through every branch until I found the bird. I slowly learned that red squirrels chatter like birds, chipmunks chip like birds, and thirteen-lined ground squirrels emit a lovely, birdlike trill. One by one, I learned to separate bird calls and songs from nonbird sounds.

One evening around sunset, a whistled song caught my ear. I searched and searched, but every time I thought I was closing in on the singer, it would suddenly shut up, and then start up again a few minutes later, often at a distance, and I'd start searching again. I gave up when it got dark, but I heard it again the next evening, and the next. I searched every night for over a week until I finally found, in the beam of a strong flashlight, a one-inch tree frog. My "bird" was nothing more than a spring peeper.

Recordings are useful for verifying birdsongs and learning new ones, and going out with experienced birders helps, too, but the only way to master bird-calls and songs is to get out there on your own and listen and search. It takes time and patience, but eventually every April song becomes a familiar greeting from a dear old friend.

Notes

April

Troglodytes aedon is a mouthful for a grown-up, but in "Mr. Rogers' Neighborhood" King Friday knows a bird by that name, and Fred Rogers even sings a song called "Troglodytes Aedon." Aedon was the Queen of Thebes, changed into a nightingale by Zeus. The scientific name is appropriate for a bird that creeps into tiny dark places like a troglodyte and sings a rich song bigger than itself.

19 House Wrens will soon return from Texas and Mexico to the North Woods. Our familiar backyard wrens and other subspecies of the House Wren are masters of diplomacy, getting along with people in every country of North, Central, and South America. They're less popular with birds—if a wren notices any bird nesting on its territory, it will puncture holes in all the eggs.

Males return first, anytime from mid-April through May. Each builds several stick nests, usually in natural cavities or woodpecker holes, or in the wren houses of very lucky people. But wrens have also nested in empty cow skulls, fishing creels, watering pots, tin cans, hats, boots, shoes, the nozzle of a pump, an iron pipe railing, weather vanes, holes in walls, mailboxes, overalls hanging on a clothesline, and even in the axle of a car that was driven every day. The female chooses her favorite among his stick nests and lines it with spider egg cases, feathers, hair, grasses, and other soft materials before she lays six to eight eggs. She incubates while he spends his nights in those extra nests he built—his "bachelor pads." It takes two weeks for the eggs to hatch.

Notes

20 "Die for adultery! No: The wren goes to 't."
King Lear may not have been an ornithologist,
but he knew about wrens. New techniques of sampling
blood in chicks indicate that many other species are also
somewhat promiscuous. Ornithologists expected this in
ducks and wrens, but were shocked to learn that some of
the most innocent-looking warblers and bluebirds also
have extramarital pairings.

When a brood of baby wrens hatches, both parents feed
them until the young leave the nest after two weeks. Then
dad often assumes responsibility as mom incubates a new
brood by him or another male. When the first batch is
independent, and sometimes before, dad often mates
again. Each female wren can lay three clutches in a season,
maximizing the number of babies. Some die from nest
parasites, many are eaten by predators or stung by wasps,
newly fledged young are poisoned by lawn sprays, and
many more are killed on their long-distance migration.
Human sensibilities may be offended by promiscuity, but
I'm glad evolution worked out some way of ensuring the
survival of a fragile bird who can't outweigh three dimes.

You can buy wren houses in garden stores or obtain building plans from libraries or state departments of natural resources. A hole one inch in diameter is fine for wrens. Chickadees can enter a one-and-an-eighth-inch hole, and may nest if sawdust covers the floor. If the hole is bigger, House Sparrows take over. Set it between five and ten feet above the ground, under building eaves or in a tree.

Notes

April

The aspen draws its energy from decay and sunshine, and a Ruby-crowned Kinglet harnesses that energy in a miracle of movement. This perpetual motion machine empowers its atom-sized body with sunshine transformed into life by an aspen. The kinglet returns the sunlight to earth in its glittering crown and the richness and warmth of its song.

21 Aspen flowers and long, cottony fruiting structures bust out in April, feeding hungry creatures even as late snows swirl about the branches. Catkins, the color of earth and sparrow, wave in the slightest breeze, concealing the abundant wildlife within.

Plump porcupines perch improbably in the delicate outer twigs, munching soft buds and flowers. A Yellow-rumped Warbler darts from branch to branch, hovering like a hummingbird at the tip of a flower, searching for the first insects, which also gather in the aspen's bountiful boughs. A Yellow-bellied Sapsucker sits patiently, waiting for sap to collect—not quite as slow as molasses in January. A Red-breasted Nuthatch hollows out a rotten spot where a branch once grew.

Until particleboard and cheap paper came along, the aspen was the weed of the dendrological world. It regenerates as fast as we can chop it down, one of the few native species that has kept its resolve to stay uncivilized no matter what. It's the Huck Finn of the North Woods—common and plain, but with a heart as big as the sky.

Notes

22 Driving along the shore to Two Harbors, I see loons everywhere. They gather on the great lake soon after the ice breaks up and make exploratory flights each morning, checking whether their own personal lakes are open yet. People with lake cabins marvel when loons appear the day of ice-out, as if the loons magically foresaw when it would happen, but it's really a case of persistence and hard work paying off.

We rejoice at their return, these haunting and evocative creatures of northern lakes. Their unique bodies give them underwater skills we can only dream of. They swim with their feet, using their wings for quick spurts and turns. In deep dives, their heart rate drops, and special physiological adaptations prevent them from suffering oxygen deprivation or developing the bends when resurfacing. Many of their bones are solid, unlike the bones of ducks, and their specific gravity is about the same as water. They often expel air from feathers and respiratory air sacs to sink slowly and quietly beneath the surface, leaving scarcely a ripple. We cannot help but watch for them to resurface—loons are always worth waiting for.

Loons can submerge for well over a minute. Although an ornithologist once clocked a fifteen-minute dive, no one has ever duplicated his observation—rarely do loons remain under for more than three minutes. Loons have been reported caught in nets as deep as 265 feet, but most scientists believe dives deeper than 100 feet are fishy tales. Perhaps loons found in deeper nets were ensnared as the nets were dropped or pulled up.

Notes

April

Hamlet's lines, "I am but mad north-northwest. / When the wind is southerly, / I know a hawk from a hand-saw," inspired a Hitchcock movie. Shakespearian scholars debate Hamlet's meaning. Some claim the hawk, like a hacksaw, was a basic tool of the carpenter. Others say *handsaw* was a corruption of *heronshaw* for a young heron. No matter which is correct, there's little argument about why Hamlet said it—he was trying to appear cuckoo.

23

William Shakespeare was born sometime around April 23, 1564, and died on April 23, 1616. He, or whoever wrote his plays, was familiar with avian folklore and mythology, and must have observed many birds firsthand.

One of Shakespeare's favorite metaphors was the cuckoo. The European species are famous for promiscuity—the word *cuckold* was derived from the cuckoo. The cuckoo is also the harbinger of spring in Europe, as our robin is here. Its song, a two-noted "cuckoo" exactly like the clock, inspired Shakespeare to write, "The cuckoo, then, on every tree,/ Mocks married men; for thus sings he, Cuckoo/ Cuckoo, cuckoo: O word of fear,/ Unpleasing to a married ear." He also wrote, "He was but as the cuckoo is in June,/ Heard, not regarded."

Shakespeare made many allusions to owls, usually as harbingers of death, though one of his owls sings "a merry note." He also refers to falconry and the swan song. Romeo and Juliet's first quarrel was about the identification of a bird—Romeo said it was a lark, but Juliet insisted it was a nightingale.

Notes

24 In mid-April, Double-crested Cormorants gather, some sitting with wings spread open, on the rocks of the breakwater where ships enter the Superior harbor. In flight, they look like all-black geese, necks outstretched and pointed wings beating steadily and fairly rapidly. They often fly in flocks, in a line or V. In water, their long, low profile gives them a loonlike appearance.

Although cormorants used to be abundant in Minnesota and Wisconsin, their numbers declined dangerously from the 1960s through the early '80s. Now, in part because they mooch at fish farms in winter, they're increasing again.

Ornithologists assign cormorants to their own family, related to pelicans and anhingas, the snake birds of Florida and the tropics. Like anhingas, cormorants have poorly developed oil glands, and "hang their wings out to dry" after a few dives, perched on a rock or buoy. Their relationship to pelicans is betrayed by naked orange skin on their throat pouches and webs between all four toes—a condition ornithologists call *totipalmate*.

Cormorants are voracious fish-eaters. The word *cormorant* comes from the Latin *corvus marinus*, for sea raven. Shakespeare said they were "insatiate," and fishermen have placed bounties on them. But, except in artificial situations, cormorants seldom compete with human fishing interests to any great extent—they seem to prefer rough fish, like carp, to game fish.

Notes

April

It's easy to observe jaw-stretching in cormorants and boobies—their upper bills flex upwards at the naso-frontal hinge. In other birds it's harder to tell whether the bird is breathing when the beak opens. By 1985, detailed descriptions of yawnlike movements had been done for penguins, ducks, geese, plovers, Old World warblers, and finches, and right this minute, an ornithologist may be taking copious notes about the movements of some poor, sleepy blackbird.

25 One of the great unanswered questions in ornithology is whether or not birds yawn. Most species open their beaks in what looks like a mammalian yawn, but a German ornithologist suggested in 1930 that this "jaw stretching" is independent of breathing movements and isn't a true yawn. In 1967, two ornithologists observed both inhalation and exhalation in yawning ostriches. In 1974, both a true jaw-stretch, without any appreciable opening of the throat, and a true yawn, with definite inhalation of a breath of air, were observed in Brandt's and Pelagic Cormorants. In 1977, jaw-stretching and true yawning were documented in the Great Crested Grebe and the Brown Booby.

The physiological function of yawning, in birds or in mammals, remains a mystery. In mammals, yawning may purge deeper parts of the lung of carbon dioxide, which accumulates during shallow, restful breathing, though some dispute this because yawning never occurs during sleep. Air travels completely through avian lungs to large air sacs, so if yawning does exist in birds, it may have a different function—perhaps as a signal to researchers that the issue is utterly boring.

Notes

26 Buffalo birds once roamed the Great Plains, following herds of bison. Their short, conical bills couldn't penetrate thick prairie sod, but the bisons' heavy hooves exposed grubs and seeds for buffalo bird feasts. In turn, the buffalo birds ate ticks and other biting insects off the bisons' backs.

Bison roamed as they pleased, staying in an area for days or weeks and then moving on. If a female buffalo bird was nesting when the herd left, she could remain, only to starve, or she could follow the bison, but then her babies would die. So, over time, she developed a strategy of laying her eggs in the nests of other, usually smaller, species, like sparrows and warblers. Their urge to incubate and feed was stronger than their recognition of individual eggs or babies, and they couldn't tell one baby from another. At each visit to the nest, they fed the hungriest baby—the one with the biggest mouth. Since the buffalo bird was biggest to begin with, it got the lion's share. When it was full grown, something suddenly clicked in its tiny bird brain and it left its adoptive parents, striking out to find its own species and the bison it needed.

Bison and buffalo birds lived together for thousands of years in mutual dependence, but settlers who appeared on the scene in the 1800s doomed the relationship. They exterminated the bison, but provided a substitute—domestic cattle. Now buffalo birds became cowbirds. The settlers burned and plowed the prairie sod, so cowbirds suddenly could obtain their own food, and the settlers also chopped down the eastern forest, so cowbirds could invade clearings where they had never before been.

Notes

April

John James Audubon, born April 26, 1785, based his Brown-headed Cowbird painting on specimens provided by his friend Edward Harris. Audubon wrote, "If we are fond of admiring the wisdom of Nature, we ought to mingle reason with our admiration." He was troubled by the fact that natural babies often didn't survive with a cowbird, but added, "This is a mystery to me; nevertheless, my belief in the wisdom of Nature is not staggered by it."

27 The strategy buffalo bird females developed long ago for keeping their babies alive is now tragically destroying whole species of other birds. The prairie victims of buffalo birds/cowbirds lost a baby or two while raising cowbird young, but weren't usually affected more than once every few years because of the cowbirds' nomadic ways. With agriculture, cowbirds became both more sedentary and more numerous, and year after year parasitized forest birds that raise only a single batch of young each year before returning to the tropics.

Brown-headed Cowbirds can invade forests only within a few hundred feet from edges. Unfortunately, road cuts and clearings for houses and lumbering have fragmented our forests into sections small enough to allow cowbirds to parasitize vireos, warblers, flycatchers, and tanagers that never encountered them in precolonial times. Cowbirds have become one of the primary causes of the decline of warblers, vireos, and other Neotropical migrants. Without cowbird trapping programs, the endangered Black-capped Vireo, of Texas and Oklahoma, and Kirtland's Warbler, of Michigan, might already be extinct.

Notes

28   T. S. Roberts tells this story:

Many years ago there stood on the campus of the State University at Minneapolis two cannons, which were used every morning in artillery drill, and from which blank charges were frequently fired. A pair of Bluebirds selected one of these guns as a nesting-site. The nest was accordingly built but of course was removed next morning. This went on for several successive days, the nest built one day being destroyed the following morning. At length one morning the cadet whose duty it was to charge the gun failed to observe whether or not the nest was there and rammed down the cartridge with a will. When he tried to fire the gun, of course it would not go off; so the load was drawn and an examination disclosed the nest and the female bird jammed into a scarcely recognizable mass against the breech. Promptly the male secured another mate and the following morning the usual nest was in the gun. This continued for a day or two, when the cannon was stored for the season in a shed near by and a cavity in an adjoining tree was chosen for the nest, where peace reigned.

Birds occasionally make poor selections of nesting sites. In 1984, a pair of Rock Wrens was discovered in a railroad yard in Bemidji, Minnesota. These birds of the West apparently built their nest in a boxcar, and hopped the freight when the train started moving. They stayed in Bemidji for at least twenty days, but ended up abandoning their nest.

Notes

April

A Chimney Swift nest is built from twigs gathered on the wing, cemented together with swift saliva—a thick, viscid glue that is actually edible. Some Oriental swifts make their entire nests of this material, the source of "bird's nest soup." Our swifts nest in hollow tree snags and chimneys—thousands of swifts can live in a single chimney or silo—but don't call them chimney sweeps unless you actually see one wearing a top hat and carrying a broom.

29 Chimney Swifts' pleasing chittering calls rising above the din of traffic carry our thoughts aloft, far above the noise and grime of the city. In spite of their drab coloring, swifts are closely related to hummingbirds, belonging to the order *Apodiformes*, which means "without feet." Both swifts and hummers do have feet, but they're reduced in size. If a swift lands on the ground, it may not be able to take off again—its legs and feet aren't strong enough to push it up. Long claws on its tiny toes and hard, sharp spines on the tips of its tail feathers help it cling to vertical brick and wood.

The flickering, jerky flight of Chimney Swifts comes from short, massive wing bones, completely different from the long, slender bones of swallows. Slow-motion photography proved that swifts don't beat their wings alternately, but at times one wing does beat harder than the other. All of a swift's courting, drinking, bathing, and gathering of food and nesting materials takes place on the wing. An ornithologist estimated that one banded Chimney Swift flew 1,350,000 miles during its nine-year lifespan!

30 By April's end, migrants arrive fast and furious—we can amass a list of more than seventy species in a day. Loons and Horned Grebes dot the big lake—during grebe migration peaks, I've counted over a thousand in a five-mile stretch. Most of the early ducks are divers, but more dabblers appear each day. Hawk migration also peaks. Many eagles return, along with Osprey, Northern Harriers, and Broad-winged Hawks. Sharp-shinned Hawks cruise along the South Shore—if the wind is right, we see one every time we look up. Yellowlegs call from every mud flat, and kingfishers rattle over streams and ponds. Phoebes call, wagging their tails and fluttering out from every country bridge. Sometimes we pick out a Barn Swallow or two among the abundant Tree Swallows.

In the woods, kinglets abound. Rubycrowns give their sharp "tch!" call and burst into bubbly, liquid song. We wonder how such richness emanates from so tiny a figure. Goldencrowns make a high-pitched sibilant lisp in triplets. Longer, single lisps come from Brown Creepers. Above all is the Winter Wren, its delicate song threading through trees and rocks, carrying spring magic to every nook and cranny of the forest.

Few tropical migrants have returned, but to prepare for the avian feast yet to come, we clean hummingbird feeders and stock up on oranges for orioles. We'll set them out early the second week of May.

Notes

May

I set a bowl of grape jelly on the picnic table each spring. When Katie was two, she had little picnic lunches there, often sitting side by side with the Peabody Street catbirds. Wild birds seem to intuitively understand that small children won't hurt them, though of course they stay well out of reach.

1 May is the perfect month, when every day promises new birds. May brings magnificent Minnesota mornings, and, along Lake Superior, deliciously dull, dreary, dank, dark, drizzly, drippy, depressing days that birders delight in. For on those awful May days, migrants settle in by the hundreds.

We spoon grape jelly into plastic bowls on platform feeders or deck railings in May for catbird, thrasher, and oriole feasts. One cold spring, three Cape May Warblers visited my jelly for two weeks before they moved on to their spruce forests. We also stick nesting materials—short lengths of twine and wads of cotton—in tree branches. We don't set out dryer lint—when lint gets wet and then dries, it shrinks and hardens. A nest incorporating lint may disintegrate after the first rain. We brush our dog Bunter in the backyard, and throw handfuls of fur to the wind for nesting birds to use in construction. We pick up white gull feathers along beaches to toss to Tree Swallows, which line their nests with them. The swallows quickly learn to pluck them from our hands on the wing—a beautiful game for children to play.

Notes

2 Some sports and hobbies require competitors or partners—it's hard to fence or play bridge or Scrabble alone. Astronomy requires a clear night sky. Wildflower watching ends with the first snowfall. But birding can be enjoyed anywhere, anytime, alone or with companions.

Sit near a window and you can take to the sky with pigeons and swifts during the most tedious meeting. Play golf, and even if no one scores an eagle or a birdie, there'll be plenty of real birds to distract and delight. We can keep lists of birds seen or heard on TV or in movies, even keeping a special list of birds seen or heard in commercials. I kept a list of birds seen during pregnancy—that's one list not even Roger Tory Peterson himself can top. Back in my junior-high teaching days, more than one kettle of Broad-winged Hawks out the window released my students and me from the intricacies of long division, at least for a while. Once birds permeate our consciousness, we discover new eyes and ears, and not even sleep overcomes this awareness. We don't wake with the first noisy crow of the morning, but a Whip-poor-will or a softly hooting owl can rouse us from deepest sleep.

Even a boring speech holds the interest of a bird aficionado. The speaker may crane his neck and tell a cock-and-bull story—then his goose is cooked. If he lays an egg, a British audience may give him the bird, or hiss at him, imitating a hissing goose. If he's chicken-hearted, he'll leave, crestfallen. Then we'll return to our nest, free as a bird, or go larking about.

Notes

May

Billie and I watch bluebirds sitting on a fence and a telephone wire and fluttering from a wet pasture to a tree. Everything about bluebirds pleases—their plump one-ounce bodies, gentle expressions, patriotic colors, rich song, tenderness toward mate and young. Scores migrate along the Lake Superior north shore in autumn, assuring us that their numbers are improving, but the handful we see in spring are more pleasing to winter-satiated eyes, ears, and hearts.

3 Spring keeps us in a constant state of agitation. If we're stuck indoors, what birds are we missing? If we're in the woods, what species are in the wetlands? If we're watching ducks, what's in the woods? So many migrants stay here for only a few days, and we can't bear to miss a single one—every blank line on a daily checklist is a rebuke.

In Port Wing, patches of snow still stand on shady roadsides and in the woods, but frog music and mud are the order of the day. Clumps of frog eggs dot roadside ditches, and an American Bittern flushes from the weeds—it's a connoisseur of frog legs and other frog parts. Ducks, geese, Great Blue Herons, and kingfishers crowd the slough. In the woods, Orange-crowned and Palm Warblers join Yellow-rumped Warblers—we enjoy harbingers of tropical migration perched in the same branches as the last redpolls.

We witness this restless avian life like children opening an early birthday present—filled with delight, yet greedy for the flood of avian gifts yet to come.

Notes

4 Little adobe birds are starting to build their clay igloos under building eaves where mud and water are abundant. Cliff Swallows have square-tipped tails and a cream-colored triangle on their foreheads, easy to observe when they peek out of their gourd-shaped nests.

Cliff Swallows have one of the longest migrations of all land birds, wintering in South America from southern Brazil through central Argentina, and nesting as far as Nova Scotia, northern Ontario, and northern Alaska. They eat flying insects, including mosquitoes, thereby subsisting indirectly on human blood.

Cliff Swallows collect mud in their capacious mouths and mix it with a generous helping of saliva to build their nests. Flocks gather at mud puddles, grabbing mud and fluttering their wings and mating in a jolly orgy. They lay four or five eggs twice each summer. Many babies die when cold, rainy periods make flying insects scarce, or when fastidious humans dislodge the mud nests from buildings. Many die in accidents or are eaten by Sharp-shinned Hawks and falcons during migration. We're always pleased to see the survivors.

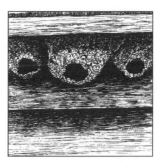

Cliff Swallows have been nicknamed eave swallows, jug swallows, and mud swallows for their nesting habits. Several books refer to them as republican swallows, apparently referring to their communities, not their politics. A careful scrutiny of voter registrations in Minnesota and Wisconsin suggests that not one Cliff Swallow is registered to vote here. The situation may be different in Chicago, where even dead old coots have been known to vote.

Notes

May

An ornithologist once calculated that each Barn Swallow flies about six hundred miles each day, zipping here and there in search of flying insects. Medieval Europeans believed that swallows hibernated in mud and marsh ooze. They observed that the swallows gathered in wetlands after breeding, and then disappeared. It took the Renaissance and world exploration to discover that they were migrating.

5 European immigrants were delighted to discover that the same Barn Swallow that they loved at home lives here, too. Shakespeare wrote of it in *Richard III*, "True hope is swift, and flies with swallow's wings." Tennyson's "Swallow, Swallow, flying, flying South," was the same species, too, though his bird was headed for Africa, not South America.

Ancient Romans birdnapped breeding swallows and brought them to sporting games to mark with the colors of the winners. On release, the birds rushed to their cold eggs or starving babies, inadvertently informing the people back home of the winners.

Barn Swallows build their mud nests on rafters, eaves, or other supports. The nest is wide open at the top, unlike the Cliff Swallow's gourd-shaped nest with its little peek-hole on the side. Both species pack as many bugs as they can into their throats, bringing about four hundred of these meals to their broods each day, amounting to about eight thousand insects per nest per day—a much better record than the finest bug zapper on the market.

Notes

6 Fork-tailed Flycatchers, elegant creatures belonging in southeastern Mexico and Central and South America, have appeared somewhere in the United States or Canada every year since 1970, usually in autumn. Sightings are as unexpected, and almost as unbelievable, as apparitions of Elvis. Three times Frank Freese saw one on his Columbia County property in mid-November 1978. He brought ornithologists to the spot, but the bird appeared for Frank alone. Fortunately, his photographs were more convincing than tabloid photos of Elvis in a laundromat, and his sighting became the first official Wisconsin record. Another forktail appeared before Robbye Johnson and Bill Penning in Douglas County on June 24, 1988, vanishing before other birders could arrive. The American Birding Association met in Duluth days later, but the bird had disappeared forever.

The first Minnesota forktail appeared before Peder Svingen in the Duluth harbor September 6, 1991. Peder photographed it, then rushed to a phone to alert Kim Eckert. Kim called a few others and we arrived within minutes, but the miraculous apparition had disappeared, leaving no trace except an image on film.

When Kim Eckert called me about Minnesota's second Fork-tailed Flycatcher, on May 6, 1992, in Grand Marais, I hustled the kids into the car, nabbed Russ at work, and charged up the shore. It was almost sunset when we arrived, but there was the bird! We ate fast food and rushed back, arriving after eleven on a school night. The children were exhausted but contented—their Mother's Day obligation was fulfilled, perhaps forever.

Notes

May

Farmers used to shoot kingbirds in huge numbers, mistakenly believing that they decimated honeybees. The U.S. Biological Survey laid that fear to rest in 1897, when they examined the stomach contents of 281 kingbirds collected in different parts of the country— only fourteen had consumed any bees at all. As enlightened farmers left kingbirds unmolested, they discovered a big advantage to having them around—these feisty birds chase hawks and crows from chicken coops.

Notes

7 If *Tyrannosaurus rex* returned to life, it would find a bird after its own heart— *Tyrannus tyrannus*, tyrant of all tyrants. The Eastern Kingbird weighs less than two ounces, but makes up for size in feistiness. These flycatchers attack hawks and other huge birds seemingly for fun. Once in Madison, Wisconsin, I watched a kingbird take on a Bald Eagle. The southbound eagle was flying high in the sky across Lake Mendota, hundreds of yards from the kingbird's territory, when the kingbird took after it and actually won the joust—it darted and pecked at the eagle's back until the eagle ignominiously turned and headed back north.

Kingbirds raise their young with the same gusto. One ornithologist wrote, "In the space of four hours, the parents made 108 visits to the nest and fed their brood ninety-one times." Another ornithologist wrote, "To my amazement, a large green dragonfly with great head and eyes, measuring across the wings at least four inches, was jammed, wings and all, into the mouth of one of the little ones. After a few minutes, as if for dessert, a large red cherry, fully one-half inch in diameter, was rammed home in the same manner."

8 In May, lovely tropical birds return to the Northland, and the oriole is one of the most exotic. The subspecies of Northern Oriole that we see in the eastern United States is the Baltimore Oriole, named for the Lords Baltimore, the family that founded and controlled the colony of Maryland, whose family crest was orange. For centuries, the Baltimore Oriole was considered a true species, but in 1973, the American Ornithologists' Union officially "lumped" it with Bullock's Oriole of the American West, after taxonomists decided that the two forms were actually races of the same species.

Orioles are related to blackbirds, belonging to a subfamily called the *Icterinae*. This name comes from the Greek word *ikteros*, for a small yellow bird. Ancient Greeks believed that if a jaundiced person sighted a small yellow bird, the person would instantly be cured, and the bird would die. If we find that our vision has become jaundiced after a long winter, the sight of an oriole may indeed cure us. And, unless one is an ancient Greek, or perhaps a cat, looking at the oriole should not be fatal to the bird.

Orioles return in early May, and we lure migrants out of the sky with oranges, cut in halves and strung up in tree branches, set on feeding platforms, or impaled with dowels on special feeders. They also eat sugar water (one cup of water to a quarter cup of sugar) from oriole feeders or plain bowls.

Notes

May

Mix one cup of water to a fourth of a cup of sugar for hummingbirds. Food coloring is unnecessary, since most hummingbird feeders have bright red parts and artificial dyes may be harmful. Don't use honey—a fungus that grows in honey water can kill hummers. Also, change the water every two or three days—fermenting sugar water causes liver damage in hummingbirds.

9 John Doe is a short, stubby American male with more than a third of his weight in his chest muscles. His heart, for his size about five times larger than a normal human heart, beats 1,260 times per minute during moderate activity, and his resting pulse is 615, though when he sleeps on cool nights it may drop to 36. He's restricted to a mostly liquid diet because of abnormal metabolism, yet each day he gorges on over twice his weight in liquids as sweet as soda pop. Is John headed for big trouble? No, he's just a typical hummingbird.

Hummingbirds are the smallest birds in the world, smaller than warm-blooded animals have any right to be. Indeed, if they maintained a normal body temperature through a long night, they'd starve, so they allow their temperature to drop by as much as 30 degrees to conserve energy. They're the only birds that fly backwards, straight up, and straight down, thanks to unique wing bones and muscles. Ruby-throated Hummingbirds winter in Mexico and Central America. Many fly nonstop over the Gulf of Mexico in early spring, and reach the Northland in early and mid-May. Setting out sugar water probably saves many of their lives after cold nights.

Notes

10 Mother's Day is an appropriate time to consider the evolutionary advantages of raising babies to adulthood over a four-month period, then taking eight months off to recover before starting afresh with a new brood. And parent birds never have to do dishes or laundry.

In Disney movies, where birds wear clothes, carry money, and lug suitcases, they use dishes only when Donald takes Daisy on a date. Pet birds use dishes, but never wash them. The only birds ever recorded washing dishes, those in *Snow White*, enjoy cleaning the dwarves' mess probably from the sheer novelty of the experience. If a real bird's house gets messy, it moves out or ignores it, easy to do with a limited sense of smell.

Disney birds do laundry assisted by cute woodland mammals, all singing happy songs. They never go from room to room collecting piles of dirty clothes enormous enough to squelch the song out of a chickadee. And they never, ever iron, though I don't, either—not since I discovered I was pushing around an extremely hot piece of metal that outweighed a Red-tailed Hawk. My new iron is called a "steam valet" and weighs less than a raven. I'd like to use it, but quoth that raven, "Nevermore!"

Birds never worry about what to wear. Loons change their outfits twice a year, choosing ostentatious checks and fancy collars in summer as a fashion statement in the land of understated Scandinavians, and changing to dull gray garb when they head to the overpopulated coast, where by downplaying fashion they perhaps reduce their chances of being mugged. Their designer combined the finest wet suit, down underwear, overcoat, and sunsuit into one neat, inexpensive ensemble.

Notes

May

Before Margaret Morse Nice, researchers were careless observers who got their "facts" from literature rife with errors. Nice traced misinformation about incubation lengths to a nineteenth-century Major Bendire, who got his misinformation from the writings of Aristotle, who had extrapolated observations of barnyard geese and chickens to wild birds. Scientists perpetuated the mistakes for twenty-three centuries, until Margaret Morse Nice set the record straight.

Notes

11 The Song Sparrow is one of the most well-researched species in the world thanks to Margaret Morse Nice, a mother of five who believed that women had more to contribute to the world than a tidy house. When she lived in Oklahoma, she wrote the definitive *Birds of Oklahoma*. When she moved to Ohio, she trapped and banded 870 different Song Sparrows near her home, and closely followed 336 individuals. She weighed and measured each one every time it entered a trap, providing her with a wealth of data. In the course of her research, she never killed a single bird. Nice's study of the Song Sparrow was "the first long-term field investigation of the individual life of any free-living wild animal," wrote Konrad Lorenz.

Nice's most famous bird, which she called 4M, remained in her study area for seven years. On May 11, 1935, she followed 4M for an entire day, beginning at 4:42 A.M.; 4M began singing two minutes later, over a half hour before the sun rose. Until sunset, Nice recorded his every action, his every food morsel, every one of the 2,305 songs he sang. There are worse ways to spend a day, or a lifetime.

12 One of the first warblers to return each spring is the Nashville—discovered in 1808 near Nashville, Tennessee, by Alexander Wilson. It's lemon yellow beneath, with an olive back, no wing bars, a bluish-gray face, white eye rings, and a secret orange crown that only the most determined birders see in the field. Wilson found only two more during his lifetime, and Audubon managed to shoot only three or four. Nowadays it's more common—I count an average of forty-four just along my Breeding Bird Survey route.

Like many other warblers, Nashvilles nest on the ground, although they feed mainly in trees. They weave their nests from moss and bits of fern on a moss hummock at the foot of a stump or bush. Rabbit fur often cushions the four or five white eggs, dotted with reddish brown. The Nashville is one of the easiest warblers for beginners to observe, since it feeds mainly in the middle story of trees, usually on the outermost branches and twigs. Yet, as with most warblers, you must be alert to the possibility—even during the peak of warbler migration, most people pass right by these avian jewels without ever knowing what they're missing.

The Nashville Warbler's song is one of the easiest to learn. It's just about always given in two-parts. I learned it as "see-bit, see-bit, see-bit, see-bit, see; weet-weet-weet-weet-weet." The Nashville is a tiny sprite—only about four-and-a-half inches long, weighing a third of an ounce.

Notes

May

Great Blue Herons nest in many different places—on the ground, on rock ledges, in dead trees or living pines, even on duck blinds. Some nest alone, others in colonies. Newly built nests may be only eighteen inches across, but older nests, used year after year, can grow to be three or four feet across. It takes the eggs about a month to hatch, and about two more months for the young to fledge.

13 John and Karen take me to a Great Blue Heron rookery one dawn. The morning is filled with early warbler music—Ovenbirds sing "Teacher! Teacher! Teacher!" Black-throated Green Warblers sing both "zee, zee, zoo-zoo, zee," and "zee-zee-zee, zoo-zee." Nashvilles sing their two-part song. These early warblers have first choice of territories, but a hungry week or two waiting for the first caterpillars to emerge on the first leaves.

In the pink dawn, Tree Swallows zip everywhere. Here the swallows nest in natural cavities in the rotting wood along the shoreline. No other sound of spring has the power of a Tree Swallow's "cheerily, cheerily" to make me smile.

Morning fog hangs over the lake, and the tall snags laden with improbable stick nests are in soft focus. Two herons fish in the water and several fly in and out, but most sit in the skeletal trees, their ungainly forms perching awkwardly, assuring us that, yes, Mother Nature still has her sense of humor.

Notes

14 Some birds, like chickadees and robins, are recognized by just about everyone. Others, like LeConte's Sparrows and Alder Flycatchers, are familiar only to serious bird-watchers. The Brown Thrasher is a fairly common bird of suburbs as well as the country, and the state bird of Georgia, yet many people don't know it exists.

The thrasher is related to the mockingbird, and can imitate many bird songs and calls, though, unlike the mocker, it doesn't imitate screeching tires and chain saws. It has a reddish brown back, heavily streaked breast, long tail, and golden eyes. It's often found noisily tossing leaves aside to uncover bugs in the moist soil. It eats many insects, including army worms and tent caterpillars. Nothing eats enough army worms to suit Northlanders, but the thrasher does its part. It also eats frogs, small snakes, sow bugs, lots of garden pests, acorns, and a variety of berries, and can be attracted to feeders with grape jelly. Thrashers may live a long time—a banded one was captured and released when it was nine years, eight months old, and another when it was twelve years, ten months old.

The Brown Thrasher's song is a series of short, musical phrases, usually sung in pairs. Farmers interpret the song as "Drop it, drop it, cover it, cover it, pull it up, pull it up." People who spend more time on the phone than in fields translate the song as "Hello, hello, yes, yes, who is this? who is this? I should say, I should say, how's that? how's that?"

Notes

May

Golden-winged Warblers sing a simple "Bee, bzzz-bzzz-bzzz." They're uncommon, breeding in openings of swampy deciduous woodlands and in old pastures overgrown with dense shrubs, and are becoming rarer as the closely related Blue-winged Warbler expands its range northward. Bluewings and goldenwings sometimes hybridize. From beneath, the goldenwing resembles a chickadee, with black bib and white underside.

15 Birdwatching can provide a surprising level of high-quality aerobic exercise. I used to bird at my favorite Madison park early each morning, leaving at seven-thirty to catch my bus to get to work. Hearing my first Golden-winged Warbler, I searched hard—we have to actually see birds to add them to a life list—but this one hid in a thick tangle of shrubbery as my bus came and left. No way could I catch a bus with a lifer singing so near. It took ten minutes, but I finally saw it, and then had to run two-and-a-half miles to school.

I didn't notice the school bus pass about a mile from school, but several kids noticed me and were taking bets about just how fast an elementary teacher can sprint. I charged into my classroom just as my sixth graders were coming in for science. My speed gave them new respect for science teachers, and my story gave them a new alibi when they were caught in a tight situation. For the rest of the year, whenever someone was late for class or caught gazing out the window, we'd hear a suspicious story about an elusive Golden-winged Warbler.

Notes

16 May nights are cool in the Northland—we aren't supposed to set out tomatoes until Memorial Day—but in a lakeside cabin we sleep with windows open. The weight of an extra blanket or two is a reasonable price for hearing the nighttime music of loons.

Loons communicate with many kinds of behaviors, but it's their calls that capture our imaginations. Judith McIntyre, the authority on loon vocalizations, interprets short, single hoots as contact calls. Tremolos, or laughing calls, which children interpret as "Let's party, dude," are actually alarm calls. Duets proclaim or defend territories. Yodels, given only by males, are aggressive territorial proclamations. Long wails seem to mean "Come here" or "Here I come." Even week-old chicks wail to beg from or call parents. We imitate wails to attract a loon closer. If it makes the laughlike tremolo, we quickly leave it in peace.

Listening to loons in bed at night, we seldom try to translate. Like all lovely music, the beauty of loon music transcends language, surpasses understanding. It simply is.

Contrary to popular opinion, the loon does not take its name from its "loony," maniacal call. The name is etymologically unrelated to *lunar*, from which we get *lunatic* and *loony*. *Loon* actually comes from the Scandinavian word *lom*, for a lame or clumsy person, and was applied to the loon for its awkwardness on land.

Notes

May

Chickadees visit feeders through summer, but far less frequently than in winter. In summer they concentrate on protein from insects and spiders. In fall they get extra vitamins from wild fruits. In winter they're limited more to carbohydrates and fats, when they scrounge for suet, carrion, seeds, and insect eggs and pupae found in bark crevices.

17 Before dawn, the sweet whistles of chickadees fill the air. The "fee-bee" song is given year-round, but least often in fall and early winter and most often in spring. Usually only males sing, but occasionally a pair duets back and forth, perhaps sealing their pair bond, acting as the Steve and Eydie of the bird world.

The romantic inclinations of chickadees increase as spring advances. They're discreet, treasuring their privacy, unlike cowbirds and gulls, which are caught in the act of lovemaking right on people's front lawns. The "come-hither" look in a chickadee is a full-body display. The male or female delicately flutters its wings and tail, and then retreats to a hidden branch to create new little chickadees. The pair excavates their own nesting hole. The nests I have found have all been in the trunks of small, rotted birches, below eye level. To find a nest, watch for chickadees carrying wood chips, and follow them. Sometimes they dig out two or three holes before they're satisfied, so it takes patience to find the real nest, where they'll rear six to eight young. Put your hand near an occupied nest and the chickadee within will loudly hiss like a snake.

Notes

18 In sphagnum bogs at dawn, Hermit Thrushes and Winter Wrens sing. John Terres describes the Hermit Thrush's song as a "clear flutelike note, followed by ethereal, bell-like tones, ascending and descending in no fixed order, rising until reaching dizzying vocal heights and the notes fade away in silvery tinkle." It harmonizes with the Winter Wren's silver-threaded song. This tiny wren, four inches from the tip of its beak to the end of its stubby tail, belts out one of the longest of all bird songs, with 108 to 113 separate notes. Its whole body vibrates with the effort.

The Hermit Thrush sings deep in the woods, motionless for minutes at a time, looking more like a dead branch than a feathered angel. But he's not shy. We watch for many minutes as he sings again and again. Winter Wrens are much harder to locate. Once, scanning the tree tops with my naked eye, I glimpsed a tiny red berry near the tip of a tall, thin spruce. I pulled up my binoculars, expecting a botanical marvel, and looked right into the open mouth of a singing Winter Wren. When my mind's eye riffles through memorable scenes, this discovery is always on top.

At dawn, as the sky is transformed from gray to pink to soft blue, we feel a oneness with the earth. Animals are less wary by the dawn's early light—I've approached deer, fox, and even coyotes that would have vanished before I noticed them in day. It's the witching hour, ours for the keeping if only we drag ourselves out of bed to accept this gift from above.

Notes

May

Unlike most sparrows, which sing from exposed perches, whitethroats usually sing in low branches, but with practice it isn't too hard to find singing birds. They respond to whistled imitations of their song, and often duet with humans. It's fun to play this game in backyards during migration, but not in the woods once they start defending territories—good human whistlers can stress the birds during their nesting season.

19 The North Woods ring with the song of "Old Sam Peabody, Peabody, Peabody." Once White-throated Sparrows cross our northern border, they change their tune, to "Oh, sweet Canada, Canada, Canada." This most pleasant of tunes is one of the true joys of spring.

The whitethroat is named for its white bib. The bib isn't as conspicuous as its black-and-white head stripes, but at least the white throat is visible in all plumages. Many whitethroats have tan head stripes—ornithologists once believed these were females and young birds, but many now believe the tan- and white-striped variations are rather like blue- and brown-eyed people.

Whitethroats often visit feeding stations in large flocks. It's possible to see fifty or more scratching the ground in their busy way at the peak of migration. They like sunflower, but also feed on mixed seed. Like most sparrows, they seldom alight on the feeder itself, but pick up spilled seeds beneath. They remain in North Country to breed, and we hear their matchless song in our forests throughout June and July.

Notes

20 The raspy song and "chick-burr" note of a Scarlet Tanager issues from a Port Wing aspen. This is poor habitat for a bird requiring mature, unbroken hardwood and mixed forests, and the firebird will soon vanish, but I'm grateful for even this brief glimpse.

Tanagers are becoming heartbreakingly scarce in eastern America compared to just a decade ago. Tropical deforestation is half the story, forest fragmentation here the other half. Roads and development cut huge forest tracts into a patchwork of smaller woods. People find small woodlots equally lovely and more accessible, and edge produced by cuts provides habitat for grouse, deer, cats, hawks, skunks, raccoons, crows, and jays. Problem is, many of these edge creatures are predators, or omnivores with an attitude, and it goes badly for the tanagers. Cowbirds don't invade unbroken forest beyond edges, but as edge grows, tanagers raise cowbirds instead of their own babies. If their first brood is lost—to a predator or a cowbird—they don't get another chance before they must head south. A world without the vivid beauty of tanagers would be a diminished world, indeed.

Dr. Sidney Gauthreaux used weather radar data to conclude that between the 1960s and the 1980s the number of birds migrating along the coast of the Gulf of Mexico declined 50 percent. Imagine that.

Notes

May

Shorebirds enjoy two summers every year, catching more sun rays than virtually any other creatures on earth. They're also exposed to more ultraviolet light than most, and may suffer long-term health effects with the thinning ozone layer. Skin cancers are probably unlikely with feather protection, but eye problems may result from prolonged exposure. So far, tiny avian ophthalmologists haven't reviewed the situation.

21 Ah, May—that fragrant month of lush grass and blooming hyacinths, when waxwings and hummers hover about apple blossoms, the time when shorebirds and birders alike are drawn to—sewage ponds. Apparently some olfactory sensibilities are more discriminating than others.

Some of the finest birding in spring is at mud flats and sewage ponds, where sandpipers and plovers pick through muck and sludge. These creatures of earth and wind are among the world's greatest travelers. The smallest, the Least Sandpiper, weighing less than a first-class letter, breeds on the Arctic tundra and winters in Central and South America. The largest, the Hudsonian Godwit, with upswept bill and long, slender neck, weighs between seven and fifteen ounces. If godwits traveled by airline, their frequent flyer mileage would bring airlines to bankruptcy—they nest in subarctic Canada, spend late summer on Hudson Bay, and then head for Argentina's Tierra del Fuego. Most shorebirds will soon vanish to the Canadian wilderness, so head on out to your nearest sewage treatment pond and enjoy these exotic wanderers while you can. Just remember your nose plug.

Notes

22 A Lake Superior May is usually punctuated with cold, steady drizzle and thick fog—perfect for watching migrants. On the shore, especially at Minnesota Point, warblers hop and skulk in the sand at the edge of the water. Apparently, bug-catching in cold weather is easier near water. It's fun to look down upon warblers for once.

When my children were little and I was housebound on cold, rainy days, I birded through the window, running out whenever a chickadee flock came in with attendant warblers. I sprinted in every two or three minutes to make sure everyone was okay, and then charged back out, praying that this would be the day when all three kids took a nap at the same time. On pleasant days the kids came out with me, but the big migration always happened during shivery drizzle, when birds advancing on a warm front were grounded by a cold front. Even with my parental responsibilities I could see eighteen or twenty species of warblers in a day. How can anyone mourn the sunshine in the presence of a flaming Blackburnian Warbler, or with a lemon and licorice Magnolia Warbler glowing in the mist?

Thrushes abound during May showers. When my binoculars get too foggy outside, I dry them off at the living room window watching Veeries and Swainson's Thrushes running along the driveway and on Peabody Street. Thrushes often sing their ethereal songs throughout a drizzly day.

Notes

May

The pintail is the only freshwater duck in North America with long central tail feathers, giving it such nicknames as sprigtail and spike tail. Males have a sophisticated beauty—their soft brown, black, and white colors may be muted but could never be considered drab. Females look like dignified, long-tailed Mallard hens. Ninety percent of their food is vegetal—mostly seeds from sedges, grasses, and pond weeds.

23 Spring migration makes us as restless as birds, and Billie and I often find ourselves at Erie Pier, where the Army Corps of Engineers piles up dredge spoils from the Duluth harbor. It's muddy, occasionally smelly, and noisy from heavy machinery. The sand on the dikes is oily, probably toxic, but we come for ducks and shorebirds, and pay little attention to anything else.

Most of the duck migration has passed, but we find nine species, and are especially pleased to see our first, and possibly last, Northern Pintail of the year. This elegant duck doesn't visit the Lake Superior area on purpose, so we never see more than a few in a year.

Pintails nest on the tundra and near prairie potholes, sometimes building their nests over a half mile from water. They produce fewer ducklings than most—only six to nine in a brood. A great many winter on saltwater. One pintail that was treated for botulism and then banded and released in Utah in 1942 was found, hungry and exhausted, on Palmyra Island, about a thousand miles southwest of Honolulu and three thousand miles from the mainland, eighty-two days later.

Notes

24 One morning every May I count Mourning Doves for the U.S. Fish and Wildlife Service. Data from over one thousand twenty-mile routes helps them plot Mourning Dove distribution and abundance throughout the country. Northeastern Minnesota is notoriously poor in doves, and my route through mostly forested country is one of the worst—I often find no doves at all, though I did find three in 1992. Despite a dearth of doves, the survey offers a pleasant way to spend a spring morning. Being alone on dark country roads has its dangers, so Billie or my dog, Bunter, comes along to keep me company.

It's dark at my first stop, always precisely at 4:55 A.M., thirty minutes before sunrise, on a calm day without rain. The temperature is usually in the thirties, rising to the forties by the time I finish. I arrive early to hear the morning's last woodcocks. Snipe aren't so fussy about light—I hear winnowing at several stops. Sedge Wrens twang, like toy rubber-band musical instruments, accompanied by the Alder Flycatchers' "we-be'-o." Robins and Veeries carol as a grouse drums. On lucky years I hear an owl, or at least see a shadowy silhouette on the drive.

When doing an official survey, I must concentrate on listening and looking for Mourning Doves once 4:55 A.M. rolls around, but singing Bobolinks, Black-billed Cuckoos, and Golden-winged Warblers always manage to catch my attention. At each stop I listen for exactly three minutes and then rush on to the next stop, one mile away. I finish at 6:52, and go home for breakfast. There are few finer ways to start a morning in May.

Notes

May

Books caution birders to wear inconspicuous clothing, but orioles approach my bright orange University of Illinois sweatshirt, and Red-winged Blackbirds bonk my head and hummingbirds fly up to my face when I wear a red hat. Research suggests that some dully colored birds shy away from bright colors, but once, in Texas, a Northern Beardless-Tyrannulet came within ten feet of me and my red hat, and there's no duller bird in the universe.

25 Walking along the dike of the Port Wing sewage ponds, I come upon a pair of Canada Geese and their nest. They stand their ground, watching my every move with wise and wary eyes, ready to beat me to a pulp, or die in the attempt, if I try anything. If I'd sneaked up on them in a camouflage suit, they'd have flown away in a flash, I think less frightened than outraged at the arrogance of any human who believes it possible to enter the wild unnoticed. My bright red hat seems to reassure birds that I have nothing to hide.

These geese allow me to come within fifteen feet of them—I don't want to disturb them, but I do want to reach a bend in the path that lies between us. The male shields his mate's body, just in case, and they honk. When I honk back, the female seems to take it as a reassuring sign and settles down on her nest. The male still doesn't trust me, but by the time I turn away on my bend in the path, he's hissing at a turtle and pretty much ignoring me. He knows I'm only human, not a part of his wild world, but he condescends to grant me a short visit.

Notes

26 Humans take from the natural world, but give nothing in return. We buy duck stamps and contribute to nongame wildlife programs to support habitat maintenance and wildlife management, but in truth, managing the wild is an oxymoron. We decide which species merit attention, usually because they make tasty or photogenic targets, forgetting that each is part of a complex web of interconnected parts, many so small we don't know they exist, yet each irreplaceable. In the last century we destroyed the Carolina Parakeet because it ate more fruit than we cared to share, and the Passenger Pigeon because it was edible and easy to shoot by the boxcarful. We smugly pretend that we are wiser and less greedy now, yet during severe droughts we kill threatened duck species for no better reason than that grown people don't know another way to enjoy autumn marshes at dawn. We take Florida vacations, flushing our sewage into the Everglades, where it fertilizes cattails that choke out the native sawgrass upon which Everglades creatures depend. We dine on all-beef patties that in life grazed on the raped and murdered tropical rainforest. Have we forgotten that the root of the word humane is human?

Species have become extinct almost since life on earth began, and the birds we know today will all eventually become extinct. Why should we bother to save them? My children will all one day be dead, too, but when my baby Joey was hospitalized with septicemia, delaying his ultimate destiny was the whole point. A world without children, or a world without birds, is an unimaginable horror worth fighting, even dying, to prevent.

Notes

May

When *Silent Spring* was published, the chemical industry viciously attacked the dying Rachel Carson as well as her work. *Chemical World News* called the book "science fiction." *Time* called it "an emotional outburst." *Reader's Digest* canceled a contract to condense it, running the *Time* piece instead. A Federal Pest Control Board member said, "I thought she was a spinster. What's she so worried about genetics for?"

27 Rachel Carson was born May 27, 1907. Before writing *Silent Spring*, she was a biologist and writer, who raised two nieces after her sister died, and then her great-nephew after one of her nieces died.

In January 1958, she received a letter from Olga Huckins of Duxbury, Massachusetts, expressing concern about pesticides being sprayed over a private bird sanctuary in Cape Cod. It took Rachel Carson four years to research and write *Silent Spring*, as she battled breast cancer. The book, first published in a three part condensation in *The New Yorker*, and then in book form on September 27, 1962, explained how life-forms are interrelated and how poisons we use to kill insects ultimately seep through the food chain to contaminate higher animals, including ourselves.

Rachel Carson succumbed to cancer on April 14, 1964, during a spring when scientists, stimulated by her work, were first learning how DDT damages eggshells of nesting birds, and were finding the toxin in human milk. Jimmy Carter posthumously awarded her the Presidential Medal of Freedom in 1980.

Notes

28 The rising sun illuminates the crown of a Chestnut-sided Warbler. Black eye markings set off its white cheeks and chestnut sides to perfection—this is truly my favorite warbler. An Ovenbird's cheery "teacher, teacher, teacher!" reminds me of my start in birding, when every bird was new and exciting. Of course I love the Ovenbird best. A sunbeam catches the glow of a Blackburnian Warbler's flaming throat, and I realize this is my real favorite. An American Redstart whizzes by—I studied redstarts in Madison, and memories jolt the realization that of course the redstart is best. Three male Black-throated Blue Warblers dart about on the bathhouse roof, their matchless beauty and elegance proof of most-favored status. A Palm Warbler wags its tail on the roof, and I remember how Palm Warblers keep me company on the wall of the Lakewood Pumping Station in fall when I'm counting birds—surely I love this one best. Then the sleepy lisp of a Black-throated Green Warbler and the buzzy ascent of a Northern Parula make me realize the truth. Just as each one of my children is irreplaceable and uniquely special, so, too, each warbler is my absolute favorite.

Warblers are returning to the North Woods at a furious pace now. They're easiest to find when we know their songs. Warblers, recorded on both record and cassette, produced by Donald J. Borror and William W. H. Gunn through the Cornell Laboratory of Ornithology and the Federation of Ontario Naturalists, is the finest and most complete recording of their songs and calls available.

Notes

May

John James Audubon wrote about an encounter with a Rose-breasted Grosbeak one night In 1834, while he was sleeping in the Mohawk River Valley of New York: "The evening was calm and beautiful, the sky sparkled with stars. Suddenly there burst on my soul the serenade of the Rose-breasted bird, so rich, so mellow, so loud in the stillness of the night, that sleep fled from my eyelids. Never did I enjoy music more."

29 One of the most pleasant of backyard birds is the Rose-breasted Grosbeak. Its song, like a robin who takes voice lessons, is a long, rich warble. Robins sing long sentences, the words often of three syllables—Rose-breasted Grosbeak sentences can't be broken into distinct words as easily. Unlike robins and most other birds, female as well as male Rose-breasted Grosbeaks sing. And, again unlike most birds, males help construct the nest and even incubate the eggs. Both sexes have been observed singing as they sit on the eggs or young, which seems somehow foolish but sweet. Females stay on the nest even when approached by predators. There are many stories of researchers or photographers who have literally picked up a female in the hand to steal a glimpse at her eggs.

Rose-breasted Grosbeaks eat as much insect as plant food—one of their common names is the "potato bug bird." Their scientific name, *Pheucticus*, may come from the Greek *pheuticus*, meaning "shy and retiring," or from the Greek *phycticos*, which means "painted with cosmetics." Either meaning seems appropriate.

Notes

30 The very first Gray Catbird I ever saw was skulking in thick shrubbery on the Michigan State University campus when its mewing calls caught my attention. I expected it to be a real cat, and was delighted to learn that at least one bird was named for a feature I could recognize. Catbirds are in the same family, Mimidae, as thrashers and mockingbirds. They sing a long string of imitations and notes, occasionally punctuated by a mew.

The catbird is long and slender, a bit smaller than a robin, with a solid gray body, black cap and tail, and rusty feathers beneath the base of the tail. It usually builds its nest quite close to the ground, in thick, brushy tangles, and is secretive about its nesting habits. Several times I've been unable to find the Peabody Street catbirds' nest until the leaves fell. It's attracted to honeysuckle, mulberries, crab apples, and other fruiting trees and shrubs. It eats a bit more plant than animal food, but does eat plenty of insects and grubs. It visits feeders for oranges, jelly, sugar water, suet, peanuts, and bread. It's feisty—if a snake, raccoon, or other predator comes near, a catbird displays ferociously and sometimes even attacks.

Predators kill many catbirds. During migration many crash into tall buildings and TV towers and are hit by cars. Although one banded catbird survived over ten years, most never see their first birthday, and few live beyond two. If someone says you're sitting in the catbird's seat, you'd be wise to find out how literally it's meant—you might be in big trouble.

Notes

May

Chickens come from four species of jungle fowl inhabiting Southeast Asia. They've been recorded in writings from India as early as 3200 B.C., China by 1400 B.C., and Egypt and Crete by 1500 B.C. Cocks are pictured on Greek coins from at least 700 B.C. Greeks valued fowl primarily for cockfights, but Romans used them for food, developing a complex poultry industry that collapsed with the fall of the Roman Empire.

31 When five-year-old Katie got chicken pox, we needed to find out how the disease got its avian name. I guessed that it came from the little bump in the center of each pock, which sort of looks like plucked chicken skin. Friends suggested that maybe people once believed the disease actually came from chickens. Folks at the St. Louis County Public Health Service didn't have the foggiest idea, but guessed it came from people scratching like chickens. Finally I consulted the highest authority on matters etymological, the Oxford English Dictionary, which demolished all three hypotheses in one fell swoop. Chicken pox is named for the fact that it's so mild compared to smallpox—such a wimpy disease is thus called "chicken."

Male domestic fowl, called cocks, have for centuries been known for their combativeness, or cockiness. But females are another matter. Despite the definite presence of both intestines and vertebrae, chickens have long been considered gutless and spineless. Fortunately, Katie quickly got better, and I concluded that it's better to be henpecked by chicken pox than hit by some more cocksure virus.

Notes

June

June

Boy, do I have egg on my face! I put all my eggs in one basket, and, like an egghead, counted my eggs before they hatched—my nest egg smelled like rotten eggs. The situation was like walking on eggs. But you can't make an omelet without breaking eggs, so I'll just keep searching for the goose that laid the golden egg and wondering which came first—the chicken or the egg.

1 June and eggs are bustin' out all over. Ordinary eggs crack open to reveal baby egrets, eagles, and Evening Grosbeaks, and each will eventually help produce more eggs—an eggstremely eggciting cycle inspiring many cultures to use eggs as symbols of fertility, regeneration, and spring itself.

Unlike reptile eggs, covered with tough, leathery skin, bird eggs are encased in a fragile calcareous shell. In spite of this thin, delicate shell, the egg is strong enough to bear the weight of the parent bird—strong enough even to withstand the force of human hands squeezing it. Reptiles, amphibians, fish, insects, and even the duck-billed platypus lay eggs, but the eggs of birds have more power over our imaginations. The public outcry against DDT in the 1960s and early 1970s was less because of its potential effect on human beings than because it causes eggshell thinning. The horrifying image of a mother Peregrine Falcon accidentally splattering her babies convinced the public, and the Nixon administration, to ban this dangerous pesticide. Eggs are supposed to be symbols of life, not death.

Notes

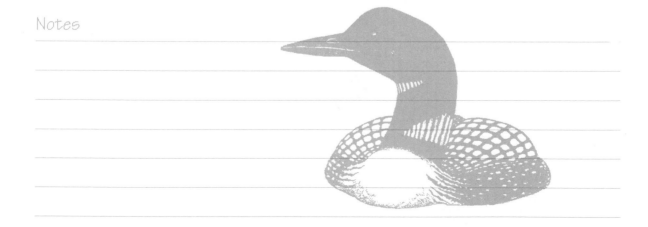

2 Birds live a dark, cramped existence within the egg—nature's starkest efficiency apartment. The embryo forms in a germinal spot between the yolk and the albumen. The yolk, like a pantry, holds a rich mixture of fats, proteins, and carbohydrates to nourish the embryo. The albumen, an all-encompassing waterbed for the ultimate couch potato, is about 88 percent water and 10 percent amino acids, with traces of minerals. It cushions the embryo, protects it from drying out, and provides structural support to keep the yolk from flattening. The albumen transfers water and some nutrients to the yolk as the chick develops. The shell, covered with hundreds of tiny pores where oxygen and carbon dioxide diffuse in and out, protects the egg and keeps it from drying out.

Wastes collect in the egg's bathroom, a chamber called the allantois, which grows as the yolk shrinks. The allantois is surrounded by a network of blood vessels. As the chick grows, these thin-walled vessels press against the shell, absorbing oxygen through the pores, allowing a developing bird to solve its waste disposal and breathing problems in one simple, elegant system.

An embryonic bird has simple needs and pleasures—its greatest excitement each day comes when it's rolled over. But the embryo, like a developing human, hardly vegetates. It can hear sounds, like the soft peepings of brothers and sisters within their own eggs. Some birds even learn elements of their species's song from the egg. Parent birds never learn to communicate with their unhatched babies by taking little avian prenatal classes.

Notes

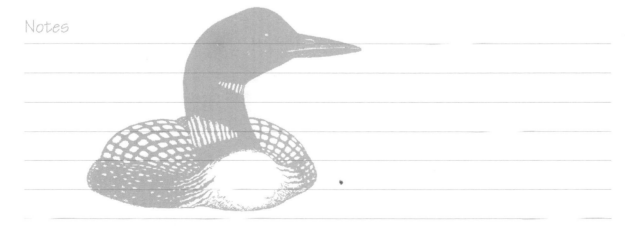

June

For such tiny birds, hummingbirds sometimes get into big trouble. They've been caught in spiderwebs, impaled on thistles, swept into lakes by high winds, snatched out of the air and eaten by frogs and dragonflies, and snapped up by praying mantises. Most hummingbirds don't survive until their first birthday. As Kermit the Frog says, it's not easy being green.

3 Once I was watching a male hummingbird when a Bald Eagle flew overhead. The hummer attacked, darting at the eagle from above like a tiny, stringless yo-yo. I doubt if the eagle even noticed, but it was moving on anyway and so the hummer returned to his perch, mission accomplished. A person looking up in the middle of this scene to see a large bird with a hummer coming up from its back might start a myth about hummingbirds riding on the backs of eagles.

The male hummingbird spends its summer brawling with bumblebees, other hummingbirds, and any other birds that get its dander up. Meanwhile, the female weaves a tight, shallow cup nest, the size of a walnut half, using soft down from ferns, milkweed, fireweed, and thistles. The upper edge curves inward to keep the eggs from rolling out. She binds it together with spiderwebs or silk from a tent caterpillar's nest, and decorates the outside with lichens and mosses so the nest blends with the branch. The two bean-sized eggs hatch in sixteen days, and the babies fly in three weeks. She doesn't seem to mind single parenthood—she often goes through the cycle twice in a season.

Notes

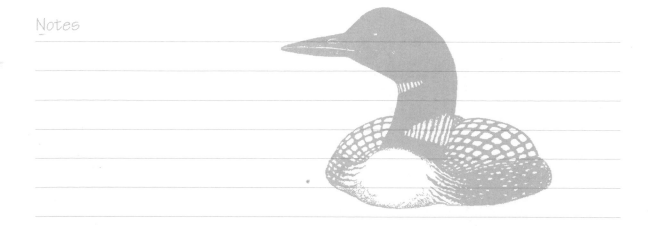

4 One of the easiest warblers to identify is the Magnolia Warbler. The strikingly handsome male is yellow with heavy black streaks beneath, a bluish-black back and tail, gray crown, black cheeks with white eyebrow stripes, and bold white patches on the wings and tail. The square white tail markings are similar to the orange or yellow on a redstart's tail, and, like the redstart, the Magnolia Warbler often fans its tail in display to emphasize the feature.

Magnolia Warblers are birds of the northern coniferous forest. On a morning stroll through Port Wing spruce woods in June or early July, I usually find ten or so males on territory, singing at eye level and sometimes approaching quite close to me. They received their inappropriate name in 1810 from Alexander Wilson, who shot some migrants in a magnolia tree near Fort Adams, Mississippi. A more recent Alexander, Alexander Sprunt, contended that naming them "Balsam or Spruce Warbler would be better by far than Magnolia." He added, "Few birds are as spectacular in their habitat as this one. Seen amid the semigloom of the silent ranks of evergreens, it seems to glow with living color."

Tiny migrants are often tossed about horribly in storms. On May 7, 1951, Texas ornithologist Pauline James wrote from Padre Island, "Over 10,000 exhausted small birds perished here this day, about 85 percent of them warblers. Of 2,421 birds actually collected, 1,109 were Magnolia Warblers."

Notes

June

In 1945, to learn whether females could raise young alone, an ornithologist shot a nesting male Indigo Bunting. The next day the female had a new mate, and the scientist shot him, too. Each day a new male appeared and was shot until the scientist had removed nine—he left the tenth in peace. Extra birds, called floaters, were once all around, waiting in the wings for available territories. Fifty years later, few extra songbirds exist anywhere.

5 The Indigo Bunting, the truest blue bird of them all, is fairly common in open areas of the Northland, but not many people notice it. Males are bright blue and sing on conspicuous perches, but without good lighting they appear black or gray. When the sun hits them full front, their extraordinary color catches the eye. Female Indigo Buntings are dull brown with faint streaks, like unusually drab sparrows.

These little birds spend about seven months of the year in Central America, coming to the United States only to raise their babies. The female weaves the cup-shaped nest from grasses, snake skins, strips of bark, and anything else handy, from feathers and hair to facial tissues. The nest is usually only a few feet from the ground in a tangle of shrubs, but she occasionally builds it five to fifteen feet high, perhaps to confuse ornithologists. While she's building, he sings to declare their territorial boundaries. The song is a long string of paired notes, some buzzy, each pair on a different pitch. Indigo Buntings may sing at any time of day, and often into August after other birds have packed up their instruments for the season.

Notes

6 A chickadee once landed on my sleeping dog Bunter and snatched a beakful of dog hair. Bunter didn't miss the fur, but it served as valuable insulation for the chickadee. Chipping Sparrows line their nests with horse hair. Tree Swallows use white gull feathers. These unconsidered trifles are snatched up by birds that value them in a behavior classified by ornithologists as *autolycism*.

Autolycism is neither predation nor parasitism—it's a type of symbiosis. Seabirds and vultures watch one another in the sky, and when one drops down for a meal, others quickly follow. African honeyguides can't get inside honeybee hives unless something bigger opens them, so when a honeyguide discovers a hive, it leads a human or the badgerlike *ratel* to it. The mammal gets most of the honey, and the honeyguide gets the comb. Cowbirds and egrets follow grazing cows, horses, and bison, eating insects stirred up by large hooves. African marsh hawks attend quail-shooting parties to pick up quarry the sportsmen don't find. Some raptors follow trains, snatching up birds flushed as the train rushes along. By all accounts, the train never notices.

In Shakespeare's play *A Winter's Tale*, a rogue named Autolycus, named for Greek mythology's Athenian scrounger, is described as a "snapper-up of unconsidered trifles." That character inspired British ornithologist Colonel Richard Meinertzhagen to name the practical uses birds make of other animals autolycism.

Notes

June

Blackburnian Warblers usually build their nests out toward the end of high limbs, where mother and babies are safe from virtually all predators. The highest nest ever located was eighty-four feet up in a spruce. Four scrawny nestlings, stuffed only with beetles, caterpillars, spiders, and other such fare, are magically transformed within weeks into exquisite Blackburnian Warblers, to delight our eyes and touch our souls.

7 On a dawn walk on the shores of Burntside Lake near the Boundary Waters, at a little footbridge, a male Blackburnian Warbler sips from a rippling stream and takes a quick bath, spraying water droplets, and then alights on a branch at eye level to preen in a ray of early morning sun. He's comfortable and at peace, utterly ignoring my presence, clearly not as fascinated with my species as I am with his. His mate flies past, and he darts off in pursuit. Within a minute he's perched at the top of a spruce, singing at a more typical altitude for his species.

To match the high notes of its song, the Blackburnian Warbler is usually a bird of the heavens, flitting among spires of spruce and balsam and in sun-dappled crowns of birch and aspen. When this quarter-ounce sprite alights on the outermost twig of a trembling aspen, the leaves barely rustle. Either to display their flaming throats to other males or to soak up a few rays of sunlight, males tend to face the sun as they sing, vivid orange against blue sky.

Notes

8 The male Blackburnian Warbler is extraordinarily beautiful, even by warbler standards. Elliot Coues wrote of it, "There is nothing to compare with the exquisite hue of this Promethean torch." The female's colors are duller, but she has a shy prettiness all her own. They breed in northern mixed and coniferous forests, especially in untouched mature spruce forests that foresters maintain are poor habitat for wildlife. In Minnesota bog country and the spruce forests of northern Wisconsin, this is one of the more common warblers. It's also found in the Appalachian mountains, mainly in oaks and hemlocks.

Despite its fairly high numbers, the blackburnian is elusive. Audubon painted three female blackburnians, labeled "Hemlock Warblers," apparently never realizing they were of the same species as the blackburnian male correctly labeled on one painting. Modern birders have little trouble identifying it by plumage, but its songs are more confusing. One is very similar to the Black-and-White Warbler's "wee-see, wee-see, wee-see." Others sound like Magnolia, Cape May, Nashville, and Yellow-rumped Warblers.

"Blackburnian" isn't a dictionary word, but it evokes the warbler's flaming orange throat, crown, and face, in contrast with shiny black facial and wing markings. The name was applied not out of the necessity to create a unique and lovely word for a unique and lovely creature, but simply to honor Anna Blackburn, an English woman whose patronage supported ornithologists during the 1700s, enabling her to decorate her home and museum with stuffed American birds.

Notes

June

Donald Duck was conceived when Walt Disney heard Clarence Nash reciting "Mary Had a Little Lamb" as a flustered duck on a Los Angeles radio station. Donald hatched on June 9, 1934, as a supporting character in *The Wise Little Hen.* The first film to explore Donald's hot temper was *Orphan's Benefit,* which catapulted him to stardom. Unlike the parents of most birds, Walt Disney didn't lay an egg with this duck.

9 The most famous duck in the world, Donald, is a Pekin duck—a white, domesticated breed of our common Mallard. The early Donald had a long bill, larger than a Blue-winged Teal's, but with time and maturity, his bill has shrunk. Donald is less portly than many domesticated ducks, but he still can't fly—he apparently limits filming to summer while he's molting.

Unlike other ducks, Donald can't swim. Fortunately, he can build boats, which he demonstrates in a few Chip 'n' Dale cartoons. He's also the only bird known to sprout facial hair—recorded in the 1945 film *No Sail.* He changes color, from livid blue when he's angry to bright red when he's humiliated in front of Daisy. And he does one thing no other wild bird has ever done—carry money.

One of the greatest complications in Donald's life is due to a natural characteristic of Pekin ducks—females often lay their eggs in inappropriate places, and overall make somewhat poor mothers. This explains why Donald so often ends up taking care of his three nephews, Huey, Dewey, and Luey.

Notes

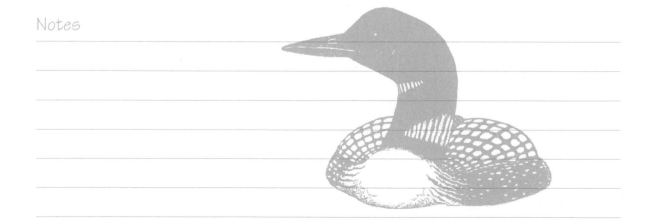

10 A newly hatched duckling is cuter than a robin in the nest because baby ducks are *precocial*—that is, they hatch with their eyes open and their bodies covered with soft down, ready to leave the nest within a couple of days, and often within hours.

Many precocial species live in marshes or near inland waters, where predators are numerous. Heavy, short-winged ground-nesters in any habitat, like grouse, are also likely to have precocial babies—they need too much landing space to alight directly on their nests, and if they continually ran back and forth to the nest feeding young, they'd wear down a revealing path for predators to follow. For birds like this, evolution favors larger eggs, and the babies complete much of their development before hatching. Ducks, shorebirds, and New Zealand kiwis lead their young to feeding areas, and the babies feed themselves. Domestic chicks get help from their mother, who scratches vigorously to unearth edible morsels. Gull and tern chicks, which are *subprecocial,* hatch covered with down, but are fed by their parents for a month before they can fish on their own.

Megapodes of Australia lay their eggs in a sand mound to be warmed by the sun, or in a mound of dead vegetation, which produces heat as it decays. Parents stir the sand so newly hatched babies can dig their way out, but then leave the babies completely on their own. Black-headed Ducks of South America lay their eggs in other birds' nests, especially grebes', and once hatched, the ducklings take care of themselves.

Notes

June

Altricial birds are helpless at first, but some are more capable of independent activity than others. Newly hatched woodpeckers are completely naked, and can do nothing but open their mouths to beg. Belted Kingfishers are also naked, but if a predator or ornithologist digs out a burrow, baby kingfishers toddle away from the light. Hawks hatch with thick down and open eyes, but are still completely dependent. They're considered semi-altricial.

11 When they hatch, songbirds, herons, and owls look like babies only a mother could love. These *altricial* species hatch pretty much naked and with closed eyes. They pop up and open their mouths like jack-in-the-boxes when the nest is jostled, and after they're fed they immediately back up to defecate on the edge of the nest, but can do little else. Baby songbird droppings are encased in strong membranes so the parents can carry them and dispose of them far away from the nest.

Large altricial species, like herons and eagles, nest in trees or on inaccessible cliffs. Egg production is fairly easy on the mother, since altricial birds don't develop much or need much nourishment within the egg. As a trade-off, once altricial eggs hatch, the parents feed and attend the nestlings constantly for weeks or even months. Altricial young don't leave the nest until they're feathered out, close to or heavier than adult body weight, and almost ready to fly. Many warblers fledge in eight to ten days. It takes about seventeen days for Blue Jays to leave the nest, thirty-five days for Great Horned Owls, two months for Great Blue Herons, and almost three months for Bald Eagles.

Notes

12 A woman calls, worried about a baby Blue Jay in her yard. When I see it, I'm horrified. Never have I seen a bird that couldn't balance, but this one lies limply on its side. One of its eyes is closed, and it can't lift its head. She tells me the yards on both sides of and behind hers were sprayed the day before. The jay's neurological damage supports my suspicion that it was exposed to high levels of insecticide.

Most lawn care companies apply fertilizers and pesticides on a schedule. Whether or not a particular lawn has cutworms, it gets insecticides. Whether or not it has dandelions, it gets herbicides. In a drought, we can recognize lawns serviced by these companies by their dead grass—they get fertilizers on schedule whether it rains or not. And these companies adhere to their schedules whether or not birds are likely to alight on wet, freshly poisoned grass. When people ask me why they don't get as many birds as they used to, I ask them if they or their neighbors hire lawn care services that apply herbicides and insecticides. Funny thing—the answer is often yes.

All pesticides must be approved by the Environmental Protection Agency. But many received "grandfathered" approvals in the 1970s and have never been tested for effects on wild birds. New ones quickly disintegrate to nontoxic chemicals, but may be highly toxic on application. Most insecticides kill earthworms, spiders, ladybugs, and butterflies—robins that aren't killed outright vanish as their food disappears. In 1992, the EPA stopped requiring most field testing before approval of new pesticides.

Notes

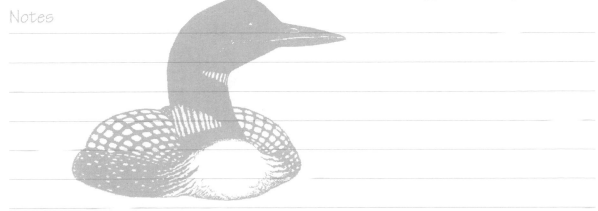

June

Birds pay a steep price for human antipathy to dandelions, but weed-haters do have alternatives to poisons. The time-honored technique of pulling weeds by hand still works. And for those without the time or inclination to do it personally, there are plenty of kids around who'd appreciate a little income. If toxic chemicals really seem the best solution, it's far better to spot-spray individual weeds than to lace every inch of lawn with poison.

13 My poisoned baby jay mews softly. It swallows well and seems comfortable in my hand, or in a tissue-lined bucket. The second day it opens both eyes, and on the third lifts its head. It can't swallow much at a time, so I feed it often. The will to live is powerful in a baby jay—life is all it will ever have. This one is curious about everything around it, and has the jay's usual good humor. I carry it about in a little sling.

It's at the itchiest stage, covered with growing feathers, each emerging from a strawlike sheath. A healthy fledgling spends hours scratching sheaths and shaking off dandruff—I do it for this one. I flex wings and legs so muscles can develop. Within a week it flaps by itself. It still can't balance, and, flopping on its side, wears away shoulder feathers, but steadily improves. After eighty-seven days, it sits upright for ten-minute stretches, and needs a roomier home than a plastic bucket. I move it to a cloth-lined aquarium when I can't carry it around in its sling. The first night, it wedges between cloth and glass, pressing a bare shoulder against the cool pane, and dies of hypothermia in its sleep.

Notes

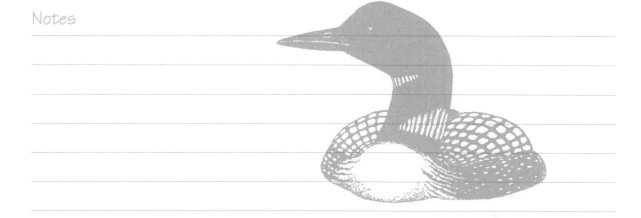

14 *Bartlett's Quotations* has over 22,000 entries—I naturally gravitate to bird references. I find 130 quotations just under the entries "bird" and "birds." Paul Laurence Dunbar knows "why the caged bird sings." Shakespeare says, "The eagle suffers little birds to sing," and "When birds do sing, hey ding a ding ding;/ Sweet lovers love the spring." *Bartlett's* authors are ambivalent about birds—there are a "clumsy dirty gray bird," a "gold-feathered bird," a "wild barbaric bird," and a "divine bird of Zeus." Lewis Carroll's Jubjub bird shows up, too.

No woodpeckers, nuthatches, vireos, or chickadees show up in *Bartlett's,* but bitterns, eagles, and hawks are all represented. Macbeth's chide to "thou cream-faced loon" is there, John Webster's "call for the robin redbreast and the wren," and Thoreau's bluebird, carrying the sky on his back. And that nasty old Anonymous gets space, too— "There was a little man, and he had a little gun,/ And his bullets were made of lead, lead, lead;/ He went to the brook, and saw a little duck,/ And shot it through the head, head, head." No Mother Goose ever wrote that one.

John Bartlett, an American editor and owner of the University Bookstore in Cambridge, Massachusetts, was born June 14, 1820. He published his first compilation of quotations in 1855, writing in the preface that "the object of this work is to show, to some extent, the obligations our language owes to various authors for numerous phrases and familiar quotations that have become household words."

Notes

June

Bobolinks have acquired such nicknames as skunk blackbirds, May birds, meadow winks, butter birds, and rice or reed birds. Southern farmers called them "Jekyll and Hyde birds"—pretty and joyful in spring, but devouring rice in late summer. Of course, those same farmers devoured the Bobolinks in enormous quantities, and shipped them to markets in Philadelphia, New York, and even Paris. On fancy restaurant menus they were listed as "reed birds on toast."

15 North Country pastures and meadows are home to the Bobolink—"Robert O'Lincoln" to William Cullen Bryant, who transcribed its song as "bob-o'-link, bob-o'-link, spink, spank, spink." One early ornithologist wrote it, "Tom Noodle, Tom Noodle, you owe me, you owe me, ten shillings and sixpence." Another transcribed it as "oh, geezeler, geezeler, gilipity, onkeler, oozeler, oo." Edward Howe Forbush wrote, "This is about the only bird that completely baffles the latter-day 'interpreters' of bird music. His notes tumble out with such headlong rapidity, in an apparent effort to jump over each other, that it is next to impossible for the scribe to set them down in the proper sequence of musical notation. Nevertheless, this harum-scarum expression of irrepressible joy is of the most pleasing character, and ranks among the finest music of the fields."

Male Bobolinks are solid black in front, with creamy yellow napes and bold white markings on wings and tail, as if they put their tuxedos on backwards. Females look like oversized LeConte's Sparrows. They pretty much stick to business in summer, so almost all the birds we see are males.

Notes

16 Walking along Port Wing meadows at dawn, I watch for snipe flying up from roadside ditches, their singing tails winnowing. An Upland Sandpiper calls its long, dramatic wolf whistle. Savannah Sparrows sing sleepy tunes, and yellowthroats conjure up a witchity spell. But the songs that thrill me most come from Bobolinks— they sing with such abandon and exuberance that my heart swells. They've inspired poetry from a wide variety of writers, including staid ornithologists. Thomas Sadler Roberts wrote in *The Birds of Minnesota*:

> In a favored place a dozen males may be in sight at once, swinging from the tops of tall weeds and flower stalks or circling in the air on fluttering wings, all vying with one another in a gushing medley of joyous, tinkling notes unrivalled among our singing birds. Ever and anon one of the circling birds sinks to the meadow below on upturned wings, fairly bursting with the ecstatic effort that pours from his vibrating body. An hour with the Bobolink in June is to the bird-lover an hour of long-remembered joy.

For centuries, Bobolinks were among the most abundant birds of the prairies and grassy meadows of Minnesota and Wisconsin, defining for many people the beauty of open country. Up here, they were considered a beneficial species because they ate huge quantities of weevils, beetles, grasshoppers, caterpillars, and the seeds of ragweed and other noxious weeds, and their joyful song ringing through the meadows was pleasing beyond compare.

Notes

June

Emily Dickinson understood the spiritual value of a Bobolink meadow. She wrote:
"Some keep the Sabbath going to Church—
I keep it, staying at Home—
With a bobolink for a Chorister—
And an orchard, for a Dome."

17 The Bobolink is a true long-distance migrant, breeding in the northern states and Canada, and, at summer's end, flying over five thousand miles to southern Brazil and northern Argentina. Bobolinks were abundant in the 1700s and early 1800s, but were so heavily hunted to provide food and to keep them out of rice fields during migration that the population was decimated. Nowadays little rice is grown along their main migration route, so they aren't shot as pests, but we've destroyed much of their breeding habitat, and they're shot for food and sport in South America. Farm pesticides claim many, and also kill the insects—beneficial as well as harmful—that make up their food supply.

It takes twenty-three to twenty-seven days for a Bobolink to develop from a newly laid egg to a flying bird, and during this critical time farm cats and mowing machines destroy them by the thousands. When farmers delay haying until baby Bobolinks are flying, they give this extraordinary species a chance to recover its numbers, and themselves the opportunity to enjoy Bobolink music for many years to come.

Notes

18 It's 3:45 A.M., June 11, 1992, as I drive to my Hart Lake Breeding Bird Survey area. Once every June I run a twenty-five-mile route, stopping and tallying birds for three minutes every half mile, taking four-and-a-half hours to complete the route. Kathy is my official assistant—I call out every bird I hear or see, and she marks each on our count sheet. Judy's along for fun—what else can a person do at 3:45 in the morning?

We pile out of the car at 4:30 and record weather conditions—50 degrees, little wind, no clouds. At 4:38, exactly thirty minutes before dawn, I start calling out birds—two Veeries, two Magnolia and three Mourning Warblers, an Ovenbird, three yellowthroats, one Song and one Swamp Sparrow, and six White-throated Sparrows— nineteen birds at the first stop. I have time for nothing but counting and rushing from stop to stop until we complete the fiftieth at 8:58. It's 68 degrees, calm and clear. Our total is 873 individuals of seventy species, with eighteen different kinds of warblers. Now we can mosey back through the route, stopping here and there to enjoy the bubbling brook, the North Woods, the beautiful day, and breakfast.

The Breeding Bird Survey, coordinated by the U.S. Fish and Wildlife Service, has monitored bird population trends in the United States and Canada since 1967. Almost 2,800 randomly located routes are run by experienced volunteers, who follow explicit instructions to provide a consistent data base. The survey has provided a body of information about declining numbers of some songbirds, especially Neotropical migrants, and increasing cowbird numbers.

Notes

June

Like humans, birds recognize their young by appearance and sound, not smell. When tiny nestlings fall from a nest, we put them right back—the parents quickly accept them. When fledglings jump out, they're as obstinate as human toddlers climbing out of a crib, so we leave them alone unless they're in danger—then we place them in a nearby tree or shrub. The parents recognize their calls and return when the coast is clear.

19 A woman brings me four nestlings that she wants to get rid of. She found them after a storm ten days before, and illegally kept them without a permit, feeding them nothing but canned dog food—protein enough to keep them barely alive, but no vitamin D_3 for proper bone growth. She didn't clean their box, and their bodies are caked in dog food and feces. She says, "I knew they would die from the start, but I wanted my kids to raise baby birds at least once. Now we're expecting company, plus I don't want the kids to be sad when they finally die." Instead, my children will get that pleasure.

I can tell they're vireos from the tiny hook already developing on the tip of their bills. One by one I dip them in a warm water bath to moisten, loosen, and tease off the caked filth. After being encased in it so long, not one knows how to preen, so I dry them with tissues, and repeat the process four times before I see feathers. One has a completely bald head—its bulging eyelids are sky blue. Their beaks are oversized for their bodies, their skulls and bodies stunted by the inappropriate diet. But they have bright eyes and eager mouths, and we hope for the best.

Notes

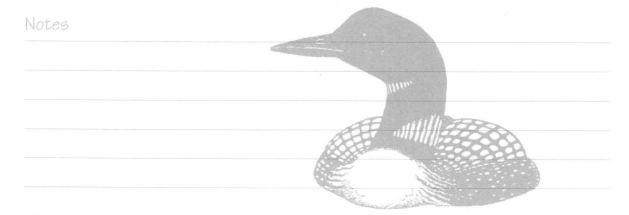

20 Our baby Red-eyed Vireos keep us busy from morning till night. The spunky bald one stretches after its bath, freed of the filthy cement that bound its body, then flitters awkwardly around my office, checking out every nook and cranny. When I place them on a sunny branch, Spunky downs a huge army worm, first piercing it with its hooked bill. Katie's favorite is "Baby"— the one with the fullest plumage and healthiest appearance. Joey and Tommy try not to fall for any of them. They know how awful it is to love a bird and watch it die.

The biggest dies first—it was growing rapidly when put on the improper diet, and survives only days. The runt lasts five days longer before suddenly fading. Poor bald Spunky dies of hypothermia that night—it had apparently survived nights snuggled between two warm bodies. Katie's Baby survives ten more days, and despite the fact that its skull is too small for its beak, we hope until the last moment that it will make it. It dies in Katie's hand, her tears consecrating its tiny body. I'm supposed to bring them to the biology museum, but Katie pleads to bury them under the lilac bush where they once basked in the warm sunshine.

Most baby songbirds eat a varied diet of caterpillars and other insects, often along with fruit, and they manufacture vitamin D_3 in sunlight. We feed them mealworms, crickets, and a mixture of ground-up high-protein dog food, applesauce, gelatin, and water, along with a mineral supplement and plenty of bird vitamins. We much prefer to return baby birds to their parents, who do a better job than mere humans ever could.

Notes

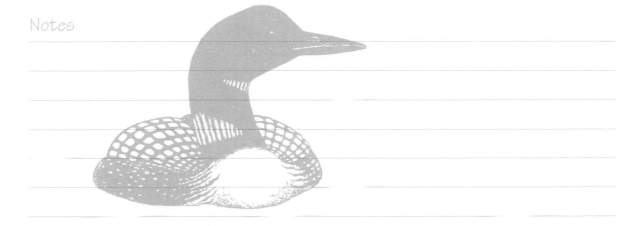

June

Birdsong will be heard throughout this longest day of the year, but the full chorus ebbs away hours after dawn. Female birds spend long June days building nests, incubating eggs, and then feeding and home-schooling their young. Males of many species help with construction work, and often share equally in day-care duties. One would think these busy birds would sleep soundly, but males often sing intermittently throughout the night.

21 Summer richness fills the air—even the muggy humidity gives us a feeling of tropical wealth. The northern forest stands cool and deep, darkly shaded with thick pines and spruces, fragrant with balsam perfume. At dawn, we listen to choir music as night's darkness succumbs to gentle light and magical shadows. We walk slowly, searching for each chorus member.

The alto section, dominated by Ovenbirds and White-throated Sparrows, sings at eye level, each member wearing a lovely, soft brown choir robe. The forest sopranos, lisping warblers and tinkling Winter Wrens, reach cathedral heights on the spires of spruces. Tenor Rose-breasted Grosbeaks show off rosy neckties and flashy tuxedos in flight over the dusty road. The basso profundo of the Ruffed Grouse reverberates along the forest floor, the performers themselves lost in the shadows of their mossy drumming logs.

This exquisite choir that never rehearses is the finest performance of the season. Tickets are given away free at the theater door, but you must arrive early—the forest choir seldom sings an encore.

Notes

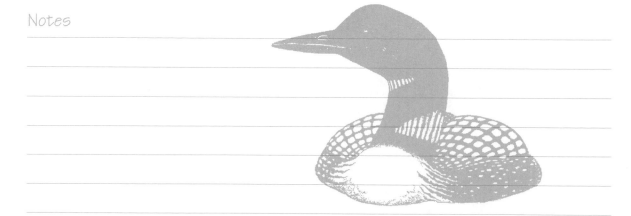

22 Bunter and I walk along Quarry Road in Port Wing. Three Winter Wrens proclaim territorial boundaries in exquisite song over our heads. At a sheltered beach, I watch ducks and shorebirds while Bunter whines impatiently, eager to play fetch. She leaps skyward as I pick up a chunk of driftwood, but I study it carefully before tossing it into the water—ladybugs cluster on driftwood here, and it would be an unforgivable sin to hurl a congregation of them to a watery death for the sake of a game of fetch.

The few people who drive past on the gravel road toward the slough wave and smile—Port Wing is a friendly place. There's always a Killdeer with eggs or young about at the slough so Bunter must heel, but she never minds, because we're headed for her favorite beach—the one that always has dead fish for rolling in. To kill the smell, we play fetch in the lake again as we follow the beach to Big Pete Road. Virgin pines tower above the dark, deep woods, and buzzy warbler song fills the air. Finally we head back along the long stretch of highway to Kinney Valley Road and Grandma's house. We're hot and tired, but our spirits are restored.

What Is It about birds that draws us to them? Donald Culross Peattie wrote, "Every human being looks to the birds. They suit the fancy of us all. What they feel they can voice, as we try to; they court and nest, they battle with the elements, they are torn by two opposing impulses, a love of home and a passion for far places. Only with birds do we share so much emotion."

Notes

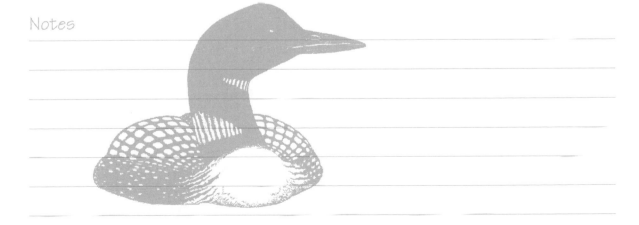

June

Early in the morning, especially during dry, warm spells, warblers are often attracted to water. Standing at a footbridge over a gurgly stream is a pleasant way to see warblers and other tree-top species at or below eye level. Warblers aren't particularly shy or afraid of us—it's their quick, busy ways that make them hard to see.

23 June is rich in warblers and mosquitoes—we can't enjoy one without coping with the other. Warbler beauty is undisputed, but on territory they're secretive and busy, spending so much time in thick foliage that few but the most patient or determined search for them. Their songs give away their presence, so once migration ends and trees have leafed out, birders check them off on daily checklists without bothering to look. But patience is rewarded—singing males or skulking females sometimes lead us to their nests.

Baby warblers fill us with wonder—their tiny, naked bodies and bulging, closed eyes quiver with life and expectation. They blindly trust that if they open their mouths when the nest is jostled, they will be filled with food. Within days, they magically transform sluggish caterpillars into feathers and quick energy, and are eager to search out their own livelihood. When they leave the nest nine or ten days after hatching, they already hold within their tiny bird brains a calendar telling them when it's time to migrate, and a map that will show them the way. We wish these tiny graduates success, happiness, and a long life ahead.

Notes

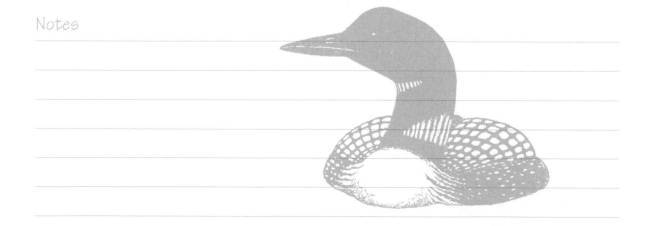

24 The word *bird* comes from the Anglo Saxon *bredon*, meaning "to breed"—*bird* originally came to mean "a chick or young bird." Chaucer used the word inconsistently, spelling it both "brid" and "byrd," and his meaning varied, too. Before his time, the word *fowl* was used for adult birds of any species, but he sometimes used *bird* as the more inclusive term. It took until Shakespeare's time for the spelling to stabilize as "bird," and even longer for the word to lose its connotation of a chick instead of any avian creature. Nowadays, the word still hasn't stabilized completely. At a family reunion, a typical grown-up might refer to an unpopular uncle as an "old bird," recount a birdie shot in a game of golf, snap a picture while shouting, "Watch the birdie," and then, when the instant photo is out of focus, complain that these cheap new cameras are for the birds. After the reunion, when a small child asks why Aunt Joanie's tummy was so fat, there might even be a discussion of the birds and the bees.

John Ciardi, the etymologist and poet, was born on June 24, 1916, and died on Easter Sunday, 1986. His lucid accounts of the origins of words graced National Public Radio for several years, sparking our interest in the origins of bird names.

Notes

June

HAWK

Orioles take their names from the Latin *aureolus*, for "golden"—the human names Aurelius and Oriel share the same derivation. Plovers are named for the Latin word *pluvia*, for "rain," in spite of the fact that plovers have no particular association with rain. *Merganser* comes from Latin for "a diving goose," and *hawk* comes from the Anglo Saxon word "to have," in the sense of grasping or seizing.

25 The etymology of common bird names is a fascinating study. The American Robin was named for the robin redbreast by homesick English settlers. *Robin* was originally a diminutive nickname for Robert, which meant "bright and famous," or "victor over all."

Sparrow comes from the Anglo Saxon word for a "flutterer," and used to refer to any small bird. Biblical references to sparrows may actually allude to our familiar House Sparrow, which has been a noticeable presence in Eurasian societies since the beginning of civilization.

The name *starling* comes from Anglo Saxon, too, and literally means "little star"—either from the five-pointed silhouette of this bird in flight or from the tiny flecks on the plumage worn through the winter. Although most people consider starlings the rabble of the bird world, sterling silver probably takes its name from it, from four birds on the silver coins of Edward the Confessor.

Notes

26 Dull little moths lay army worm eggs in late summer—150 to 400 eggs on a single twig—and the eggs hatch the following spring into dark, hairy caterpillars that munch leaves as they crawl, en masse, through their arboreal birthplace, literally eating themselves out of house and home. Once they've defoliated one tree, they move on to another, and another, exposing nests and baby birds to rain, the hot sun, and the view of hawks, crows, and other flying predators, seriously reducing nest success. In three weeks the caterpillars pupate, metamorphosing into dull brown moths that each lay hundreds of new eggs. They prefer fruit tree and aspen leaves, but eat many others as well. Fortunately, most trees store enough energy to survive even severe army worm damage.

A close look at an army worm reveals a striking metallic blue back, with a row of keyhole-shaped gold spots. Most Northlanders, avian as well as human, prefer to keep their distance. I've watched orioles and jays peel off the hairy skin to eat the soft innards, and crows take road-killed ones, but, except for Black-billed Cuckoos, most birds prefer fasting when the alternative is downing one of these guys.

Many American forests are now managed for paper and wood fiber rather than saw lumber. Aspen grows fast and is relatively soft—perfect for pulp. As more northern forests are managed for aspen on short rotation cycles, birds requiring mature or old-growth forests, like Saw-whet Owls and Blackburnian Warblers, vanish. Army worms have cyclical population fluctuations. Increasing their aspen food supply raises both the peaks and the valleys of their cycle.

Notes

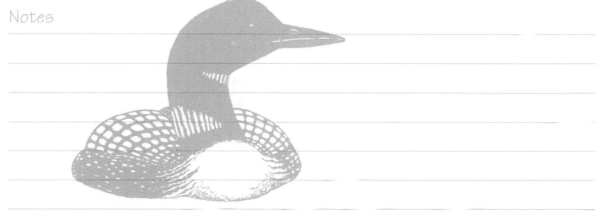

June

Many people call for widespread spraying in army worm invasion years, forgetting that pesticides kill honeybees, ladybugs, spiders, earthworms, and other beneficial invertebrates, and often poison birds and mammals, too. *Bacillus thuringiensis* kills caterpillars indiscriminately—where it's used, sphinx moths and butterflies disappear, along with caterpillars that are vital food for warblers and tanagers. Army worms are an ugly nuisance, but the alternatives are even uglier.

Notes

27 The only good thing about army worms is the Black-billed Cuckoo, which increases when its favorite food is abundant. Our Northland cuckoo eats both army worms and their close relatives, tent caterpillars, and can often be found perched right on their cottony tents, scarfing down caterpillars as fast as they emerge.

The Black-billed Cuckoo's eating habits add a level of meaning to the word *cuckoo*. It's related to the cuckoos of Europe, but, unlike them, makes its own nest and raises its own babies. The European species says "cuckoo" exactly like the Black Forest cuckoo clocks it inspired. Our cuckoo's call is a soft "cu-cu-cu." Although the frequency is well within the hearing range of most people, for some reason it's usually unconsciously filtered out. Our cuckoo is a shy, secretive bird that usually stays hidden in foliage. You must be patient to see one—it may hold still, parallel to a branch, for many minutes at a time, so the trick is to carefully search every branch. It has feet like Disney birds, with two toes in front and two behind, and belongs to the same family as the roadrunner.

28 I wake before dawn to walk in Port Wing. In my in-laws' wet meadow I hear a tiny, high-pitched buzz, like an anemic insect—it's a LeConte's Sparrow. This bug-sized bird with a buglike song is as lovely as a butterfly. T. S. Roberts wrote:

> It is one of the prettiest of the smaller Sparrows, being arrayed in a garb of subdued but beautifully disposed chestnut, gray, black, and tawny color, having the general effect of a warm old-gold suffusion. One correspondent, enthused by his first sight of the bird sitting close at hand on a mat of broken-down, dead vegetation, remarked that his first thought was of a twenty-dollar gold piece! . . . It is . . . inclined to mount to the top of a little willow or tall weed and there, over and over again, deliver its amusingly squeaky little ditty.

One dawn I watched a LeConte's Sparrow at the Port Wing sewage ponds. It sat on a barbed wire fence not ten feet away from me, reaching out and shaking dew from the leaves above it, for all the world as if it were a tiny camper taking a shower. Then it leisurely preened, a sparkling golden jewel in the rosy sunrise.

Audubon named LeConte's Sparrow for John L. LeConte, a young medical doctor who became one of the world's leading entomologists. About half of the American insects known in the mid-1800s were named and described by LeConte. It's fitting that such an insect-like bird would be named for a man so involved with bugs. On an entomological expedition to the southwest in 1850, LeConte collected a new species of thrasher, which was also named for him.

Notes

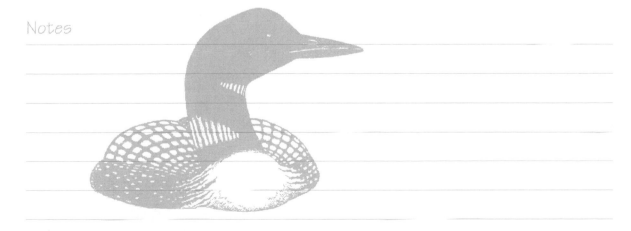

June

The LeConte's Sparrow is found in meadows and wet, weedy fields with Northern Harriers, Upland Sandpipers, Sedge Wrens, and Bobolinks, and suffers greatly from loss of habitat. Some authorities write that it sings only at dawn, dusk, and night. I've heard it singing throughout the day, but it's frustratingly unpredictable. It often stays on one perch for many minutes, so when you finally locate one, it's easily studied through a spotting scope.

Notes

29 I loved LeConte's Sparrow the first time I ever saw it, May 1, 1976, at Whitefish Point in upper Michigan. I spotted the tiny migrant on the dunes and rifled through my field guide to identify it—number 150 on my life list. It was an unusual migrant for Whitefish Point, so the bander asked our group from Michigan Audubon to circle it and walk it into a mist net. When he extricated it from the net and held it up, I was struck by the attitude of defiance in that tiny mite. It didn't seem the least bit frightened of the mass of people surrounding and staring at it, nor of the man holding it in his enormous hand, maintaining its dignity in the face of the terrifying unknown, enduring the awful ordeal of being weighed, measured, and banded without flinching, ever glaring at us like Ahab facing Moby Dick himself. In the matter of weight, a LeConte's Sparrow compared to a human is even smaller than a ship's captain compared to the Great White Whale. I'll never forget the grim anger in that little Ahab's eyes as it piped tiny avian obscenities at us, and perhaps at the universe itself.

30 When the American Ornithologists' Union met in Madison, Wisconsin, in 1979, I finagled an introduction to a scientist who had worked on the complicated taxonomy of LeConte's Sparrow and its relatives, discovering that LeConte's is strongly territorial while the Sharp-tailed Sparrow defends no territory at all. I was thrilled to meet the man who had dedicated years of Ph.D. research to understanding it. I studied his papers thoroughly before the meeting so I could comprehend his every word. And then the moment came. The first thing he said to me was, "You actually *like* LeConte's Sparrow? God, if I never see another one it'll be too soon. After chasing them around on hot summer days in those buggy fields, the only way I like to see them anymore is in museum drawers, stuffed." I hightailed it out of there in a hurry. Walt Whitman wrote, "You must not know too much, or be too precise or scientific about birds." Fearing he might have been right, I've never read another scientific paper about LeConte's Sparrow.

LeConte's Sparrows often sing while hidden in grasses. When approached, they don't usually flush—they drop to the ground and run like mice. But they do often pop up on a perch somewhere near, as if trying to get a look at the intruder. They're easiest to find with the help of a dog, which explains why they're sometimes called "stink birds."

Notes

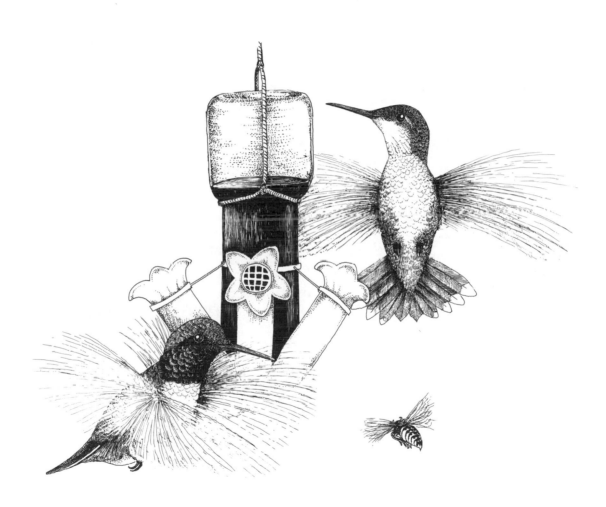

July

There are two ecological races of Savannah Sparrows. Ours lives in fields. The Ipswich Sparrow, long believed to be a distinct species, lives in salt marshes. Its kidneys concentrate salt—the salinity in its urine is more than four times the level in its blood plasma, more than twice as concentrated as in most birds—a handy adaptation for thirsty summer days when all there is to drink is salt water.

1 The soft, dreamy buzz of the Savannah Sparrow evokes the pleasant joys of lazy summer days. This little sparrow is common or abundant in open country over most of North America—the only place on the continent where it doesn't breed is in the southern United States. Ironically, it's named for Savannah, Georgia, where it was found and christened by Alexander Wilson in 1811, but which is one of the few places where it never breeds.

Savannah Sparrows sing all day, even in the heat of the afternoon. Many people seeing them mistake them for Song Sparrows, since both have streaked breasts with a larger central spot. I tell them apart by their faces—the Savannah has more streaks, especially on the crown and behind the cheek patch, and a little yellow mark above the eye. Song Sparrows prefer trees and water on their territories while Savannah Sparrows often choose fallow fields beside freeways, undaunted by the noise and pollution. Even at high noon, while the wimps of the bird world conserve their strength, Savannah Sparrows lisp their pleasing little buzzes and hiccups, grace notes of tranquility in a discordant and harsh world.

Notes

2 Lake Superior, the world's largest air conditioner, does its best to keep the Northland's temperature well within two digits, but eventually it reaches the nineties. Sure enough, these sweltering summer "dog days" make my dog, Bunter, uncomfortable. Dogs can't sweat except on their foot pads, and their best method for cooling down, labored panting, seems cruel and unusual punishment. Fortunately, dogs are as stupid as they are good-natured, and in the blazing midday sun, Bunter happily chases any sticks the kids might throw. When she finally lies down in exhaustion, her panting resounds throughout the house.

Heat affects birds worse than it does dogs—birds are more heavily insulated, and not even their feet sweat. If birds sweated, saturated down feathers would soon be plastered against their skin. Many birds pant, but they don't loll out their tongues like golden retrievers. Nighthawks and herons flutter their throats to maximize evaporation and circulation around the head, cooling them efficiently. Some birds splash in water to cool off, and others bide their time in leafy shade, considering how dog days are really for the birds.

To survive hot days, birds need plenty of water—birdbaths help enormously. Parent birds sometimes bathe themselves and then moisten their babies with their wet belly feathers. Without adequate moisture on hot, sunny days, cavity nesters may literally roast to death, especially in metal birdhouses.

Notes

July

Alexander Wilson discovered the Connecticut Warbler in Connecticut in 1812. It took seventy years to find its nest, in Manitoba. Its scientific name, *Oporornis*, comes from Greek for "bird of autumn," when most New England sightings are made. In spring it leaves South America and flies across the Caribbean to the Appalachians, across to the Mississippi Valley, and north to its breeding grounds. In fall it migrates east, following the Atlantic coast to South America.

3 The Connecticut Warbler, also known as the bog blackthroat, swamp warbler, and tamarack warbler, nests in tamarack bogs in northern Minnesota and jack pine forests in Douglas County, Wisconsin. Birders come from all over the United States to see it, though it's actually more abundant in central Canada.

The Connecticut Warbler is a shy, elusive bird, big for a warbler—almost six inches long and weighing about one-half to three-quarters of an ounce. It has a bright yellow underside, a solid brownish gray back and wings, and a gray hood with conspicuous white eye rings. Its yellow undertail coverts are extremely long, helping humans to distinguish it from the similar Mourning Warbler, which occasionally sports eye rings despite what the field guides say.

The Connecticut spends much of its life on or near the ground. It doesn't hop, but walks on long pink legs, bobbing its head and holding its tail up as it forages for insects and spiders in the crevices of bark. Its habits are poorly understood—it lures birders to its boggy habitat, but the bugs quickly drive them away.

Notes

4 When people learn that Ben Franklin wanted the turkey as our national emblem, they naturally wonder whether the shock from flying that kite didn't somehow affect his brain. Franklin, John Adams, and Thomas Jefferson were appointed by the Second Continental Congress to bring in a design for a national seal. It took time for the design to evolve, but from the beginning an eagle always formed part of it, against Franklin's objections. "The turkey is a much more respectable bird, and withal a true original native of America," he complained.

The Wild Turkey was domesticated in Mexico in Neolithic times. Conquistadors brought it to the Middle East for trade, and the turkey was introduced from the Middle East to Britain between 1525 and 1532. In Walt Disney's *Sleeping Beauty*, King Hubert pigs out on a turkey drumstick—an anachronism, since this story supposedly takes place in the fourteenth century. Turkeys were of vast economic importance to the colonists—small wonder that Poor Richard loved them. The turkey was also honored by John James Audubon as the very first number in his *Birds of North America*. Audubon gave the eagle the number two position.

Benjamin Franklin wrote in a letter to his daughter, Sarah, in 1784, "I wish that the bald eagle had not been chosen as the representative of our country; he is a bird of bad moral character; like those among men who live by sharping and robbing, he is generally poor, and often very lousy."

Notes

July

North Carolina originally designated the Carolina Chickadee as its state bird. Unfortunately, one colloquial name for this bird is the tomtit. State legislators bristled when people started calling North Carolina the Tomtit State and organized a vote among schoolchildren to find a better bird. Predictably, the kids were swayed by the color red and chose the cardinal, in spite of the fact that it's also the official bird of six other states.

5 For many years, the goldfinch was Minnesota's state bird, though never officially approved by the state legislature. In 1949, to rectify this grievous omission, legislators appointed a commission to name an official state bird. They recommended that the bird be fairly well known, found throughout the state during the nesting season and preferably during the entire year, and strikingly marked, with a pattern lending itself for use in insignia. The commission also recommended that it hold special significance for Minnesota, and not be the state bird of any other state.

The commission submitted a slate of eight candidates—Pileated Woodpecker, Wood Duck, Belted Kingfisher, Killdeer, Scarlet Tanager, Rose-breasted Grosbeak, Mourning Dove, and Common Loon. Schoolchildren overwhelmingly chose the tanager for its vivid color. But the Minnesota Ornithologists' Union, concerned about water quality in a land of 10,000 lakes, waged a campaign for the loon, and in 1961, the legislature officially appointed it. The refrigerator magnet industry would never be the same.

Notes

6 One lazy afternoon as I amble along near Burntside Lake, I come upon a male Pileated Woodpecker and his daughter in a big old pine about twenty feet from me. They pay me no mind, so I plop down on the mossy ground to watch. He pecks at the diseased wood and pulls something out. She watches intently, then begs for the treat. He pops it in her mouth and probes again. She gets two insects on her own and suddenly begs again. Whenever she flutters her wings and squawks, he patiently feeds her, but she's finding her own meals, too. Every now and again I hear a distant pileated yell. He turns and yells back. I wonder if it's the mother with another baby.

Later I come upon an adult female in flight. She yells and lands in a dead spruce. Whenever she hears a pileated call as she sits here, she turns her head but remains quiet. She preens her right wing, picks a few bugs, and moseys along the trunk, furtively peeking at me. She may be studying the behavior of adult female humans—how they laze about on the edge of a dusty road, not doing much of anything on a hot afternoon.

Birds teach humility. Mostly they avoid humans, and those coming close usually ignore us. Brooks Atkinson wrote, "Although birds coexist with us on this eroded planet, they live independently of us with a self-sufficiency that is almost a rebuke. In the world of birds a symposium on the purpose of life would be inconceivable. They do not need it. We are not that self-reliant. We are the ones who have lost our way."

Notes

July

A baby jay held in a cupped hand is surprisingly hot. With the jay's normal body temperature of about 106 degrees and its unfeathered abdomen, the feeling on the hand is of pulsing hot skin. Bird skin is thinner than the flimsiest cellophane. When a nestling jay preens its shoulder, we see red muscles right through the skin. I'm always amazed that a clumsy baby just learning to preen never accidentally pierces that fragile membrane.

7 Sneakers the Blue Jay came to Peabody Street July 7, 1991, as a tiny nestling. A Cloquet couple had discovered the fallen nest after a storm. One baby was dead, but four survived. The nest was completely destroyed, so they put the babies in a small box near the tree in hopes that the parents would take over, but the parents couldn't figure it out, so when it grew dark, they brought the babies to me.

A single baby jay raised in captivity is likely to imprint on humans. Minimizing handling helps, but jays need interactions, perhaps even affection, to develop properly. And it's hard to resist a baby jay, with its tiny stub of a tail, eager eyes, and bright red mouth opening wide to beg for food or squawk for attention. Four babies usually interact enough with one another to develop into proper wild jays, but not Sneakers. While the other three snuggled together to sleep, Sneakers followed me or the children about. If she couldn't sleep on someone's lap, she snuggled against a shoe—that's how she got her name. She had decided from the start that she was a person, and wasn't about to let anybody change her mind.

Notes

8 The inside of a baby jay's or crow's mouth is bright red. The intense color, which I can see from fifty feet without my glasses, provides an excellent target for parent jays to stuff food into. When baby jays are hungry, they make little mewing sounds, flutter their wings, and open their mouths wide. Parents find this irresistible—it keys them up to search for food just to stuff it into those bright gaping mouths. Somehow, a baby jay can communicate hungry desperation to mammals, too—few people can resist a begging baby jay, and even my dog, Bunter, looks concerned.

Rooted to the bottom of a baby jay's red mouth is its tongue. The upper surface is lance-shaped, anchored by a tubular stalk. The tip of the tongue has three barbs. Once they fledge, baby jays, like toddlers, taste everything they see, first touching it with the sensitive tip of the tongue and then taking it into their mouths. If it's soft and tasty, they swallow it. But I've never known a fledgling or adult jay to take a second bite of an unfamiliar item for at least ten minutes. This may be how these omnivores learn new food sources without getting poisoned in the process.

A baby songbird's beak has soft tissue at the sides, widening the gape to make a bigger target for parents. This tissue atrophies and hardens as the bill grows longer. Most songbirds have brightly colored gapes—usually yellow or orange. Jay and crow mouths remain red for months, and, especially in nondominant birds, sometimes for more than a year, but eventually grow black.

Notes

July

When Merlins nested on Peabody Street, local songbirds quickly adapted to the constant danger. Robins and Chipping Sparrows sang at half-volume. On three occasions I saw Blue Jays hover, peeking into the falcon nest, before going to a nearby anthill for a formic acid fix. I couldn't tell from the ground whether the female was on or off the nest, but the jays seemed satisfied that the coast was clear.

9 One of the hardest-to-find hawks in North America used to be the Merlin—a little falcon nicknamed the pigeon hawk. In 1932, T. S. Roberts wrote in *The Birds of Minnesota* that he saw it "not over a half a dozen times during fifty years."

But suddenly Merlins are on the increase. Since the mid-1980s, they've been nesting in cities and towns along Lake Superior. In Duluth they've nested above a bus stop on a busy road next to a junior high school, and in both business and residential neighborhoods. Merlins nest in abandoned crow nests, so crow population increases have helped their success. Near the nest, Merlins are noisy, sounding like hyperactive Killdeer.

The Merlin is dark and streaked—not colorful like a Kestrel—but a Merlin in flight is a thrilling sight. It cruises by like a bullet, chasing down birds from kinglet to jay size. I don't usually mind its killing ways, but once a Merlin streaked through my backyard and snatched a baby red squirrel that I had raised—to this day I begrudge it that supper.

Notes

10 When a Yellow-rumped Warbler is about, its loud chip and bright yellow rump patch make it pleasingly conspicuous. It often perches on branches overhanging a pool of water, flying out to catch flying insects—when mosquitoes swarm about a group of birders, the yellowrump fortifies itself with protein from our blood. Its song, a nondescript trill, is pleasant if dull, and my day is always brighter when one is near.

Other warblers are not so impressed with the yellowrump, perhaps because of its wimpy song. On the warbler social dominance ladder, the yellowrump is pretty much on the bottom rung. If a yellowrump nests near a Black-throated Green Warbler, the yellowrump always gets the lesser territory. Fortunately, yellowrumps are generalists, taking flying insects and fruits in addition to the normal warbler diet of leaf-eating bugs, so even if they're driven from the best foraging spots they manage just fine. They're especially successful on their wintering grounds, seeming to prefer slash and second growth—habitats that are becoming increasingly, and tragically, common in Mexico and Central America.

Taking early morning walks through the North Woods in June and early July is like panning for avian gold. Warblers aren't as numerous as during migration, but every pocket of habitat has several. I see or hear an average of more than six different warblers at every stop along my Breeding Bird Survey route.

Notes

July

More effectively than Macbeth does a Whip-poor-will murder sleep. Nineteenth century American ornithologist John Burroughs counted 1,088 consecutive calls by a single Whip-poor-will—counting these noisy calls is clearly less effective than counting sheep. Some Whip-poor-wills are fairly tame, allowing close observation as they call from a low branch, rooftop, fence, or the ground. Their eyes shine red in the beam of headlights or a flashlight.

11 One night along Burntside Lake I hear a Whip-poor-will, its song so exuberant, so filled with enthusiasm about love and reproduction and home ownership and life itself, that it's hard to believe it comes from so staid a creature. Like Clark Kent transforming into Superman, the unassuming Whip-poor-will takes on magical powers as darkness descends upon the forest. As Veeries settle down for the night, when only frog music and a distant robin are heard, a sudden "whip-poor-will!" rings out with more power than a locomotive, and this bird, able to leap tall buildings in a single bound, rescues the forest from a dull, silent night.

We set out with flashlight to catch this mysterious being in the act, with as much success as Lois Lane trying to discover who Superman really is. Blundering through the night woods, we repeatedly reach the sound only to see a shadow wing past and the call resume further on. We spy it on a rooftop, but before we can pull up binoculars to actually view the utterance, it flies away, leaving us wishing we had some kryptonite handy. Does it call with throat puffed up? Beak open or shut? Perhaps some mysteries are better left unsolved.

Notes

12 "That man is the richest whose pleasures are the cheapest." Henry David Thoreau was one of the world's first birdwatchers. He was hardly the first to understand or write about birds, but he was among the first to enjoy them, not for intellectual or literary advancement, but simply because they were natural and true. "Life consists with wildness. The most alive is the wildest. Not yet subdued to man, its presence refreshes him." Thoreau was also one of the first people to feed wild birds for his own pleasure, setting out corn at Walden Pond. Naturally, squirrels arrived first, shy but eating the corn as if they knew it their right. He disliked Blue Jays—they seemed sneaky. "At length the jays arrive . . . in a stealthy and sneaking manner they flit from tree to tree . . . They were manifestly thieves, and I had not much respect for them."

Thoreau treasured intimate moments with birds. "I once had a sparrow alight upon my shoulder for a moment while I was hoeing in a village garden, and I felt that I was more distinguished by that circumstance than I should have been by any epaulet I could have worn."

Henry David Thoreau was born July 12, 1817, and died of tuberculosis on May 6, 1862—in the short time he was given he tried to "live deep and suck out all the marrow of life." He lived a simple, mostly vegetarian life (though he occasionally ate meat, including a wood-chuck that he killed at Walden Pond), a nonhunter who accompanied a moose-hunting expedition to Maine as "chaplain" and "conscientious objector."

Notes

July

Tar on rooftops can become extremely hot—nighthawks often move the eggs to a spot of shade at midday. To cool themselves, they practice gular fluttering, rapidly vibrating their throats to increase evaporation.

13 Walking through downtown Duluth at night, we hear nighthawks *peenting*. The buzzy call can be heard any time, but most frequently near dusk and dawn. We hear nighthawks in open country as well as in the city— they're the most commonly heard bird in the movie *Dances with Wolves*. They nest on beaches, bare, gravelly fields, burned-over tracts, and flat rooftops. They don't build a nest or even scrape the ground—they simply lay two eggs in what seems to be a suitable spot, and if conditions change, they move the eggs to a more favorable place. Some writers suggest that they carry eggs in their capacious mouths, but my captive nighthawks can't even learn to pick up food from a dish—their beaks are too weak and their tongues reduced and useless. They probably tuck their eggs toward their breast with beak and chin and roll them.

Adult male nighthawks have a lovely nuptial flight, in which they dive down toward the ground at high speed, making a booming sound at the bottom. They don't crash into the ground, but sometimes crash into telephone and power lines, mangling their wings—I receive many injured adult males in June and July.

Notes

14 Our baby jays thrive. As they approach the age when they would start making tentative steps from the nest, we start taking them outdoors a few times each day. They're a delightful mixture of curiosity and fear of the unknown. If a shadow passes overhead—a gull, an airplane, or a child walking past—they crouch low and pull their wings out and up over their faces, looking like bizarre, feathered spiders. But they're too curious to maintain this posture for long—when I was photographing one jay, another crouched, afraid of the flash, but by the time I turned to photograph its fear display, it was already craning its neck to get a better look at the camera.

A Blue Jay's neck is surprisingly skinny—not much thicker than a drinking straw. When a baby without many feathers stretches its neck, we clearly see the white tracheal rings beneath the skin. Avian neck vertebrae articulate differently than mammalian vertebrae, allowing them to stretch their necks like E.T.

When Ludwig, a baby jay I once raised, tasted his first ant, he immediately spit it out and shook his head violently. Then he suddenly rubbed his tongue against the roof of his mouth, grabbed the ant again, and rubbed it against his wing and back feathers. Ants are laced with formic acid. Anting may be the avian alternative to bug spray, or the tingle of acid on skin may simply feel good.

Notes

July

Although our Ovenbird is a true wood warbler, the word *ovenbird* is also applied to the Latin American family *Furnariidae*. These birds build large clay nests that resemble an oven much more than our little Ovenbird's leafy structure.

15 The song of the Ovenbird still rings out in the woods, but not as often as in May and June—adult males are so busy searching for insects to feed their growing babies that they have little time for singing now. The teacher-bird, a fine ventriloquist, is heard much more often than seen, but if we patiently search the branches when we hear a male singing, we can often find him on the ground or on a low, usually horizontal, branch. Finding the female poses a trickier problem, but, again, patient searching sometimes reveals her.

An Ovenbird makes a pleasing sight, the rusty cap, white eye ring, and pretty pink walking shoes giving an understated touch of finery to the simple plumage. The Ovenbird's modesty and simplicity extend to its home—this true warbler spends most of its time on the ground or low branches. The nest is somewhat sunken into the ground and arched over with dead leaves—the bird received its name because of the resemblance of its nest to a dome-shaped oven. Even when it associates with mixed warbler flocks during migration, it stays beneath the others, lurking about the leafy forest floor, hidden in the dappled sunshine.

Notes

16 A woman brings me a hummingbird with an injured wing, which appears sprained rather than broken but is too tiny for me to be absolutely sure. This is a female, with a rounded tail, spotted with white, and a white throat. We call her Esmerelda.

The woman who found Esmerelda by her cabin accidentally allowed sugar water to drip on her—she's all sticky, and at least twenty belly feathers have torn out, stuck to her feet and the perch. I bathe her twice to get her feathers in order. It takes six hours for her droppings to return to a normal color—she'd had nothing but sugar water laced with food coloring for two days. Food coloring may not be harmful, but there's no good reason to use it.

Esmerelda spends her days perched on a tiny twig in an open shoe box set in a sunny, screened window, with sugar water fortified with vitamins always available. She also sips drops of sugar water right off my finger. Her tongue, which can protrude a full inch beyond her beak, looks and feels as delicate as gossamer.

Hummingbird wings are translucent, as if made of the most delicate silk in the world. These tiny, fragile structures beat seventy-eight times per second during regular flight, and up to two hundred times per second during a display dive. Few cameras can capture beating hummingbird wings as more than a blur.

Notes

July

It's a big responsibility keeping the tiniest of birds alive, but also a big pleasure. In nature, hummingbirds can live longer than ten years. We wish we could release Esmerelda to a natural life again, but her wing doesn't heal properly. My rehab permit doesn't allow me to keep unreleasable birds, and hummingbirds aren't listed on my education permit, so Esmerelda ends up at the Lake Superior Zoo.

17 Esmerelda the hummingbird has a tiny brain, but she's an intelligence worth reckoning with. Her bright eyes take in everything around her. Hummingbirds are so tiny and vulnerable that you'd think they'd be scared of everything, but they're amazingly fearless. Maybe Esmerelda figures since she can't protect herself anyway she might as well enjoy life as long as she can.

She sits on a tiny twig—her feet are much too small to reach around even a toddler's finger—and we wedge the twig at the top of an open box so she can look all around. When we take her outside to real flowers, she sips nectar and grabs microscopic insects. Her beak is too tiny to manage mosquitoes or even big aphids—she takes red spider mites, gnats the size of dust particles, and critters too small for me to identify, sometimes too small to even see. As we carry her about on her twig, she holds herself like a queen borne by servants. Even as she rests quietly, the stick vibrates furiously from her racing heart and rapid breathing. We marvel at this tiny stick, almost alive itself with the incredible life force of a hummingbird.

Notes

18 Surrogate motherhood exists in both humans and birds. Brown-headed Cowbird mothers foist their children on others to raise. A cowbird doesn't trust a lawyer to select adoptive parents—she spends weeks studying her neighbors' nesting habits, and selects ten or twelve suitable couples herself. There's no legally binding requirement that the adoptive parents raise the young cowbirds, and some refuse. Robins and catbirds toss out cowbird eggs, House Wrens puncture them, and Yellow Warblers occasionally cover up a foreign egg with new nesting material, throwing the baby out with the bath water since the warbler's eggs are buried, too. One Yellow Warbler made a five-layer nest, covering eleven cowbird eggs and quite a few of its own.

Cowbirds relinquish custody but retain visitation rights, and mother cowbirds may keep track of their babies. In one instance, a banded cowbird fought off a domestic cat that had attacked one of her banded young. Once grown, cowbirds seek other cowbirds, abandoning their adoptive parents forever. But at least they never add insult to injury, bringing their dirty laundry home or asking for money for a mortgage down payment.

A screech owl once adopted a clutch of flicker eggs in a nest box. Although owls normally eat woodpeckers, this one tenderly brooded the eggs, and when they hatched, brought the babies a mouse—they didn't have the foggiest idea what to do with it. Meanwhile, their natural parents fed them ants and other insects. The screech owl finally conceded that the natural parents provided a more suitable home environment and peacefully relinquished custody.

Notes

July

Virtually all birds seem to believe there is security in numbers. Even the most aggressive of crows won't come too close to a sitting hawk or owl until other crows join it. But hummingbirds and kingbirds are so feisty they'll take on a predator as large as a Bald Eagle entirely on their own.

19 This time of year I get dozens of calls from people wondering why Red-winged Blackbirds chase crows. Especially during nesting season, the very sight of a nest predator elicits this mobbing. As more and more birds squawk and attack, others join in until it's quite obvious how the term came about.

Everyone knows Blue Jays steal eggs and baby birds, so we're not surprised to occasionally see a robin chasing a jay. But except when a Blue Jay actually approaches a nest, most birds don't seem to mind having it around to warn of more dangerous predators. Gray Jays are another story—it's virtually impossible to find a whiskey jack in summer without a dozen littler birds, especially warblers and vireos, in angry attendance. Gray Jays eat more meat than Blue Jays, and don't provide a warning service in exchange for their plunder.

The mere sight of a crow is enough to elicit mobbing by many birds, especially robins and redwings. Large hawks and owls don't usually eat songbirds, but often steal baby crows. When one of these predators appears, the sound of mobbing crows may carry over a mile.

Notes

20 *Piracy,* or *kleptoparasitism,* is what ornithologists call the behavior of one bird stealing food from another. It's rare in songbirds, though House Sparrows have been recorded stealing katydids from female digger wasps. It's known in only one duck, the American Wigeon, but it's very common in Bald Eagles, which steal fish from Osprey, and in Herring Gulls and jaegers, which harass other gulls until they regurgitate their fish.

The most specialized of all avian pirates are the frigatebirds. These oceanic fish eaters have such reduced oil glands that their dry, light feathers give them the largest wingspan-to-body-weight ratio of all birds, enhancing their aerobatic flight and making them the fittest of all pirates—but at a cost. Unoiled feathers prevent frigatebirds from ever entering the water to catch their own fish, or even to rest.

A Merlin in Europe was once recorded stealing a catch from another hawk. The Merlin was in turn robbed by a Honey Buzzard, which was robbed by a Peregrine Falcon. Apparently there really is no honor among thieves.

Folklore has it that crows and jays steal shiny objects. Actually, wild corvids seldom if ever hide inedible items, but captive or tame ones do pick up and hide all kinds of things, and seem especially attracted to shiny or glittery objects.

Notes

July

Spotted Sandpipers sleep on shore, vulnerable to cats, skunks, raccoons, and foxes. They migrate by night, and are sometimes killed at TV and radio antenna towers. They've drowned when mussels have grabbed them by the leg and held fast, and have been killed flying into guy wires, which are invisible to birds even in day. All in all, we're lucky to live in a world that has any Spotted Sandpipers at all.

21 Of the eighty species of shorebirds in North America, the most well-known is probably the Spotted Sandpiper. The teetertail can be found along lakes, streams, and rivers in fresh water throughout the continent. It's the likeliest shorebird to be seen on piers and sandy beaches in summer. Its distinctive and constant habit of bobbing its tail has given it an abundance of nicknames, like the seesaw bird, tilt-up, and teeter-peep, and makes it easy to identify even when it loses its spots in late summer. Spotted Sandpipers fly with their wings held stiffly down-curved, vibrating in a shallow arc. They often call "peet-weet" as they take off. Females are larger and more aggressive than males—both sexes incubate and care for the young, but the female spends more time displaying and defending the territory.

Spotted Sandpipers are capable swimmers from the day they hatch, and may even dive into water to escape hawks. They sometimes perch on trees and wires, sometimes visit cultivated fields to eat insects, and aren't above eating a few army worms. In the water they eat small fish and a wide variety of crustaceans.

Notes

22 A Bovey man writes with a question. His mother spread mothballs in her green beans to keep a rabbit away, and now blackbirds are picking up the mothballs and rubbing them under their wings and on their wing and back feathers. Is this unusual? Why are they doing it?

This behavior is a variation of *anting*, probably to help keep lice, mites, mosquitoes, and ticks off birds. Although few birds other than flickers and Pileated Woodpeckers eat ants, many pick them up and rub the bitter-tasting bodies on their feathers. Some birds ant passively, sitting on an ant hill, wings spread, allowing the ants to crawl over their feathers. A mothball's strong taste or odor may also elicit anting behavior. Birds have been recorded wiping beetles, pieces of lemon, coffee grounds, vinegar, beer, hot chocolate, soapsuds, sumac berries, and cigarette and cigar butts on their feathers. A flock of grackles in Milwaukee was recorded using mothballs exactly as my correspondent describes. It all gives new meaning to the expression, "ants in your pants."

Many hawks are known to "decorate" their nests with sprigs of fresh greenery, and to add fresh sprigs throughout nesting. Although the purpose is unknown, some ornithologists speculate that since some plants produce chemicals to repel insects, the green vegetation may help minimize parasites like lice in the nest.

Notes

July

It's easy to kill baby birds with kindness. Once I cared for a baby robin whose throat had been pierced by a toothpick when well-meaning people tried to feed it. We can virtually never do as well with baby birds as their own parents could. Some people keep nestlings alive for weeks, but unless the babies thrive, their growth may be stunted, they'll eventually die, and the people will be heartbroken.

23 One summer in Madison, Wisconsin, a sixth-grader brought me a baby robin she'd found two days before. "I found it in the middle of the road. It hasn't been hungry—I put six worms in the box and they're all still there." It's hard for most people to realize that baby songbirds can't eat anything at all unless a parental unit stuffs the food into the baby's mouth. It didn't take more than a cursory examination to figure out what had happened—the bird's legs and feet were horribly misshapen from rickets. That summer we had a huge crop of buckthorn berries—I guessed the parents had fed this baby mostly berries rather than balancing the diet with insects, worms, and other kinds of fruits. Then they must have tossed this poor, deformed baby out of the nest.

The baby was so weak from hunger it couldn't open its mouth. I'm scared to force-feed baby birds, so using the blunt end of a flat toothpick, I teased in tiny amounts of applesauce, trying to build up its strength until it could beg for more substantial fare. I was still inexperienced at rehabbing, but I was pretty sure this one would never survive the night.

Notes

24 By the next morning, my baby robin was still weak but feisty, and within a day was eating well. But its ankle joints were horribly swollen, and its legs and feet misshapen, unable to support its weight. I couldn't find anyone who knew the proper dose of vitamin D$_3$ for a robin with rickets, so I gave it two or three drops right from the dropper several times a day—it grew eager every time it saw the dropper.

It thrived despite its deformities. It could fly around our apartment before it learned to walk or even stand, but even its legs steadily grew stronger. The toes were gnarled to begin with, but within a month, one foot straightened completely out. Two toes crossed on the other foot, but the little robin got quite good at perching. When I started letting it outdoors, it quickly adapted to our yard, and although I continued to subsidize it with food, it taught itself how to find worms and caterpillars and berries. It started spending nights outside, hanging around with other robins. It quickly stopped taking food from me, and when migration came, it disappeared.

A single baby robin doesn't make a whit of difference to the robin population, but it meant a great deal to a little sixth-grade girl, and it meant a great deal to me. Making meaningful connections with individual wild creatures is the first step in learning to care for a world of wild creatures—first we care for individuals, then populations, and finally whole ecosystems and biodiversity.

Notes

July

Fiction is rich in attack birds. In a Garrison Keillor Buster the Showdog sketch on "A Prairie Home Companion," a California Condor menaced Timmy the Sad Rich Kid and his faithful companion Buster, but real condors are shier than Keillor himself. If they can't escape danger, they throw up. Condor vomit is at least as unpleasant as a tern's all-out frontal attack, but it wasn't enough to protect the species from annihilation by humans.

25 People generally have the upper hand in battles with birds—after all, we have guns, pesticides, chain saws, automobiles, and predatory pets on our side. But occasionally birds win a minor skirmish. When Blue Jays nested in my friend John's yard, the female looked so pretty and docile sitting on the nest that John photographed her. The moment he snapped the shot, she flew up and stabbed him in the head hard enough to draw blood. Jays average two-and-a-half ounces, and John a thousand times that, but she was the undisputed victor.

Birds defend their young fiercely—many ornithologists bear deep scars from tangling with owls and hawks at the nest. I used to take my students hiking near some nesting Black Terns—every time, the birds flew straight in for our eyes in a truly Hitchcockian manner. Since terns aren't kamikaze pilots, they always veer off at the last moment, but before that moment could arrive, the students always crouched, covered their heads, and ran like crazy. I never chickened out, so a single field trip was guaranteed to win me the respect and admiration of every seventh-grader—a handy trick they never teach in university education classes.

Notes

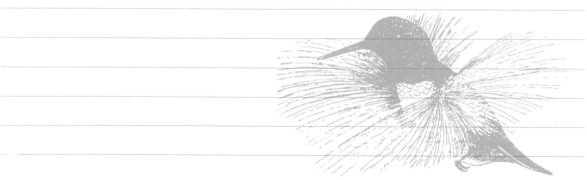

26

When a person approaches too close to a Black-capped Chickadee's nest, the chickadee hisses like a snake. I doubt if a chickadee has ever stabbed anyone, but I've heard many tales of them alighting on deer hunters and nibbling at dried blood on a scab. If chickadees weren't so cute, they'd be known as vampire birds.

The flesh, feathers, and skin of the Hooded Pitohui of New Guinea contain a nerve toxin, homobatrachotoxin, identical to that of poison-dart frogs. The Pink Pigeon of Mauritius, the only native pigeon surviving on that Indian Ocean island, has toxic flesh which discourages hunting. Ruffed Grouse become toxic after feeding on mountain laurel leaf buds. Carcasses of poisoned pigeons are usually toxic. Probably the most dangerously toxic birds are poorly prepared domestic chickens and turkeys, which spread salmonella.

When a mockingbird attacks people in Washington, D.C., it makes national news, and the bird appears the victor. All in all, though, in battles between birds and humans, I root for the birds, but I'd put my money on the humans.

Although birds rarely hurt humans, many people have a deeply rooted fear of them. When wild birds get into a house, even adults can be genuinely terrified. The fear of birds is called *ornithophobia*. Fear of feathers is *pteronophobia*. If someone panics when hearing a thrush sing, it could be a case of *aulophobia*—the fear of flutes.

Notes

July

When young Black-and-White Warblers leave home in late July, each joins a loose flock of warblers, kinglets, chickadees, and nuthatches—usually with no more than one black-and-white per flock. They mosey on south at a leisurely pace, some going no farther than the Gulf states, others all the way to Ecuador and Venezuela. Their unhurried pace through life is perhaps the secret to their longevity—banded birds have survived more than eleven years.

Notes

27 The first living warbler I ever identified was the Black-and-White Warbler. This aptly named bird is striking proof that beauty is a matter of design, not color. The adult male gleams black and white in a bold pattern, with no shades of gray to dull the effect. The female's beauty is more subtle, with soft browns on her cheeks and flanks, yet even she has a unique, soft loveliness. As if to aid our appreciation, these elegant creatures feed mainly on trunks and large, low branches of trees and shrubs, in the manner of creepers and nuthatches, and so are usually seen at or below eye level. They move along twig or trunk with a switching motion, tail sweeping from one side to the other.

Black-and-White Warblers can be found in woodlands throughout much of the Midwest, but are most common in North Country, especially in moist woodlands. Their scientific name, *Mniotilta*, means "moss plucker" in Greek, though they are more likely to be plucking insects within moss than the moss itself. The black-and-white nests on the ground, usually at the base of a tree or shrub, often hidden under an arch of dead leaves.

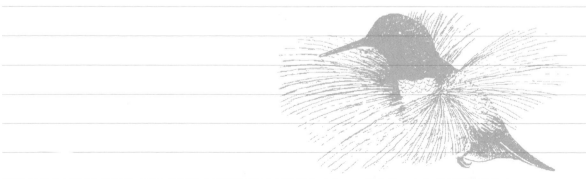

28 A woman brings me a baby Pine Siskin—a tiny feather ball. Finches often hatch while it's still quite cold, and always feather out quickly. The parents don't feed them insects, as do most songbirds, but regurgitated seed, and they nest whenever conifers have cones.

This baby looks at me through bright eyes and begs for food. I feel good about its prognosis until it raises its wings. On both sides are punctures from a cat's bite. I don't know the dosage of amoxicillin to prevent bacterial infection in a bird this tiny, and I don't know what to feed it—I'm not prepared to regurgitate seeds. I don't let my children see it—they would fall in love with it and clearly it's not going to survive. I feed it bread dipped in condensed milk—I don't know what else to do because my normal baby mixture won't do, yet I can hardly let it die on an empty stomach. I give it a drop of amoxicillin every hour, and stay up late cradling it in my hand. At midnight I kiss it and tuck it in a blueberry pint box with tissues. I turn out the light knowing it will never wake up.

True finches—siskins, redpolls, goldfinches, crossbills, Purple Finches, and Pine and Evening Grosbeaks—aren't related to cardinals, Rose-breasted Grosbeaks, buntings, and American sparrows. Finches have subtle morphological and biochemical differences, and also differ in their breeding behavior, nesting in colonies rather than on territories, and feeding their young seeds instead of insects.

Notes

July

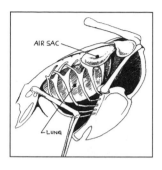

A fresh tide of oxygen passes through avian lungs as air is both inhaled and exhaled. As a bird breathes in, air rushes through the flat lungs into balloonlike air sacs. Then, as it exhales, this air circulates back through the lungs on the way out, providing an exceptionally efficient respiratory system to fill the heavy oxygen requirements of rapid metabolism and flight.

29 I wake up early to attend to my avian charges. I feed a baby jay and clean its enclosure, and tend a nighthawk with a broken wing, dreading going into my office to dispose of the dead siskin. But it isn't dead—it's bright-eyed and hungry as ever. I rack my brain trying to figure out a better diet than bread, and suddenly think of cockatiels. They aren't in the same order as songbirds, but they do feed their young regurgitated seeds. I get a parrot hand-feeding mixture from a pet store and feed it through a medicine dropper. The baby scarfs it down greedily, its crop bulging with satisfaction. It takes its medicine well, too.

Everything looks great until I peek under the wings. Scarlet raw air sacs protrude from both puncture wounds, pulsing with every breath. By the next day they're huge—each over an inch in diameter, as big as the body itself, holding the wings at a contorted angle. They keep growing and pulsating, looking like they'll explode at any moment. The baby's eyes are twinkling, yet it's dying right before my eyes. I hate cats.

Notes

30 Grotesque raw air sacs protrude from the baby siskin's sides ten days after a cat attacked it. As I work in my office, it perches on my shoulder, toying with my hair or sleeping quietly. I try not to love it.

One day the sacs seem smaller—I must be getting used to the repulsive wounds. The next day I know they're shrinking, and within a week they're gone. I keep it indoors as the wounds close, but my kids play with it now. When it starts going outside, it stays near five-year-old Katie, and sleeps in a cage in her room at night. It meets other birds, and as it learns siskin ways, it takes less food from Katie and me. One night it doesn't return. We think it has left for good, but next morning, when we're letting out the dog, it zips in and flies through the house and up the stairs to Katie's room, rushing into its cage where it swings and swings in a frenzy. It refuses to go out all day, but next morning it does, never to come in again. It still flies to Katie and me, but takes no more food from us. One lovely September day it vanishes with a migrating siskin flock.

Almost every cat-injured bird I've treated died within three days. Sometimes birds with horrible injuries should be euthanized, but I can't always be sure, not after one improbably warm March morning when my six-year-old Katie rode her tricycle in the driveway. A familiar little siskin flew in on a spring breeze and alighted on her head. From the moment of human or avian conception, we spend our lives fighting odds. And sometimes winning.

Notes

July

Both kingbirds and waxwings eat flying insects and fruit, though they time their meals differently. Waxwings eat fruit whenever it's available, from raspberries and cherries in summer to mountain ash berries and crab apples in winter, and they take insects whenever they find them. Kingbirds dine almost exclusively on insects on their breeding grounds, and almost exclusively on fruits in the tropics.

31 In late July, Cedar Waxwings swirl through the sky in flocks or rest on snags, crests erect and feathers sleek, even facing a big wind. They flit out to snatch insect treats in midair, and return to the snag like avian yo-yos. And Eastern Kingbirds fatten up before their journey to the tropical rain forest.

If waxwings are a study in soft browns and yellows, kingbirds are a study in black and white. Both species have a striking terminal tail band visible from quite a distance, the waxwing's vivid yellow, the kingbird's white. Tiny crimson tips on secondary wing feathers punctuate muted waxwing colors; a tiny crimson crown sets off the kingbird's stark colors. Waxwings display their bright markings year-round, but it takes patience and a well-timed gust of wind to reveal the red streak of a kingbird's crown this late in the season.

Kingbirds and waxwings are diametrical in personality, waxwings peaceable and docile while kingbirds are ever itching for a fight. Kingbirds are feisty and handsome, waxwings gentle and lovely, and our world would be diminished if we lost either one.

Notes

August

Migrating birds are reluctant to cross large bodies of water, so they follow shorelines. During the autumns of 1988–1990, a group of Duluth birders, while sitting on the wall of the Lakewood Pumping Station just northeast of Duluth, maintained a daily count of migrants following the north shore. Starting at dawn, we counted for at least one, and up to five, hours. Our three-year total was 755,087 birds cruising along the shore.

1 In this soft and quiet month of August, Cedar Waxwings lazily wing through the skies and alight in trees, fluttering out to daintily snatch insects on the wing. Now that most songbirds have dropped out of the choir, there's little music in the air, but waxwings snore sleepily, swooping goldfinches call "perchickory," and Red-eyed Vireos occasionally preach monotonous sermons punctuated by dramatic pauses. The only other sounds are dry grasshopper wings rasping, locusts trilling, crickets stridulating, and an occasional flicker calling "kyeer!" Every telephone wire and power line near water is decorated with swallows, as evenly spaced as strings of Christmas lights.

Human calendars claim we're in the middle of summer, but avian calendars mark the autumn migration already underway. Shorebirds from the Far North collect in ponds. Swallows, warblers, and adult male hummingbirds are on the move. A few robins still feed late babies, but many are joining migratory flocks, spending their time fattening up against the fuel requirements they will soon face. Summer is fading, autumn is coming, and our tomatoes are still green.

Notes

2 We usually start August with slow migration days at the Lakewood Pumping Station—time to ease our way back into identifying and enumerating migrating birds. But some years migration is well underway when we start. My first day in 1989, I counted 1,815 migrants in two hours. I saw 894 blackbirds, mostly redwings, flying in tight, fast flocks and shifting positions to make counting tricky. I also tallied 516 Cedar Waxwings. Waxwings always seem more leisurely than blackbirds, and their sweet snoring is just the right sound for lazy August days.

Lots of Evening Grosbeaks—321 to be precise—flew by, along with a couple of Eastern Kingbirds, their shallow, flat wingbeats pleasing and familiar. Two loons hurried by, almost leaving their feet behind them. Seven Cliff Swallows stayed around the old building, flying out and then yo-yoing back. Whenever swallows cruised past, I had to check to see if they were truly migrants or my local seven on a short feeding flight. Summery warmth filled the air, but the eight crossbills that flew over intimated that winter was lurking not far away.

One August day, an individual Merlin flew by the pumping station several times every hour. He and his mate nested in the trees behind us, and he was in charge of hunting. I didn't see him make any kills—resident birds near a Merlin nest are wary, and migrants mostly move in dense flocks—but he apparently knew of other hunting grounds because he lugged in three birds as I watched.

Notes

August

Yellowthroat females incubate the eggs, but males play an important role in feeding and raising the babies. When a male takes more than one mate, he ends up feeding eight or even twelve babies, busy from sunrise to sunset. During the most frantic stages of childrearing, parents can lose 50 percent of their body weight. Well-fattened yellowthroat migrants weigh more than half an ounce, but exhausted parents may weigh barely a quarter of an ounce.

3 The jolliest and perkiest little fireball in the Northland is the Common Yellowthroat. This five-inch warbler has one of the loudest songs of all birds, and a spunky, noisy call note as well. Most people interpret the song as "witchity, witchity, witchity," though I usually hear "looky here, looky here, looky here!" The yellowthroat's plumage is as attractive as its song—brown above, bright fiery yellow beneath, with a black mask outlined with white around its face.

Unlike most wood warblers, this little bandit isn't found in mature, deep forest, but nests in cattail marshes and shrubby edge, usually staying well-hidden in the thick vegetation. Females find males more easily than we—sometimes two or more females both find the same little songster, and he's happy to oblige as many as he can attract. The pair builds its nest on the ground, and then spends much of its time trying to keep cowbirds away. Yellowthroats raise many cowbirds instead of their own young every year. On the rare occasions that a yellowthroat recognizes a cowbird egg, it sometimes buries it under a new nest lining, but more often than not it raises the interloper as its own.

Notes

4 One of the most beautiful and graceful of all water birds is the Common Tern, also called the sea swallow for its long pointed wings and forked tail, displayed to perfection as it darts and hovers above lakes and oceans, catching fish in breathtaking dives. Although terns are in the same family as gulls, terns are much more slender and fairylike, with a black cap above their white head, and a blood red bill and feet. These ballerinas of the skies may be elegant in appearance, but they have raspy, harsh voices—they would never have made the transition from silent films to talkies.

Four-and-a-half-ounce anglers can have a remarkably long life span and travel far and wide. One Common Tern banded in Great Britain was recovered when twenty-five years old. A nestling banded on Long Island, New York, was recaptured alive off the Ivory Coast of Africa later that same year. Terns, which often fish in large groups, take only small fish, but are attracted to spots where mackerel and tuna drive smaller fish to the surface, so commercial fish catchers often set their nets near a big tern-out—a strange tern of events, leading us to the point of no retern.

Because terns are high in the aquatic food chain as fish eaters, they collect and concentrate pollutants. They're also extremely sensitive to human encroachment and development of their nesting grounds on beaches, and so have declined dangerously in the past few decades—the Common Tern is classified as endangered in Wisconsin, Illinois, and Ohio, threatened in Michigan and New York, and a species of special concern in Minnesota.

Notes

August

The word *auspicious* comes from the Latin *auspicium* for "the art of foretelling the future from birds." The Latin word itself came from *avis* for "bird" and *spex* for "a watcher."

5 Virtually all Northland wild birds are born under the astrological signs of Taurus, Gemini, Cancer, and Leo, though some owls are Aries. An ancient science more auspicious than astrology is augury—the practice of watching signs and omens, especially birds, to predict the future. People once likened the movements of birds to the departure of the human soul from earth. This mystical interpretation of bird flight led to the familiar portrayal of angels with bird wings.

If a bird fed in a grain field, it was a pigeon, portending evil. If the identical bird appeared anywhere else, it was a dove—harbinger of peace and good luck. Some folklore, like modern horoscopes, covered all eventualities. The call of a Whip-poor-will portended death, but if you made a wish when you heard the first one of spring, your wish came true. Hearing that first Whip-poor-will also meant that you'd be in the same place, doing the same thing at the same time, the following year—unless you died first. European cuckoos were conspicuous enough to portend *something*, but whether it was good or evil was anybody's guess.

Notes

6 Ancient Europeans believed swifts and ravens colluded with Satan. Both European and American robins brought good fortune. Brant geese were the Gabriel hounds, a night-flying pack baying to foretell a funeral. A songbird tapping on a window or a woodpecker tapping on a house predicted a death. If a bird crossed one's path from left to right, the person was in big trouble, but if it crossed from right to left, happy times were ahead. In early American folklore, if a bird flew into a house, it was carrying a message. If it couldn't get out again, it was a sign of death—presumably its own if the homeowner was accurate with a broomstick. The croakings of ravens predicted death and other disasters. Even today the British government protects and fosters ravens because an unspeakable disaster would supposedly befall England if the ravens were to leave the London Bridge rookery.

We no longer read bird entrails to divine the future, as people once did, but we still use the expression "a little bird told me." The Biloxi Indians of the Gulf of Mexico spoke to hummingbirds, which not only answered but always told the truth.

In America's Deep South in the 1800s, many people believed that the Blue Jay was the devil's messenger. They thought it was impossible to see a jay on Friday, when the birds carried sticks down to Satan, along with news of the world. The jays finished their devilish duties and returned on Saturday, when they were gay and noisy, relieved to be free from hell for another week.

Notes

August

Double-crested Cormorants nest in colonies, on cliffs or in trees. Arthur Cleveland Bent wrote of them, "A populous colony often contains young birds of all ages from naked helpless chicks to full-sized birds, and presents a most interesting, if not an attractive, picture. Such a colony is the filthiest place imaginable, for no other birds can equal cormorants in this respect."

7 People have used cormorants for fishing since ancient times. Japanese and Chinese bred them in hatcheries for commercial fishing. The birds formed a circle around a school of fish and worked their way inward. They wore collars to prevent them from swallowing the catch, but carried their take to the basket of their own accord. After the hunt they were given some freedom. Discipline was enforced by the birds themselves—if one dropped out of formation, the whole flock screamed and beat it with their wings, and the dominant cormorant sometimes bit it. This dominant bird sat on the bow, and the others lined up by rank. A well-trained bird could catch 150 fish in an hour.

The Dutch brought cormorant fishing to Europe in the sixteenth century. Henry IV and Louis XIII enjoyed it as a sort of underwater falconry. Louis built canals at Fontainebleau for the sport. In Japan today, cormorant fishing is merely a tourist attraction, and trainers no longer have the skills of ancient times. The cormorants are kept on leashes, and the trainer chokes them to get them to cough up the fish—not a pleasant sport for trainer or bird, to say nothing of the fish.

Notes

8 Everyone knows that some birds—like loons, eagles, Osprey, kingfishers, herons, gulls, and terns—eat fish, but not everyone knows that fish take revenge. The angler fish of the Atlantic is also called the goosefish because of its dietary preferences—a single angler fish had the remains of seven wild ducks in its stomach. The thresher shark attacks and swallows loons. Huge pelicans aren't safe—sharks sometimes sever their wings. Fish in the oceans have even managed to take land birds. A Yellow-billed Cuckoo was found inside a tiger shark in the Gulf of Mexico, and a Ruffed Grouse in a cod off Newfoundland.

Freshwater fish also take birds. Pike in Canada eat enormous numbers of young waterfowl in June and July, when baby ducks swim in shallow water. One northern pike leaped out of the water in Lake Minnetonka in Minnesota and caught a flying Black Tern, which it dragged underwater to eat. Pike are also known to take kingfishers. Bass often jump up and swallow small birds flycatching near the surface, especially warblers and hummingbirds. We wonder if they ever swim home with fishy tales about the one that got away.

In North Carolina, a male cardinal who lost his brood noticed seven goldfish in a pool. The color pattern of the fishes' mouths, similar to that of baby cardinals, apparently triggered his paternal instinct, and he stuffed a beakful of bugs into the pleasantly sur-prised fish. After that, whenever he called, the fish crowded near, sometimes leaping out of the water in their eagerness to be fed. The temporary bond between fish and bird satisfied everyone except the bugs.

Notes

August

When my sister-in-law Jeanie and I visited Yellowstone National Park in 1979, our first mission was to see Trumpeter Swans. We found a pair in the misty sunrise the first morning, and stopped to enjoy the perfect vision. Dozens of other early risers slowed down or stopped to check out what we were looking at—and every one hurried on after realizing that we were just looking at some birds.

9 Trumpeter Swans, the largest swans in the world, were once abundant in the Great Lakes area, but were brought to the edge of extinction by market hunters for their tasty meat and their skins, which made warm coats for settlers. They were also shipped abroad by the tens of thousands to furnish Europeans with powder puffs, quilts, pillows, and mattresses. Their quill feathers made popular writing instruments—John James Audubon favored Trumpeter Swan feathers for drawing the fine detail his work is famous for.

The Trumpeter Swan was gone from Minnesota, Wisconsin, and Michigan by the late 1800s—by 1933, only sixty-six were known to exist in the United States and Canada, wintering in the Red Rock Lakes of Montana. Aggressive protection and management saved them, but they still suffer from habitat degradation and destruction, diversion of water from their wintering grounds, and hunters who mistake them for Snow Geese. Many swans reintroduced into Minnesota succumbed to lead poisoning during the 1988 drought, when low water levels exposed lead pellets on the bottom. These majestic symbols of fidelity and love deserve our love, respect, and protection—not our toxic detritus.

Notes

10 When frightened, Blue Jay nestlings crouch, but once they fledge, escape from danger becomes the plan. If they fly across the open, they're vulnerable to hawks, and cats or squirrels may grab them in lower branches, so their best strategy is upward mobility, and jay parents know how to find them in high branches. But the poor babies I raise are stuck with an earthbound mama.

Before they can fly, jays are easy to keep track of. For days after their first tentative flaps, we can set them on a tree branch and they'll stay put for hours, looking all about, preening themselves and one another, stretching legs and wings, and dozing in the dappled sunlight. But as time goes by, they become more adventurous. They know they mustn't leave the tree without a grown-up, but one by one they start hopping around. Baby jays believe in "monkey see, monkey do." If one eats an army worm, the others sample one, too. If one falls into a sink of hot, soapy water and almost drowns, the others are sure to try the new game, too. And if one hops to the very top of a box elder tree, every other little jay will, too. Problem is, they don't have the foggiest idea how to get down again.

To tell our four babies apart, we borrowed some food coloring from our emergency auxiliary grandma, Mary, and identified each bird by the tiny spot on its tail. Sneakers, named for Mary's shoe, wore blue, Jake red, and Shake green. Bake's was left natural white. Jake was the biggest and most adventurous, Shake and Bake the wildest, and Sneakers the most curious about people and the least interested in its siblings.

Notes

August

Inexperienced people are often reluctant to let baby birds out when it's fledging time. The babies are dependent, but need to develop their muscles and explore the outdoors at this critical time or they'll never properly adapt to a natural life. It's hard work to successfully release baby birds—some days we spend hours rounding them up. But helping them become wild is the whole point in raising wildlings.

11 When our four baby jays first started exploring our box elder tree, we retrieved them by holding out a badminton pole—one by one they'd hop on and ride down to me. But one afternoon, Jake and Sneakers both made it up too high to reach before I noticed. I'd fed them at four o'clock and figured they'd come lower when they got hungry—there was plenty of time before dark. I wasn't taking into account just how deeply ingrained is a jay's desire for upward mobility.

By five, they mewed desperately whenever they heard my voice. I fed Shake and Bake beneath the tree and called to the other two, but they kept hopping higher, where they expected I could find them more easily. Sneakers looked down reproachfully, but poor Jake kept looking skyward, knowing darned well that any mommy worth her salt could look down and see him. By six they were calling constantly, and hopping even higher. By seven they were close to the crown of the tree, and had even attracted a neighborhood jay, but they weren't the least bit interested in her. They wanted their real mommy—me.

Notes

12 By eight o'clock the night of Sneakers's and Jake's big adventure, I was more desperate even than they to get them down out of the box elder and fill their tummies with food. Finally, Joey and I tried tossing a blue frisbee back and forth, hoping they'd instinctively follow it across the yard to us, or at least to a shorter tree. Sure enough, after a dozen tosses, Sneakers flew into a young sapling. Joey climbed up and Sneakers jumped on his head for the ride down. I fed her outside, hoping Jake would get the idea and come down, but he was stuck in that upwardly mobile mode—he hopped to the very crown of the tree, pleading with the great Blue Jay in the sky to send his mommy to him.

Finally, as it started to get dark, Russ got a big ladder and climbed as high into the branches as he could, then reached out with the badminton pole and brought down poor, desperate Jake, who pigged out and then slept until morning.

The wonderful mixture of intelligence and instinct is part of what makes baby Blue Jays so much fun—and so utterly exasperating.

Our babies soon figured out how to cope with an earth-bound mama, and came whenever we whistled. Within a few weeks they were flying free all around Peabody Street, returning to our house and squawking whenever they wanted an easy meal. Jake stayed in the neighborhood for weeks, mingling with other jays, many in migratory flocks, and coming home less and less. Sneakers never left our yard for long—she preferred human company.

Notes

August

Not all species are ready to say good-bye to summer. Some robins still care for eggs or babies; House Sparrows, which will breed in December if they have a warm nursery, are busy with child care, and so are Evening Grosbeak extended families. Goldfinches, needing thistledown to line their nests, can't begin to breed until many others are done with children for the year, but even they've finished singing.

13 Deferring pleasure is not part of a bird's mental makeup, perhaps because the future is too uncertain in a world where hawks and cats and picture windows lurk around every bend. In spring, birds eat every seed they unearth, trusting, like children dipping into chocolate chip cookie batter, that there will be a reasonable harvest despite them.

Now it's time for them to feast on that harvest. Robins attack strawberries with gusto, carelessly wiping their bills on the wood sides of our raised beds. Raspberries attract Purple Finches as surely as snow lures Will Steger. Grackles take bets about whether our tomatoes will turn red before the first frost, planning to share the fruits of our labor. We won't begrudge them a few tomatoes, since they've been dutifully combing the garden every few days for slugs. Evening Grosbeaks collect in box elders, pigging out on the seed-laden branches in an early Thanksgiving feast.

Too soon these careless days of August will pass into the responsibilities of September. We enjoy the avian riches while we can.

Notes

14 Even though we named a violet after them, few people pay attention to the feet of birds. Hardly anyone even misses the feet on store-bought turkeys and chickens. Domestic fowl have a sharp growth on their legs called a spur, a potentially lethal weapon that helps roosters enforce their pecking order. In ancient Asia, where cock-fighting originated, owners made the natural spurs even more lethal by fitting them with iron spikes.

The powerful, muscular toes and claws of hawks and owls are called talons. Osprey have pads under each toe with sharp spicules to grasp wet, slippery fish. Swifts have an opposable back toe, so when they're clinging to a chimney or hollow tree all four toes can face forward to hold them securely.

Ducks, gulls, and loons have webs between the front three toes, pelicans and cormorants have webs between all four toes, and Semipalmated Sandpiper and Semipalmated Plover toes are webbed halfway, giving them their names. Grebes and coots have separate lobes on each toe, which allow them to paddle reasonably well. Instead of two big paddles, they swim with eight little oars.

Herons and egrets have a long back toe, enabling them to perch and nest in trees. Cranes look a bit like herons, but a crane's tiny back toe, placed high on the tarsus, makes it impossible for it to perch. Cranes spend their lives on the ground or in the air, never in between.

Notes

August

Official counting of hawks at Hawk Ridge begins August 15—banding usually begins earlier. Our rule of thumb: "When the wind's from the east, hawk numbers are least. When the wind's from the west, hawk numbers are best." Hawk counters don't get rich—my earnings for August 1992, amounted to $4.46 per hour, or nineteen cents per bird. It may not sound like much, but it's more than Donald Trump ever made birdwatching.

15 In mid-August we plead with tiny green tomatoes to start growing, buy school supplies, pull out sweaters and warm jackets, and look skyward for migrating hawks. There are many fine places to observe them—Cape May in New Jersey and Hawk Mountain in Pennsylvania are the most famous, but many spots along ridges or coasts are good. One of the most modest and unassuming of all, Hawk Ridge in Duluth, boasts perhaps the largest fall hawk count in the inland United States, averaging fifty thousand raptors every year.

Hawk Ridge is an odd tourist attraction. The only way you know you're even at the right place on the dirt road is by the wood sign that reads "Hawk Ridge Nature Reserve, managed by Duluth Audubon Society." Behind some bushes another wood sign shows trails, and that's it. Some boulders along the roadside provide seating, and sometimes two portable potties are set up down the road a ways, but those are the only amenities. The thousands of visitors who gather each fall don't mind the lack of facilities—they're there to see hawks, and the hawks that gather at Hawk Ridge are plenty good enough.

Notes

16 Beginning in mid-August and continuing through October, Broad-winged Hawks follow the shoreline of Lake Superior on their southward migration. These forest raptors eat cold-blooded vertebrates like snakes, frogs, and salamanders, and must fly to Central and South America before their food disappears in fall.

Broadwings belong to a group of hawks called buteos, recognized by their short, broad tail and long, broad wings, designed to maximize surface area. As wind strikes a ridge line, it forms an updraft, and as the sun warms the earth, heated air rises in columns called thermals. When a migrating buteo feels either of these columns of rising air, it circles within it, rising effortlessly, higher and higher. Rising air cools, eventually reaching equilibrium with the atmosphere—at this point the hawk sets its wings and rushes forward, slowly losing altitude as it searches for the next thermal or updraft. To conserve energy, migrating buteos watch one another, and when one rises, others join it. Swirling masses of hawks look like steam rising from a teapot, and so are called kettles.

Hawks are reluctant to fly over water—no thermals or updrafts hold them aloft, they have nowhere to rest or hunt, and gangs of gulls may drive them into the water for lunch. So when migrants reach Lake Superior, they follow the shoreline down, collecting in huge numbers by the time they reach the tip of the lake, near Hawk Ridge. On September 18, 1993, an amazing 47,919 Broad-winged Hawks were counted from the ridge.

Notes

August

People sometimes place plastic owl decoys on power poles to deter squirrels or woodpeckers from destroying the wood, or on buildings to discourage pigeons and starlings from roosting. But squirrels and birds both eventually figure out that they're fakes. To make ours appear a bit more real, sometimes we affix real feathers to flutter in the wind.

17 One of the daily rituals for the Hawk Ridge counter is setting an owl decoy on a pole on a ledge below the main ridge. New visitors are taken aback to see a Great Horned Owl down there until they realize it's the plastic variety. We set it there to trick our avian visitors—passing hawks often circle back for a better look, occasionally even dive-bombing it, providing human visitors with satisfying looks.

Hawks attack Great Horned Owls for the same reason crows do—owls kill and eat large birds in their roosts. When Peregrine Falcons were reintroduced to Minnesota, the biggest problem they faced was from Great Horned Owls. Many birds quickly figure out that our owl is a fake, and most pay it no mind at all, but we trick enough birds to make it worthwhile. Harriers, redtails, and kestrels have all swooped at it, and Merlins and Sharp-shinned Hawks are often taken in. Even after Merlins figure out it's not real, they may swoop in more than twenty times, these feisty little shadowboxers of the sky. The owl just sits there and takes it.

Notes

18 Nighthawks are on the move, silently winging their way toward South America. They're in no hurry—they flutter this way and that, as randomly as the bugs they're chasing, their capacious mouths opening to scarf down a myriad of insects from moths and dragonflies to aeroplankton—airborne creatures too tiny for us to notice. Flying twenty miles per hour, nighthawks don't swallow—the insects just go down the hatch. Despite the atmosphere's abundant entomological distractions, these two-and-a-half-ounce aircraft make steady progress southward—if they wore T-shirts, they'd read "Brazil or Bust." A few stop in Central America, but many continue all the way to Argentina.

The nighthawk's dependence on flying insects explains why it migrates so far—it must be guaranteed a constant food supply, and by avoiding Central America, where the majority of North America's insect-eaters winter, it also avoids much of the competition. We watch huge flocks disappear into the pink, twilight sky on long, graceful wings, fluttering like moths. Even the lovely etching of their feathers is mothlike. Perhaps they have become what they eat.

Tens of thousands of nighthawks migrate along the north shore of Lake Superior every August and September—Mike Hendrickson counted 43,690 in a single two-and-a-half-hour period from the Lakewood Pumping Station on August 26, 1990. Distracted by flights of nighthawks over soccer fields, I've missed some of the best plays in Tommy's late afternoon games. On Peabody Street we sometimes count thousands per hour.

Notes

August

During my two-week stand as counter at Hawk Ridge, perhaps a dozen hawks that I would have missed are tallied thanks to Fred and Annie. They spot a peregrine so far off that I can barely identify it through 10x40 Zeiss binoculars, and a sharpshin so high in the ozone that even with binoculars I can't find it. I must use my spotting scope to see what nighthawk eyes see with no help at all.

19 I'm hawk counter at the ridge today, along with my two assistants, Fred and Annie the night-hawks. The moment I open the pet carrier, Annie scurries out onto the sunny ground beside my stool. Fred is more cautious, but he emerges in a minute or so.

Annie is young, and filled with youthful enthusiasms. Fred prefers comfort to novelty. When a redtail circles overhead, studying our nearby owl decoy, both night-hawks instantly look up. Fred, who has experienced hawks during his long life in the wild, makes a soft, guttural "rit, rit, rit" call. Annie, who was injured on her maiden flight, probably never saw a hawk before taking this job. As she gazes at the redtail, I can almost see the gears in her mind turning, calculating just how big she'd have to open her mouth to swallow this one. The hawk descends almost imperceptibly, considering whether or not to strike at the owl. Fred crouches and then waddles under my stool. Annie's eyes grow bigger and bigger. As the hawk flies off, her gaze follows him beyond the horizon.

Notes

20 A Peregrine Falcon sees the world through the most highly evolved organs in all creation—its eyes. Hawks and owls weighing less than five pounds have larger eyes than adult humans. A nighthawk's eyes are heavier than its brain. A chickadee's cornea—the part not hidden by feathers and skull—is small to reduce heat and moisture loss, but those beady little eyes are just the tips of enormous masses inside the chickadee skull.

Bird eyes don't move at all, and each works independently of the other. Many birds turn their heads to study objects with one eye when making difficult discriminations. The two optic nerves are completely crossed—each side of the brain receives information from just one eye, but a unique area of the bird brain called the Wulst may integrate information from the two nerves, permitting stereoscopic vision. Birds have a sharply defined pit in the retina called a fovea, which is absent in mammals except humans and other primates. The avian fovea is more highly developed than ours, with extremely fine, tightly packed cones, each connected by its own ganglion to the optic nerve. No wonder birds seem like such visionaries.

It isn't quite correct to refer to a bird's "eyeballs"—most avian eyes are flat or globular. Owl eyes are tubular—almost cylindrical—and fixed, facing forward in the sockets. To compensate, owls can rotate their heads well over 180 degrees in either direction. When you see a picture of a cute little owl with eyes demurely cast to the side, you know the artist has never seen a real owl.

Notes

August

Eagle, hawk, and falcon eyes have more nerve cells in the upper half of the retina than the lower, increasing the bird's visual acuity when flying or sitting in a tree or other high perch to look down upon the ground. When a captive hawk is set on a low perch, it often turns its head upside down to see a person at or above its eye level, focusing the image on the part of the eye with the greatest visual sensitivity.

21 Because of the placement of their eyes, most birds have better lateral than forward vision. Penguins and songbirds use one eye at a time to examine nearby objects—that's why robins feeding on a lawn cock their heads when studying the ground. Since monocular vision isn't three-dimensional, birds often bob their heads quickly to see an object from different angles. Bitterns have binocular forward vision when pointing their beaks up. Woodcock and nighthawk eyes are set far enough back to see above and behind themselves. Birds apparently can survive at least for a time with a single eye—David Evans once banded a Snowy Owl missing an eye that survived the entire winter season in his study area.

In most birds the iris is dark brown to black. Baby crows and jays have blue eyes that change to brown as they mature. Many hawks and owls have bright yellow or yellow-orange eyes—in some bird-hunting hawks called accipiters, the color changes to ruby red with maturity. Loons', Red-eyed Vireos', and Black-crowned Night-Herons' eyes also turn ruby as they mature. Cormorant eyes are green, gannet eyes pale blue.

Notes

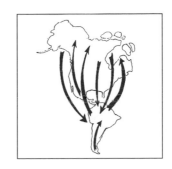

22 Hawk Ridge visitors ask why birds migrate when so much food is still available. This abundant food fuels their long journey. Birds couldn't migrate if they waited until food supplies were exhausted or frozen, though some return in spring before food supplies are adequate, in their haste to claim land and a mate.

Do birds leave because of the cold winter? Many birds that nest in the North Woods are really tropical species that leave their ancestral home during the breeding season to escape the heavy competition for tropical nest sites and food. By heading away from equatorial twelve-hour days, they also capitalize on the longer day length of the northern summer, and raise their babies more quickly, shortening the vulnerable nesting period. And fewer snakes and other nest predators live in the Far North than in the tropics. Down feathers are good insulation, but to keep the furnace going, birds need food. Those that eat cold-blooded animals or seeds that might get snow-covered can't fuel their metabolic furnaces through a Northland winter. Migration is a clever strategy to have been invented by a pack of bird brains.

Migration is fraught with peril as birds pass through unfamiliar areas, where unexpected dangers lurk on all sides. Spring and fall weather is unpredictable— storms kill huge numbers of migrants. Most nocturnal migrants navigate by the stars, and city lights may disorient them so they become helplessly lost. Lighted radio and TV towers and strong spotlights lure millions of migrants to their deaths each year.

Notes

August

Falcons are designed for high-speed chases. Accipiters, like the Sharp-shinned Hawk, catch birds, too, but take them by surprise. Accipiters often startle a whole flock of birds in the woods and then seize one as it flies upwards. Buteos and eagles, with their big surface area and short tail, are the finest thermal riders in the sky.

23 Many birders have trouble with hawk identification, with good reason, so beginners shouldn't worry if, like Hamlet, they have trouble telling a hawk from a handsaw. Few hawks have the conspicuous field marks of songbirds, and many species have great variations in plumage. It's often hard to judge how far away a hawk is under blue sky—it's either big and far away or small and near. No wonder some people despair, appreciating Ogden Nash's wistful words, "I sometimes visualize in my gin/ the Audubon that I audubin."

But identifying hawks is hardly impossible. Observe flight. Does it flap quickly or slowly, or soar with no wingbeats at all? If the wings are long and pointed, it may be a falcon. If the wings are long and round, and the tail short and round, a buteo is more likely. If the wings are short and round and the tail long, it's either an accipiter or a Blue Jay. Of course, sometimes buteos and accipiters set back and point their wings for rapid cruising, and sometimes falcons hold theirs wide to soar. Field guides are helpful—the only problem is, hawks don't know what's expected of them because they never read those books.

Notes

24 I'm sitting on the wall of the Lakewood Pumping Station, watching the sun come up over Lake Superior and listening to my favorite meteorologist's comfortable voice giving the weather data on my weather radio. A swirling flock of Cedar Waxwings flies leisurely past, and the first Blue Jays appear. During the first three hours of this pleasant day, I count 5,893 migrating birds, including 3,268 Blue Jays, 982 Cedar Waxwings, 712 blackbirds, 625 warblers, and various and sundry other dickey birds—we call this job "Dawn Dickey Duty."

A visitor asks how we identify flying songbirds. We sort them out more by shape and flight technique than by field marks. Blue Jays fly slow and even, with labored wing beats. Their long, slender tail and rounded wings are easier to see than their white underside and blue upper parts. Jays fly in long, narrow flocks. Cedar Waxwings fly in big, round flocks. Their pointed wings and swirling, lazy flight are easy to recognize, and just about every flock helps us out by calling. Their mouselike snores are quiet and high-pitched, but somehow pierce our consciousness over other sounds.

Robins fly fast, pulling pointed wings back with each stroke as if paddling a canoe. The red breast isn't noticeable, but the white area just below the tail is easy to see, even from a distance. Blackbirds have more rounded wings, which they pull up and down as jays do. Redwings undulate, but grackles fly straight, almost like robins. Siskins and goldfinches fly in swirling flocks that zip along much faster than waxwings.

Notes

August

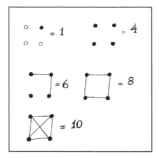

To tally our numbers, we write down multiples of one hundred, but use a dot and line system to keep track of smaller numbers. Each hour we write down weather data from the U.S. Weather Service and begin a fresh count column. At the end of a busy day, it can take over an hour to tally up all the figures for the day.

25 Counting migrating birds may never take the place of night baseball, but it's the sport for me. Hawks look like tiny specks in the ozone at midday, but at least they're bigger and slower than warblers. As hawks spiral upwards on a thermal or updraft, they form a kettle—some in front, some behind, all in constant, confusing motion, impossible to count. But one by one they reach an equilibrium point where the air no longer rises, and they stream forward in a countable line. Counters keep track of kettles in the sky, and count each only as the birds stream out the top.

Crows and Blue Jays are easy, too. They migrate in flocks of up to two hundred, but fly slowly and stay in formation as they go. Grackles and robins move fast but straight. Other blackbirds and Evening Grosbeaks are trickier because they swirl about as they go, but we can usually count them one by one. Hardest to count are waxwings and siskins. Both fly in flocks of up to several hundred birds, with each shifting position within the flock as they go. They often vanish from sight before we've counted half—then we estimate what fraction of the flock we counted, and multiply.

Notes

26 Kestrels are migrating now. They fly over Hawk Ridge from August through September, heading for the southern states and Mexico. On peak days as many as 250 may cruise over, darting by on quick, slender wings, occasionally snatching a dragonfly as they glide past. Then they gain altitude and pull their talons forward to take a bite in midair, these creators of the concept of fast food.

We usually see one kestrel at a time. These solitary birds live alone most of the year, and often defend a winter territory as well as a breeding one. Sometimes kestrels that hatched over the summer join in small flocks, which stay together through migration, but they soon outgrow the need for companionship. Some ornithologists believe kestrels mate for life, but they may be wedded more to their territory than to each other. A pair of kestrels lived relatively harmoniously in the Lake Superior Zoo until zoo keepers moved them from a small cage into a larger enclosure. The female felt a surge of territoriality, and harassed the little male until zoo keepers took pity and moved him back into the small cage again.

About 75 percent of kestrel deaths take place between August and November. A few are killed in Blue Jay attacks, many by cats, automobiles, lightning, picture windows, other hawks, and even locomotives, but most of the banded ones found dead have been shot. In captivity they have lived for more than seventeen years, but their life expectancy in the wild is only a year and three months.

Notes

August

Bears visit Hawk Ridge every fall, causing problems for the songbird bander. Although he never leaves his mist nets unattended for more than a few minutes before removing warblers for banding and release, one autumn a bear figured out the system and found the little morsels clinging to the nets right tasty.

27 One afternoon when I'm alone at Hawk Ridge with my nighthawk assistants and no car, a large bear ambles in, sniffing purple flowers right across the narrow dirt road from me. It has a glossy coat and bright eyes, and I'd just as soon keep watching it if I didn't have two little birds along, and if I did have a car—just in case. Fred seems alarmed, so I put him and Annie in the pet carrier. The bear looks up and sniffs at us with interest. I don't want to frighten it, but then again, I don't want it to frighten me, either. Now, when it comes right down to it, bears are pretty much like third graders, so I give this one my standard lecture about nighthawks—how to distinguish adult males from females and immatures from adults, their migration habits and food requirements, and on and on. Sure enough, like any third grader, it's bored silly by the lecture, but, like any well-raised child, is too polite to say so. It waits for a lull in my discourse, and then politely turns around and waddles into the woods. Knowing how and when to cultivate boredom can be a mighty useful skill.

Notes

28 In the early 1800s, Audubon watched as two nighthawks were struck and killed by lightning. In 1941, a bolt blasted four Double-crested Cormorants from a flock. All four were dead, though their feathers weren't scorched. In another 1941 storm, more than fifty Snow Geese were struck by a single lightning bolt. At least one was badly burned, but autopsies revealed that many of the others died from the impact as they hit the ground. In 1939, lightning killed thirty-four pelicans. Bald Eagles and Osprey have been struck while sitting atop nests in tall trees, and more than one tree struck by lightning has been found to contain dead woodpeckers, owls, or other birds.

Hail bonks countless birds. In 1953, two hailstorms in Alberta killed 150,000 ducks and geese and countless birds too little to document. In 1960, thousands of Sandhill Cranes were beaned by hail in New Mexico. Again, even more small birds were killed. A bluebird pelted by hail in Iowa in 1931 had both wings broken. These are the effects of normal thunderstorms. I'm not even going to think about what happens to birds in tornadoes and hurricanes.

When the Statue of Liberty asks us to send the homeless, tempest-tossed to her, she's not lifting her lamp for a pack of birds, but maybe someone should. In 1938, a biologist discovered two dead California Condors that had been beaned by hailstones while eating a horse carcass. Considering how few condors remained in the world at the time, hail represents a significant cause of the species' decline.

Notes

August

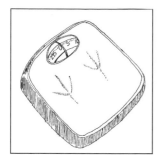

A bird doesn't have a flight crew to check its fuselage or certify that its wings and rudder are in top condition, but a bird brain serves as well as the best airline maintenance crew. Most birds molt in summer, replacing every one of their feathers after the exhausting breeding season is over but while food is still plentiful. Feathers make up about 10 percent of a songbird's weight—replacing them takes a lot of energy.

29 Migration in fall is more leisurely than in spring—the drive to mate and establish a territory hastens birds northward at a more frenetic pace than their less-urgent need to retreat south. The swallows of Capistrano and Hinkley's buzzards arrive within a few days of when they're supposed to in spring, but their return trip isn't predictable enough to celebrate.

Fueling up is cheaper for a southbound bird than for a jet plane. A bird gases up with fat in order to fly long distances. A hummingbird that normally weighs two-and-a-half grams must add two grams of fat to fly nonstop over the Gulf of Mexico each spring and fall. An eleven-gram Blackpoll Warbler balloons to twenty-three grams each fall in order to strike out from New England across the open Atlantic for the Lesser Antilles or Venezuela. Blackpolls usually fly nonstop, but a few killed in a fatal attraction to a Bermuda lighthouse were found to have lost about 17 percent of their original body weight. At that rate of consumption, they could have flown for 105 to 120 hours without a pit stop.

Notes

30 In *Casablanca*, Rick and Ilsa will always have Paris. Russ and I will always have Sand Point—a lovely little beach tucked away on Wisconsin's mainland near the Apostle Islands, discovered Labor Day weekend, 1975, in those sweet, simple years before children.

The smooth sand was dotted with footprints—raccoons, a mink, sandpipers—but showed no sign that humans had ever been there. A Lapland Longspur leisurely strolled along the beach, giving me plenty of time to thumb through the pages of my field guide trying to match it to its mug shot. That was the only lifer I added, and I saw only twelve species altogether. Now I'd easily get over forty under the same circumstances, but although birds are fewer for the inexperienced, they're also more precious. The glowing redstart I identified more than made up for four warblers I couldn't figure out at all. Delicate Barn Swallows swooping and twittering and occasionally slicing an incision into the water's smooth surface made up for Cliff Swallows I didn't realize were there, too. Russ had his fill of wild flowers and mushrooms, I of birds, and both of one another on this tranquil late summer's day.

Migrating flickers fly along the shoreline in swooping flight and sun themselves on dirt roads. Overhead, we see their bright yellow wing linings, and as they fly away, the white rump patch. Their yellow-shafted feathers dot the shoreline—hawks find flickers as attractive as we do, and tastier. Before I came upon Sand Point in 1975, I had somehow never noticed flickers collecting on roadsides. Since that day, I've never been able to ignore them.

Notes

August

Phalarope females are larger and more boldly colored than males. Males, not females, develop a brood patch and incubate and care for the young, and females produce as much testosterone as males. This *reverse sexual dimorphism* may occur because phalaropes nest in habitats with relatively little food. If the female both produced and cared for the young, she might not survive on the sparse diet. This way male and female expend similar amounts of energy.

Notes

31 As August draws to an end, Bunter and I enjoy late summer riches in Port Wing. On the grassy path to the sewage ponds, redstarts and Wilson's Warblers dart out, harvesting mosquitoes. Kingbirds and redwings scold. I tie Bunter to a fence post—settling ponds hardly provide a healthy swim. A dozen Wood Ducks bring their babies to the ponds every summer, and I worry about them. I often find shotgun shells in the tall weeds here—one would think even poachers would think twice about taking birds from sewage ponds.

On the edge of the water, two tiny synchronized swimmers, Wilson's Phalaropes, spin like toy tops. *Phalarope* comes from the Greek *phalaris* for "coot" and *pous* for "foot"—their toes have fat lobes and partial webbing, enabling them to paddle better than other shorebirds. Their legs are laterally flattened to reduce drag, and their belly plumage is dense and ducklike, providing a layer of trapped air on which they float as lightly as corks—they're so buoyant that strong winds may pluck them right out of the water. These exquisite shorebirds spinning about on this lazy afternoon make a memorable end to a lovely month.

September

September

Martha, the last Passenger Pigeon in the world, died September 1, 1914, in the Cincinnati Zoo. She was twenty-nine. Her body is displayed at the Smithsonian Institution in Washington, D.C. The last Passenger Pigeons definitely seen in the wild were one shot in Babcock, Wisconsin, in 1899, and one shot in Pikes County, Ohio, in 1900. Theodore Roosevelt reported a small flock in Maryland in 1907, but his sighting was rejected because the species had already been declared extinct.

Notes

1 The extinction of the Passenger Pigeon, the "blue meteor," was a tragedy beyond comprehension, for this was once the most abundant bird species on earth. Probably three to five billion Passenger Pigeons lived in North America when Columbus landed.

When Passenger Pigeons moved over an area, they darkened the sky—a single flock could cover an area over a mile wide and three hundred miles long. People, eagles, and falcons had an inexhaustible food supply until Europeans entered the scene. Railroads and the telegraph sealed the species' fate—as soon as a nesting colony was discovered, market hunters descended in droves. In 1874, after the species had been decimated in the east, seven hundred thousand were netted in a single month at a Michigan nesting colony. In New York, tons were shipped to market daily from another colony.

Nobody believed the pigeons could ever disappear—there were too many of them. It wasn't until 1905, after the species had been officially declared extinct in the wild, that Michigan even changed the Passenger Pigeon's status from a game to a nongame bird.

2 Chief Simon Pokagon, last Potawatomi chief of the Pokagon Band, wrote of the Passenger Pigeon:

It was proverbial with our fathers that if the Great Spirit in His wisdom could have created a more elegant bird in plumage, form, and movement, He never did. When a young man I have stood for hours admiring the movements of these birds. I have seen them fly in unbroken lines from the horizon, one line succeeding another from morning until night, moving their unbroken columns like an army of trained soldiers pushing to the front, while detached bodies of these birds appeared in different parts of the heavens, pressing forward in haste like raw recruits preparing for battle. At other times I have seen them move in one unbroken column for hours across the sky, like some great river, ever varying in hue; and as the mighty stream, sweeping on at sixty miles an hour, reached some deep valley, it would pour its living mass headlong down hundreds of feet, sounding as though a whirlwind was abroad in the land . . . Never have my astonishment, wonder, and admiration been so stirred as when I have witnessed these birds drop from their course like meteors from heaven.

Chief Pokagon wrote in 1895, "I would most prayerfully ask in the name of Him who suffers not a sparrow to fall unnoticed, what must be the nature of the crime and degree of punishment awaiting our white neighbors who have so wantonly butchered and driven from our forests these wild pigeons, the most beautiful flowers of the animal creation of North America."

Notes

September

Even when not searching for food, Sharp-shinned Hawks remain in attack mode. We often see them darting at hawks high in the sky—other sharpies, redtails, even eagles. These feisty little characters are our bread-and-butter birds at Hawk Ridge. During their heaviest migration, from mid-August through mid-October, we often count hundreds in a day.

3 When little birds start smacking into windows in Duluth, we know that Sharp-shinned Hawks are migrating. Sharpies can be found wherever there are birds to eat, from warblers to pigeons. These accipiters—hawks specially adapted for hunting woodland birds on the wing—have long tails for quick maneuvers, and short, wide wings for rapid flight among dense trees. Females begin migrating before males of the same age, and their migration peaks right as warblers and other tiny songbirds are moving. They catch their prey in flight with their strong, sharp talons. When one of these excellent hunters appears on Peabody Street, all the birds at the feeders scatter in a panic.

Just as sharpies are adapted for killing little birds, those same little birds are adapted for getting away, which means a lot of hungry hawks are flying around every fall. Early in the morning, sharpies fly low over the ridge, searching through the trees for breakfast. As they find sustaining morsels, one by one they move higher in the sky—those kettling with broadwings have temporarily satisfied their hunger, and can concentrate on moving south.

Notes

4 The skies of autumn pulse with the wing beats of migrating birds, coursing through their arterial flyways like the blood of life. In migration is such mystery, and such miracle. Imagine a hummingbird rushing along, stopping for a snack whenever it eyes a patch of jewelweed or a promising feeder, but ever pressing onward. It travels over a thousand miles down to south Texas, which is amazing enough without even considering that once it arrives there it must fly six hundred miles more, nonstop over the Gulf of Mexico, without refueling. Its heart throbs at least 936,000 times during that journey over treacherous water, while its wings beat at least 6,048,000 times without a rest. And all this happens at the peak of hurricane season. Marathons, and even ultramarathons, look like pretty tame accomplishments in comparison.

Most tiny birds migrate by night, with the advantage of fewer predators, less wind, and cooler temperatures to keep them from overheating, but hummingbirds migrate by day, whizzing along on their long journey like oversized bumblebees.

Many people take in hummingbird feeders by Labor Day, but we keep them available as long as hummers come. Virtually all adult hummingbirds have already left the Northland despite abundant flowers and feeders. The year's young have an urgent instinctive need to go, too, but can't leave until they have fat deposits to fuel the flight. Many starve after early frosts. This is nature's way. The human way is to give them a hand.

Notes

September

When an extremely rare Yellow-billed Loon turned up in Duluth on October 17, 1987, three other experienced birders and I found it far out in the lake—upturned pale bill and all. When, on more careful inspection, we discovered it was really a Double-crested Cormorant, we sheepishly drove down the shore to where the real loon was, vowing never to breathe a word of our mistake to another living soul.

5 A woman calls with an identification problem— she's already talked to a biologist at the university, but he clearly knows nothing about tropical hummingbirds. She's sure I can help her. She recently saw a bird the size of a Ruby-throated Hummingbird or even smaller in her garden. It had rosy oval wing patches, a down-curved bill that rolled in and out, and two feathery antennae. I break it to her that her rare tropical hummingbird is really a sphinx moth, adding that it's a very common error—many people mistake both this species and the cecropia moth for hummingbirds. But the woman is furious, and shocked that I don't know any more than that so-called biologist. She vows to report me to—to somebody, and hangs up.

The next day when I get a call from another woman with a rare hummingbird, I brace myself. This bird has a reddish brown back, but otherwise looks pretty much like a rubythroat. I breathe a sigh of relief—it's a Rufous Hummingbird. There are three records of this western species in Wisconsin and several in Minnesota, all since 1974. She won't have to report me to anyone.

Notes

6 Yellow-bellied Sapsuckers are common migrants right now. They make a sharp mewing call in spring and summer, but are fairly silent in autumn, so they aren't very noticeable. As many as a dozen at a time have visited our backyard in fall, quietly digging little holes in the trunks of the box elder and spruces, then eating the inner bark and lapping up sap with their brushlike tongues. A couple have taken nectar from our hummingbird feeders, and one hung out with robins and Cedar Waxwings, eating berries in our mountain ash. But we have to pay attention to notice them.

Most woodpeckers peck holes only to pull potentially damaging insects from trees. Yellow-bellied Sapsuckers actually serve as agents, allowing diseases and insects to infiltrate ornamental trees. Their preferred food is the sweet running sap that flows in healthy trees. Even much of their insect food is composed of flying bugs that get mired in the sticky fluid, rather than the grubs that damage trees. But sapsuckers provide an important function in nature—hummingbirds, kinglets, warblers, phoebes, and many other birds feast on sap made available by these avian little maple syrupers.

To discourage sapsuckers from a valued tree, we can wrap aluminum sheeting around a ring of fresh sapsucker holes—sometimes the sapsucker will leave, but occasionally it will drill a new circle of holes above or below the metal, making us repeat the process. I've seen many perfectly healthy trees riddled with healed-over sapsucker holes, so unless I had a financial or sentimental stake in a particular tree, I wouldn't worry.

Notes

September

The "bait birds" used to lure hawks into the nets at the ridge are raised by David Evans for seasonal employment, and kept in a coop in his yard the rest of the year. One domestic dove that worked on and off for Dave since 1978 was retired from active duty in 1992.

7 The Hawk Ridge Research Station, created by David Evans in 1972, is one of the finest raptor-banding operations in the country. Volunteer and professional banders trap about four thousand hawks and owls each year, luring them into nets with a starling or pigeon tethered safely behind. Banders weigh and measure each hawk and place a numbered metal U.S. Fish and Wildlife Service ring around its leg before release, sometimes also drawing a blood sample or collecting other information.

Sharp-shinned Hawks hunt as they migrate—from 1,100 to 3,175 are lured into the nets each year. Few are ever recaptured, but those that are provide important clues about sharpshin migratory habits. Some winter in the Midwest, but they've been recovered from almost every Central American country and even from South America.

Emaciated hawks are fed before release, and twice Dave has netted sharpshins impaled by a branch sticking through the breast and out the back. In both cases the wound appeared healed—he cut off the protruding ends and applied antiseptic before release. Maybe that's why my sympathies are as much with the hawks as with their meals.

Notes

8 Strong westerly winds were recorded for five straight days from September fifth through ninth, 1988, and the Duluth sky grew a hazy yellowish brown, which the National Weather Service attributed to smoke from the devastating fires at Yellowstone National Park. On the smokiest day, September 9, a record thirty-four Swainson's Hawks appeared at Hawk Ridge, well east of their normal range. The prevailing westerlies also blew in a little Western Kingbird, who stayed in the same north shore area for at least two days, one of the easiest rare birds I've ever seen.

Western Kingbirds once ranged in the same areas as bison, nesting in thickets along western rivers and streams and lining their nests with thick, felted bison wool. They've adjusted to settlement by nesting on buildings, windmills, utility poles, and water towers, and now substitute cattle hairs and sheep wool for bison fur. Western Kingbirds aren't as feisty as their eastern counterparts—two or more pairs have often been found nesting in the same tree, and they've also nested within a few feet of Swainson's Hawk and Golden Eagle nests.

Western Kingbirds are found regularly in western Minnesota, though breeding locations are spotty on this eastern edge of their range. Every year, a handful of individuals turn up in Wisconsin and other eastern places—the first one I ever saw was at Point Pelee in eastern Ontario. Western Kingbirds winter in southern Mexico and Central America.

Notes

September

Jays are usually noisy, but they migrate silently. With their labored wing beats, they tire easily—flocks frequently land in trees to rest and snack. When a Sharp-shinned Hawk darts into trees harboring a flock of jays, we hear a raspy "rit-rat!" If it's a close call, or if the sharpie actually gets one, the whole flock chatters noisily, perhaps the Blue Jay equivalent of an Irish wake.

9 Why do some Blue Jays go south for the winter while others stick around? In 1988, the best migration year ever recorded at the Lakewood Pumping Station, we counted 6,733 Blue Jays the whole season, less than half the 13,750 counted the year before. We've tallied over 6,000 jays in a single day migrating over the pumphouse, yet many stay in the Northland all winter.

No one knows exactly what causes one Blue Jay to light out for the territory while another endures the winter. It may have to do with food supplies—some ornithologists have noted that jays are more abundant in years when acorns are also abundant. But food is probably not the only variable in the Blue Jay migration equation—some evidence from banded bird studies indicates that young birds are more likely to migrate than older ones. I suspect that individual choice plays as big a role in a Blue Jay's migration as it does in the annual flight of humans from the Northland to the Sun Belt.

Notes

10 My baby Katie took her first tentative steps on this planet to draw closer to the window to see Blue Jays. There were plenty of them that fall of 1984. Scores of migrants gathered at the sunflower seed to fill their tummies, while the Peabody Street regulars swooped in and out, stuffing their gular pouches and carrying the seeds off to eat in a sheltered branch or to hide against winter shortages.

Several gray squirrels came regularly to the front porch to take peanuts from my hand, and the neighborhood jays took to following them. No sooner could a squirrel hide a peanut under a leaf or bury it in a shallow grave than a jay would swoop down and dig it up again, but pretty soon the jays decided to skip the middleman and started taking the peanuts from my hand, too. Katie's eyes shone whenever they flew in, these creatures that were bigger and brighter than any birds she'd ever seen, and easier for little eyes to watch than sparrows and finches at the feeder. She'd clap and giggle with delight as the cooperative birds flashed vivid blue and white wings right next to the window. Her second word, after "mama," was "boo jay!"

It's easy to distinguish local Blue Jays from migrants. Those passing through are both hungry and unfamiliar with the neighborhood, so they chow down right at the feeder, holding a single seed in their feet and hacking It open like overgrown chickadees. Jays staying the winter don't usually eat at the feeder—they stuff their throat pouches and carry the seeds away. One jay's restaurant is another jay's grocery store.

Notes

September

Most backyard birds, including flycatchers, are passerines, or perching birds—three-fifths of all bird species are passerines, which have three toes in front and one behind, with leg muscles and tendons arranged to tighten if the hold on a perch becomes precarious. Most have muscles in their syrinx that insert into the ends of the upper bronchial half-rings, making them oscine passerines, or true songbirds. Flycatchers lack this unique song-producing apparatus.

Notes

11 An Olive-sided Flycatcher sits upright in a dead box elder limb. This oversized pewee wears dull autumn colors year-round—its erect posture, solitary ways, and somber plumage give us the impression of rigidity and righteousness until we hear one shout "Quick—free beer!" Hormone levels are at low ebb in autumn—this one is silent except for an occasional "pip-pip."

The olive-sided summers in bogs and coniferous forest of Canada and the northern tier of states—it is frequently heard in the background on the Canadian Broadcasting Corporation's "Anne of Green Gables," filmed on Prince Edward Island. Most summers a pair nests in Port Wing, and in autumn I always find a few on Minnesota Point and usually one in my yard, which can be counted on to stick around all day but disappear for good when darkness falls. Today's bird flutters out periodically, fattening up on flying insects in preparation for the long journey to the Andes Mountains. Olive-sideds are not rare, but the distances these one-ounce birds travel twice a year, their loner ways, incongruous song, and proud bearing make them birds of quality and distinction.

12 In September, little sandpipers dot the beaches of Lake Superior, scurrying along the waves, sometimes allowing us to approach within ten or fifteen feet before they take off in unison, showing off bold white wing stripes as they stream along. Soon they alight again, and tirelessly resume beachcombing, which is hardly just an amusing pastime for them—it's their livelihood.

The Sanderling's pale plumage and wing bars are its best field marks. Its comical habit of running in and out along the waves while constantly probing for food makes it doubly pleasing to watch.

Every Sanderling is raised in the Arctic Circle nursery, on tundra or rocky deserts of northern Canada, Alaska, Greenland, or Siberia, and its childhood is as ephemeral as the arctic summer. By July, babies are full-grown, powerful long-distance fliers already heading south. Some winter along North American coasts, but most go to southernmost South America, Africa, and even Australia. There's probably not a sandy beach in the world that has never been visited by a Sanderling.

Sanderlings are unique in the sandpiper family in lacking a hind toe. This feature isn't mentioned in field guides, but it's not hard to see, even from a distance, and makes it easy for beginning shore-bird watchers to clinch its identification. Without the support of a hind toe, a Sanderling balances a little more forward than its relatives, and runs differently—almost like a wind-up toy.

Notes

September

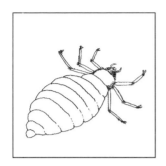

Dozens of shorebirds were found dead or dying in Duluth in the fall of 1990, but hardly anyone cared until I got sick. Issues of human health naturally cause greater concern to humans than issues of bird health, but that hardly means we should ignore the needs of our avian brothers and sisters. People value gold more than silver, but only a foolish miner would toss out silver nuggets because they weren't gold.

13 One September, after a series of storms washed raw sewage into Lake Superior, three Sanderlings were found, weak and emaciated, on Minnesota Point, and brought to me. All three had lice and mites—these parasites multiply quickly when a bird is too sick to preen properly—and one louse bit me. A couple of days later, I got sick. After running a high fever for two days, and remembering the louse bite, I went to the doctor. My white count was normal, as were two smears, so I went home reassured that it was just the flu.

By the next day, one Sanderling had died, my fever was still climbing, and I was having trouble breathing. When I was sleeping on the sofa, Bunter licked my face and I knew she was really a wolf there to eat my dog—Russ hustled me back to the doctor. Psittacosis, or parrot fever, causes the same symptoms I had, and victims show normal white counts and smears. My doctor sent in a blood titer to be analyzed. Meanwhile, a healthy nighthawk with a broken wing that I'd been caring for also died. We were in trouble.

Notes

14 After catching a mysterious disease from a sick Sanderling's louse, I was getting weaker by the hour. I had a vague recollection that the nighthawk who also died had been getting amoxicillin, which obviously didn't work, so I told my doctor to try tetracycline instead. The fever climbed, and my breathing became so shallow that Russ stayed up all night making sure I didn't stop breathing altogether. Before dawn, the fever broke, but it took weeks to get my strength back.

As horrible as this was for me, it was the Sanderling and nighthawk that ended up dead. In the 1990s, it's a lot harder to survive if you're a bird than if you're a human. Lake Superior is the largest, and was once the cleanest, lake in the world. Migrating shorebirds resting on her shores have enough worries trying to find food and avoid Peregrine Falcons and foxes without having to lug around water purification kits besides. Meanwhile, we humans continue to swim and boat in the big lake, and to draw our drinking water from it, all the while leaking our wastes into the water and trusting that human beings will prove in the long run a bit sturdier than Sanderlings.

Of three sick Sanderlings I cared for in September 1990, only the weakest one died. Necropsy results implicated lead poisoning, but didn't explain the infection or what made me and the nighthawk sick. The other two Sanderlings felt a whole lot better after eating twenty-four dollars worth of brine shrimp and taking over our bathtub. Russ released them a week later.

Notes

September

Migrating birds rush along the Lake Superior shoreline in huge numbers in mid-September. Shorebirds, unusual gulls, and a huge variety of songbirds are seen whenever we draw our eyes from the hawks. Early morning field trips during Hawk Ridge Weekend provide visitors with a balanced list of birds. For information about Hawk Ridge Weekend or the Nature Reserve, write to Duluth Audubon Society in care of the Biology Department, University of Minnesota, Duluth, MN 55812.

15 Hawk Ridge Weekend is scheduled every year for the second weekend after Labor Day, when birdwatchers gather in Duluth from throughout the Midwest and points beyond to thrill at the flight of the hawks. Peak broadwing migration falls in mid-September, but the actual dates of the best flights are unpredictable, depending entirely on wind direction and weather. Our biggest migration day ever, September 18, 1993, when we totaled 49,560 hawks, fell on a Hawk Ridge Weekend, but many years people outnumber birds, and a couple of times our Saturday hawk count has been less than twenty.

Whether we gather in cold, steady drizzle or under blue skies dotted with raptors, it's the congregation of people that makes the weekend special. Faces of friends that we see but once a year are as welcome as Swainson's Hawks. Rituals of the weekend—trying to predict whether the field trip up the shore or the one to Park Point will produce the best birds, guessing the number of hawks for the Saturday night contest—each little part is as vital to our sense of autumn as the changing leaves, reaffirming our faith that all is right with the world.

Notes

16 Warblers almost always migrate by night. We hear their "seep" call notes in the starry sky; and radar studies, moon observations, and birds killed at ceilometers and lighted buildings and towers prove the point. We often see warbler flocks moving in the right direction in daytime, but usually below the tree canopy, feeding as they wend their way. Only after dark do they take off on serious flights, high in the sky.

A tiny warbler flying at night along Lake Superior with winds from the west would be likely to get pushed over the water—a dangerous prospect, since warblers don't put on large fat deposits until they get farther south. So on autumn days when the wind has a westerly component, they apparently override their instincts and migrate by day—on the best days we count well over one thousand warblers per hour from the Lakewood Pumping Station. It's hard to imagine tiny warblers calculating weather conditions and proximity to the lake, making cost-benefit analyses to determine the best time to migrate, but these little bird brains adapt to strange places and novel situations throughout their long migration. Perhaps they're smarter than we think.

When the autumn wind has an easterly component, which would provide favorable tail winds, virtually no warblers migrate by day along Lake Superior. It's when there's a southwest headwind or west or northwest crosswinds that warblers can be seen migrating by the thousands. Peak flights occur between August 23 and October 7.

Notes

September

Osprey are well-adapted to a piscine diet, with a reversible front toe and sharp spicules on the bottom of their talons for grasping slippery fish, and oversized wings to pull heavy fish out of the water and lug even a four-pound load through the sky. Only one Osprey seen at Hawk Ridge bore cargo—they're headed for fishing waters far south of here, from the southern states down to Peru and Brazil.

17 As the sun rises at Hawk Ridge, a still, winged form floats on the distant horizon over Moose Mountain. I can't make out its shape as it cruises, steady as an airplane, straight toward me in the opalescent sky. No matter—long before I make out the crook in its long wings, its white forehead reveals that it's an Osprey.

Of all birds, the fish hawk is the wildest, the least able to compromise with civilization, often refusing to eat anything in captivity—many with minor injuries die at even the best rehabilitation facilities. We see hundreds each year at Hawk Ridge, but the banders have never caught one of these single-minded piscivores. Osprey, which weigh between three and four pounds, can catch, and sometimes drag to shore, enormous fish, but in their singleness of purpose, they're sometimes dragged underwater and drowned.

My dawn Osprey glides closer and closer, then overhead, then vanishes into the distance. I thrill at the vision, but it never even notices me. Perhaps if I were a Pisces instead of a Scorpio?

Notes

18 On September 18, 1992, an Air National Guard F-16 taking off out of Duluth crashed. In the few seconds he had, the pilot steered the plane away from houses, ejected, and parachuted to safety. Thanks to his quick actions, there were no human fatalities.

That same day, over eight thousand Broad-winged Hawks, and countless other migrants, flew over Duluth. Birders figured a bird had to be involved, and sure enough, two weeks later a pair of aviation investigators came to Peabody Street with a mangled wing fragment—dull brown primary feathers without markings. By their small size and glossy, ducklike texture, we could tell they came from a shorebird. The pointed feathers, with outer primaries much longer than inner, were consistent with a long-distance migrant. We speculated that it might be a Solitary Sandpiper or a Lesser Golden-Plover, but had no references on hand with wing-chord measurements. When the investigators came back a couple of hours later with photos of carcasses, we made a definite identification, later verified by the Smithsonian Institution. This was the first aircraft collision with Lesser Golden-Plovers ever recorded.

On October 4, 1960, an Eastern Airlines Electra jet taking off from Logan International Airport in Boston struck a flock of starlings, consequently clogging the engines and crashing the plane. Sixty-two people died. The scorched feathers were sent to the Smithsonian Institution and identified by Roxie Laybourne, the world authority on feathers. She also verified the identification of the plover feathers involved in Duluth's F-16 crash.

Notes

September

Perhaps related to the artistic rule that there are no straight lines in nature, most birds simply don't see wires strung out in their airspace, even in daylight. In 1987, The U.S. Fish and Wildlife Service published a technical paper indicating that 68 percent of migrant birds flying toward power lines in the Great Plains don't respond to the lines, and those that do often flare up, hitting the wire above the one they're avoiding.

19 The night of September 19–20, 1957, twenty thousand migrating songbirds, mostly warblers, thrushes, and tanagers, were killed by crashing into a single TV transmission tower in Eau Claire, Wisconsin. One foggy fall weekend in 1963, thirty-five thousand birds were killed at the same tower. Millions of birds die at radio and TV towers every year—transmission towers may represent the largest single cause for the decline of some nocturnal migrants.

The Federal Aviation Administration requires tall towers to be lighted at night and during periods of poor visibility to safeguard airplane traffic. But nocturnal migrants, who normally use the stars to navigate, become disoriented when flying within view of artificial lights, especially high in their airspace, and are attracted to the lights like moths to a flame. Moving toward the lights, they crash into the tower, guy wires, and one another. People seldom find the carcasses unless they specifically search for them—crows, squirrels, and other scavengers carry them off as fast as they can find them. For birds, a lighted tower is one horrifying window of vulnerability.

Notes

20 Dragging myself out of bed in the cold, pre-dawn darkness, I wonder why on earth I don't just go back to sleep—Bunter, usually exuberant even by golden retriever standards, looks as tired as I feel. But you can't earn $3.00 an hour counting dickey birds if you laze around in bed. The whole house is in a strange, slow-motion time warp. The ticking cuckoo clock is loud and slow, the sleeping children's soft breathing slow and steady, even Bunter's tail wags andante tempo. She climbs wearily into the car, her muscles still idling, and off we go.

Shadows of Mourning Doves and a few crepuscular thrushes and sparrows loom in the headlights as we pull out of the driveway. Once we reach London Road, the glimmer of moonlight on the lake awakens a slim memory of other dawns, and by the time we reach the mouth of the Lester River, it all seems worthwhile. I see a loon sinking into the cold, deep water in search of breakfast, reminding me of the banana in my backpack. Bunter shares the thought—she sniffs at the pack, wondering how many dog biscuits it holds.

Skies are pinker when you're not in a hurry, the lake more luminous. The upright, proud silhouette of a Red-necked Grebe breaks the water's stillness, the pine trees sway gently, and the soft clouds grow imperceptibly brighter. Autumn should always begin this way.

Notes

September

Every morning before the sun rises, I listen to my weather radio and record the National Weather Service's data. The familiar voice of my favorite weatherman sounds friendly and warm as he shares the morning's meteorological secrets with his unseen listeners. The air seems still here, but Dave says the airport has a north wind at five. The barometric pressure, like my hopes, is already high and still rising.

21 When I climb the slippery, dew-covered slope to the Lakewood Pumping Station's brick wall, the eastern clouds bear a razor edge of gold. Circling above is an Osprey—an auspicious sign. A little male sharpshin swoops in and dives at a waxwing flock. They stay in tight formation as he veers off, and all survive. He looks for easier pickings beyond the trees.

Three Palm Warblers alight on the wall, bobbing their tails in a friendly way. Bunter charges through a clover patch and stops short as she smells a creature in a hole. She checks out that hole every time we come but nothing ever emerges. A monarch delicately opens and closes its wings at my feet. Goldfinches twitter above, and warblers make seeping sounds way up above the clouds. A Great Blue Heron flies along the shore, slowly beating heavy, down-curved wings. A whitethroat sings in his feeble autumn voice, and a yellowrump tisks at the pitiful attempt. A flock of Blue Jays materializes beyond the trees, moving along like a parade of ghosts. I'm already up to seventy-four birds as the sun slices the horizon. It's going to be a good day at the pumping station.

Notes

22 On September 22, 1989, after a week of southeasters, the wind shifted overnight. I woke to an endless stream of robins coursing over Peabody Street, and fifty pigging out in the mountain ash. The big day was here.

Children, however, need grown-ups no matter which way the wind is blowing. You can't tell a three-year-old to fix his own breakfast because Mommy's looking at fall warblers, and kids don't magically disappear after breakfast—Tommy wanted to paint and Katie wanted help reading as urgently as I wanted to watch migration. The ephemeral nature of a good migration day seemed like a legitimate excuse to plant them in front of the TV for the morning, but the ephemeral nature of childhood itself was a better reason not to. And I had a writing deadline and injured birds to care for. All morning I rushed about madly—as soon as I started one thing, I'd spot something through the window and charge out. Swarm after swarm of broadwings flew by, along with swooping flickers and swirling siskins. The air itself was alive, and me a wishbone, pulled in two directions at once.

Walking is a fine way to enjoy children and birds both. Katie and Tommy observed broadwings filling the sky for thirty seconds before making friends with a ladybug. Looking over robins in a mountain ash, my eyes just about popped out to see a Townsend's Solitaire—Katie and Tommy declared robins prettier. They made a fine collection of sticks and leaves while I counted over three thousand hawks, and a satisfying afternoon was had by all.

Notes

September

Peregrine Falcons were completely exterminated from eastern North America because of shooting and, especially, DDT destroying their eggs. Thanks to the efforts of falconers working with peregrine reintroduction programs, this excellent bird has been restored to much of its former range, but unless the water birds and other migrants that it depends on for sustenance fare as well, eventually the peregrine will disappear once again, this time forever.

23 Walking along the dikes at Erie Pier one quiet morning, Billie and I suddenly spot a winged arrow shoot toward us at high speed—a Peregrine Falcon bent on scrambled shorebirds for breakfast. I've used binoculars for so long that I pull them up without a thought and watch the adventure close up, the peregrine's helmet glowing ebony, its eyes gleaming with hungry intent.

Billie's 7x35 binoculars aren't as powerful or deluxe as my Zeiss 10x40s, and she hasn't yet been graced with as many peregrines as I, so I offer her my glasses, but she's already grabbed my spotting scope. Now a scope is wonderful for swimmers, waders, perched sparrows, and other birds that stay put, but it's nigh near impossible to catch a cruising falcon, much less keep it in view—especially one swooping and climbing and swooping again with shorebirds scrambling everywhere. But, as if drawn by the peregrine's sheer power, or her own desire, she centers the scope and follows most of the falcon's roller coaster maneuvers until it gives up and flies out of sight, leaving us almost as exhausted as the relieved sandpipers, grinning at each other. All we can say is, "Wow!"

Notes

24 A friend brings me a bird found on a sidewalk in downtown Duluth—the tiniest bird she's ever seen. It's a warbler, but so caked with mud that I can't be certain which species. Despite the mud, its eyes seem perky and its intact wings flap hard—I can't figure out why it can't fly until I pick it up. I'm amazed to find that its feet are encased in mud balls the size and weight of big marbles. Apparently it hit a window and fell into a puddle, and as it flailed about, stunned, the sticky mud coating its feet built up into balls.

I bathe it three times and slowly soak the mud off its feet. I quickly determine that it's a female Magnolia Warbler, but clean up takes over an hour. Meanwhile I offer her mealworms—she can manage only the tiniest—and grape jelly, which she quickly accepts from my hands. When she's clean, dry, and well fed, I set her free in my backyard, where she feeds in trees and shrubs—her flight is fine and she seems in good spirits. When warblers fly in with a chickadee flock, she joins them, and tries her luck at migration one more time.

Warblers often end up on downtown sidewalks— Duluth's tallest buildings aren't that tall, but the lights bewilder these nocturnal migrants, especially in the autumn fogs that Lake Superior provides in abundance. Over the years, several businesses have called me to pick up little birds found on their sidewalks—redstarts, Nashvilles, yellowrumps, one Canada, and two Magnolia Warblers.

Notes

September

During autumn, cats near Lake Superior kill countless warblers. Grounded, hungry warblers are less wary than usual. One British researcher estimated that bird populations are harmed when the average cat kills fourteen birds a year—barely more than one a month. In September 1991, Peabody Street cats killed dozens each during a two-week period. Scores of carcasses littered the sidewalks as I walked Tommy to kindergarten each day.

25 Every now and then we get such hard September frosts that warblers suddenly have trouble finding food to fuel their migration. The same cold temperatures that turn our leaves lovely colors cut off the warblers' primary food source—crawling and flying insects. Trees draw the nutrients out of their leaves before cutting off circulation and triggering the color change. Caterpillars must pupate before the leaves change, cutting off warbler food supplies. The swarming insects that Yellow-rumped Warblers specialize in are also hard to find in cold weather.

On frosty mornings, when the soil is warmer than the air, yellowrumps and Palm Warblers gather on lawns and roadsides, picking up insects and being picked up by cats in huge numbers. When they're grounded under these conditions, they're also killed by cars. On September 25, 1991, in the "Great Highway 61 Warbler Massacre," thousands of inexperienced pedestrians were killed as they followed the lakeshore and were attracted to the sun-warmed pavement. Warblers are fairly good at evading most falcons, but they're simply not equipped to deal with the Ford variety.

Notes

26 The first Harris' Sparrows known to ornithology were collected in Missouri by Thomas Nuttall on April 28, 1834, and in Nebraska on May 13, 1834, by Maximilian, Prince of Wied, but it took these laid-back discoverers over six years to publish their accounts. In 1843, Audubon shot some in Kansas, naming them for his companion, Edward Harris. The American Ornithologists' Union accepted Nuttall's scientific name since he described it first, but kept Audubon's common name because his book put it into general use.

The following century, George Miksch Sutton finally discovered a nest, after a long, frustrating search in northernmost central Canada. He wrote, "As I knelt to examine the nest a thrill the like of which I had never felt before passed through me. And I talked aloud! 'Here!' I said. 'Here in this beautiful place!' At my fingertips lay treasures that were beyond price. Mine was Man's first glimpse of the eggs of the Harris's Sparrow, in the lovely bird's wilderness home." Sutton had the soul of a poet but the reflexes of an ornithologist, so he shot the female and collected the nest and eggs for museum specimens.

Harris' Sparrows, tall, dark, and handsome, visit feeders regularly at our end of Lake Superior, and are abundant migrants through the Dakotas, but are rarer farther east. They breed in the stunted boreal forest west and north of Hudson Bay. Long ago, many probably lived their entire lives without ever seeing shade trees, but now they're hard pressed to find their proper habitat where it belongs.

Notes

September

The role of humans in nature is one-sided. We forage on berries that would otherwise feed insects to sweeten the diet of swallows. We trample warbler nests on the forest floor to photograph a grouse drumming. To ethically walk through any wild place, we must remember that we are uninvited guests and treat our hosts, wary geese on their nests or fragile frogs hiding in the weeds beneath our feet, with respect and gratitude.

27 Unlike hawks and wolves, humans hunt on full stomachs. Hawks feel death in their talons, wolves taste it in their jaws, never distancing their consciences with arrows or bullets. They don't carry prey in bags to keep blood off their hands, or tied to car roofs to prevent hernias.

Hawks and wolves earn their hunting licenses by exposing themselves to the inconveniences and dangers of nature, armed only with their wits and their bodies, paying for the right to take from nature by giving themselves in death. Chickadees pick at the suet clinging to a dead wolf's bones. Insects eating the carcass are in turn eaten by warblers, or by frogs that feed herons and cranes. Few of us would choose so natural a fate, we who spray ourselves with chemicals to keep from donating blood to mosquitoes that feed kingbirds and nighthawks. None of us can survive without taking from nature, and those of us who don't hunt mustn't forget that the vegetables we eat also come from the earth. We, too, wear fibers and leather, and wash soaps and filth down the drain. The best any of us can do is to limit our plunder to what we need.

Notes

28 Once there was a Blue Jay named Sneakers. She was a good little jay, but she was always curious. One morning Sneakers saw a big hole in her house where some workmen were going to put a new window. The sun shone brightly, and Sneakers was curious, so she flew through the hole to investigate. She had nobody to play with—her mommy and daddy were gone for the morning—but she saw some children walking down Peabody Street, so she followed them all the way to Lakeside School.

The playground was filled with noisy, happy children, and Sneakers sat on the fence and shouted with them. One boy was eating a candy bar. Sneakers opened her wings and begged, but he apparently couldn't understand Blue Jay talk. She flew onto a little girl's shoulder, but the girl waved her hands in a most unfriendly way. Some fifth graders called out to her and laughed cheerfully. This was turning into a jolly adventure, when suddenly a bell rang. All the children lined up and disappeared into the school, leaving Sneakers all alone. What was a little jay to do?

Even imprinted Blue Jays are usually wary of strangers, but Sneakers once alighted on our neighbor Bob's shoulder as he weeded his garden, and she visited a day-care center and even let a boy "capture" her for a pet. Fortunately, he couldn't keep her—she returned home the next day, her tail frayed but no worse for the experience. We finally had no choice but to apply for a permit to keep her permanently as an education bird.

Notes

September

Sneakers can't play piano—the keys are too heavy for her—but she types on our computer. Her words come out garbled and incomprehensible, but she seems pleased with the result. She's curious about books, especially picture books, and can even turn pages. I don't know if she makes sense of drawings, but bright colors please her—she's especially taken with color illustrations of proteins in my biochemistry textbook.

29 When the children disappeared into Lakeside School, Sneakers looked in the windows. The children were so busy putting away coats and lunch boxes and pulling out homework that hardly anyone noticed the little jay peeking in.

Sneakers liked the bustle and the children. She decided school might even be worth sitting through math, so she flew through the first open window she could find, into a first-grade class. The teacher wasn't expecting a Blue Jay that day, so she lined up the children and marched them out of the room. Sneakers was checking out the thumbtacks on the bulletin board when a teacher named Mr. Ritchie came in and gave her a treat. He carried her around the school, talking to her in a nice voice and feeding her crackers—she decided school was a good place for a lonely little jay. But then he brought her to a door. It was so sunny and bright outside that before she knew what happened, she had flown into a tree. She found another open window, and again Mr. Ritchie carried her around, but again he sent her outside. Sneakers was ready for school, but apparently school wasn't ready for Sneakers.

Notes

30 Ten Turkey Vultures float in the sky above Hawk Ridge, their wings, dark in front, pale silvery behind, held in a shallow V called a dihedral. They glide effortlessly, often not flapping for many minutes at a time, riding thermals and updrafts with greater ease than any mere hawk could do.

Vultures require meat for survival, but virtually never kill—they eat decayed meat from animals that are not just merely dead, but really most sincerely dead. Such fare hidden beneath the forest canopy can apparently be detected high in the sky through the vulture's sense of smell. Decaying meat is soft, so vultures have no need for strong, sharp beaks or killing talons and strong necks. A vulture's wimpy, undersized, naked head and neck are easy to wash up after a goopy meal. The small size and bare skin of its head add to the Turkey Vulture's ungainly appearance when it sits in a tree or picks at a road carcass. Vultures can survive on their putrid diet apparently because their digestive system is able to destroy many dangerous germs, including cholera. As we watch them float in the blue sky, we try not to think about their meals. Perhaps they do, too.

The Turkey Vulture, affectionately known as the "TV," belongs to the family Cathartidae, the name derived from Greek *kathartes*, for a purifier, reflecting the usefulness of the vulture's scavenging habits. The medical meaning of catharsis is purgation, especially of the digestive system—vultures defend themselves by vomiting on an attacker, and protect themselves from excessive heat by wetting their legs with urine. We much prefer to see them in the sky.

Notes

October

October

October is an intense month in North Country. The leaves are virtually all gone, but we start the month with occasional summery weather, the last mosquitoes, the biggest songbird migrations, lots of bluebirds, and children still wearing shorts to school. The month ends with winter—the biggest snowfall ever recorded in Duluth, thirty-six inches, began October 31, 1991—shorts are packed away, replaced by snow pants and pack boots.

1 The last week of September 1988 was gloomy and wet, but a cold front moved in on the thirtieth. I was hopeful about what I'd find at the Lakewood Pumping Station when I headed there October first.

The dark, overcast sky looked ominous, and for a few minutes I was afraid I'd be rained out. Cars on the Scenic North Shore Drive kept their headlights on for over an hour after the sun supposedly rose.

A few warblers made seeping notes overhead as I wrote down the weather data, and when I started officially counting at sunrise, I had to scramble to count small flocks of robins and warblers flying inland along the ridge. It took a few minutes for me to realize that something extraordinary was happening. The flocks of robins didn't stop. Normally I write down individual marks for each bird, or numbers like 50 or 100 for flocks that I count one by one. But now I found myself writing down numbers like 2,000 and 2,500. I was still managing to count most of the flocks by twos, but more and more I was counting by fives and tens. The first hour total was 7,133. And the birds kept coming.

Notes

2 October 1, 1988, was the closest I've ever come to wishing I'd never see another robin or warbler. The flight was still mounting after an hour. I was getting most of the birds cruising over the ridge line to the north, but then I realized that the sky overhead was also streaming. I searched for the beginning of that flock, but it extended beyond the western horizon. After I counted thousands, I rushed back to scanning the ridge line—robins were still cruising there nonstop, plus I had to keep track of thousands of warblers and the odd sharpie and kestrel. I missed an awful lot of birds, but I counted an awful lot, too.

Kim Eckert came with his bird identification class at 7:15. He took the robins along the ridge as I counted warblers along the ridge and everything overhead. Kim would call out things like "two thousand robins. Do you have those three hundred warblers? Two sharpies. Three thousand robins. Nine hundred warblers over the tower." We counted a greater percentage this way, but Kim had to leave after three hours. Molly Evans came for a while, but the last half hour I was soloing again, my eyes seeing specks everywhere, my brain reeling with quantification.

Our five-hour total for October 1, 1988, was 95,948 migrants, including 62,707 robins, 29,330 warblers, and a smattering of longspurs, siskins, crows, ravens, geese, eagles, etc. If Kim could have stayed, we would easily have topped 100,000. When I got home, still in a daze, I walked smack into a bag of sunflower seeds. Sweeping them into a dustpan, I reached 738 before I realized I was still counting.

Notes

October

Mayflies, stoneflies, and dragonflies, which swallows and other birds depend on for food, require clean, well-oxygenated water during egg and nymph stages. Many butterflies and moths are habitat-sensitive. We'll always have mosquitoes, flies, agricultural pests, and army worms—like rats, they flourish in our altered environment and quickly adapt to control methods. No insecticide or bug light kills just one species, and the ones worth saving are often the most vulnerable.

3 Bzzzzt! Though it's late in the insect season, my neighbor's bug zapper is still heard occasionally, mindlessly luring moths, mayflies, crane flies, and other insects to their deaths. Running twenty-four hours a day from spring until fall, it zaps a lot of mosquitoes, but even more of the countless other creatures that fuel avian life.

Ten years ago, when the light was new, it zapped furiously all night long, keeping us awake. Back then, moths gathered on screened windows every summer's night, in huge numbers when a porch light was on. I consider moths nighthawk food, but even when I had an injured nighthawk depending on me, I was hard-put to whack these porch moths with a fly swatter—every one I targeted turned into a vulnerable individual rather than an edible abstraction. Zapper lights don't see insects at all. They don't key them out by species or make a philosophical determination about which should be saved and which fried. Hardly any moths have showed up on my screens the last few years, even when I've left a light on for them. The zapper doesn't work so hard anymore, either, its mission accomplished. Bzzzzt!

Notes

4 Bunter charges into a Port Wing pasture and flushes a late Sedge Wren. It makes a couple of scolding notes, then perches atop a goldenrod as if checking the air to see whether tonight's weather will be right for setting out on a long journey.

I could look at this bird all day, if only it would let me. It's prettier than a House Wren, with delicate white eyebrows setting off curious black eyes, and dark streaking on the back and crown. It's lively and spirited, an avian Tinkerbell, and, like Tinkerbell, it's also an elusive prankster—it took me over two years to add one to my life list. The first specimen known to science was found near Rio de la Plata in Argentina, and Audubon searched long and hard before finally finding his first in 1832. Once it's on a life list, most birders are satisfied simply to hear it, without ever bothering to look for it again. I'm fond enough to search the weeds often, but my love is unreciprocated. Even the little mite flushed up by Bunter perches for less than a minute before whizzing off like an oversized bumblebee, to hide once more in the weeds.

The Sedge Wren is one of the tiniest of North American songbirds, about four inches from the tip of its beak to the end of its stubby tail. It's as secretive as it is tiny, living in big wet meadows frequented more by cows than people. It has a wonderful summer song, twanging like a toy rubber band musical instrument, but the song is too quiet to penetrate the awareness of anyone but a birder.

Notes

October

Three species of jaegers have appeared in Minnesota and Wisconsin—the Pomarine, Parasitic, and Long-tailed Jaegers, the only species belonging to the genus *Stercorarius*, from the Latin "having to do with dung." Most Great Lake sightings are of Parasitics in autumn, but each species has been recorded at least once in spring. Closely related skuas are much more restricted to the ocean. Across the Atlantic, both genera are called skuas.

5 An ill wind blows from the east, rattling windows and pilfering rain hats. There'll be no hawks today, so I head out to Minnesota Point. Along Lake Superior, east winds often push birds along the Great Lakes system from the Atlantic Ocean all the way to Duluth.

Standing on the beach scanning above gray, turbulent waters, shivering hard and wiping rain off eyeglasses and binoculars every few minutes, I watch gulls blown about like avian confetti. They would swarm up if a jaeger came in—these storm-tossed birds have more control of their flight than it appears. Jaegers were named for the German *jager*, wild hunters who plundered and robbed along the Rhine, and true to their name, jaegers' eating habits are even more unsavory than those of gulls. They scavenge on dead fish and birds, and offal, and harass gulls and terns until the victims disgorge half-digested stomach contents, which the jaegers devour. All three jaeger species have been found in October in Duluth, but during my ninety-minute search today I don't find a single one. Later I hear on the hotline that birders found two this morning from other vantage points. An ill wind, indeed.

Notes

6 When Joey was four and three-quarters years old and Katie called herself "two and two-quarters old," Russ and I suddenly needed to learn all about dinosaurs. We learned that *Triceratops* ate plants, *Tyrannosaurus Rex* ate *Triceratops*, and *Deinonychus* had huge claws that could rip out the insides of *Brachiosaurus*—every gory detail of which delighted our sweet little children. But their bird-watching mommy was most fascinated with the idea that dinosaurs may well have been unfeathered, four-legged birds. The skeletons of "bird-hipped" dinosaurs were more similar to birds' skeletons than to reptiles'. Some scientists consider *Archaeopteryx* more than just a bridge between reptiles and birds—it's one link in a long chain of evidence that dinosaurs were primitive, earthbound birds. *Stenonychosaurus* was so swift a runner that it was almost certainly warm-blooded, and may even have had an insulating cover of feathers.

It's hard to explain extinction to a small child. Even if dinosaurs were true reptiles rather than birds, it's appealing to look at a tiny chickadee and imagine that it embodies the spirit, and maybe something of the physical presence, of lumbering *Brachiosaurus*.

Even dinosaurs unrelated to birds have interesting avian parallels. Struthiomimus's name means "ostrich mimic," and many duck-billed dinosaurs had hollow bone structures on their heads, which may have served as resonating chambers for amplifying their voices, working like the long, coiled trachea of the Trumpeter Swan today.

Notes

October

Three-year-old Tommy used to come to my bird presentations, sitting in a corner coloring. Once a man asked if birds have teeth. I said no, modern birds are toothless. Tommy walked on stage, took the microphone, and said, "Archaeopteryx had toofies." I explained that archaeopteryx, a transition between dinosaurs and birds, had both teeth and fully developed feathers. My shy little boy took the mike and added, "Tyrannosaurus rex had BIG toofies!"

Notes

7 Robert Bakker, paleontologist at the University of Colorado, believes that dinosaurs walk the earth today. He wrote in the British journal *Nature*, "One group still lives. We call them birds."

The *pterosaurs,* or flying reptiles, didn't follow the same evolutionary line as Bakker's dinosaurs, but they were the most birdlike animals in the world for much of prehistoric time. They were probably warm-blooded, with birdlike feet and skull features. Their hollow bones and large brains allowed maneuverability in flight. They caught fish with beaklike mouths, and had throat pouches like pelicans. But there were great differences between pterosaurs and birds, too. The feathered wing of a bird is framed by arm bones, but the membranous wing of a pterosaur was framed in part by enlarged finger bones, similar to bat wings. Some pterosaurs may have had fur.

The last flying reptile fossils found have been in rock layers 63 million years old, which also hold the bones of other prehistoric creatures that may have flown in the same skies as the pterosaurs—modern birds.

8   I like to believe that humans are at the pinnacle of evolution, perhaps because I happen to be a human, as are my husband and children. But I must admit that birds have keener vision and hearing, and more efficient vascular and pulmonary systems. Feathers are more complex, and prettier, than hair. Albatrosses and frigatebirds reign as lords of the sky and oceans, alighting on land only to breed. Penguins master Antarctica, ravens the Arctic, sandgrouse the desert. Loons dive deeper, ostriches run faster. Crows outswear us, thrushes outsing us. Territorial defense with song seems more advanced than our method of duking it out. And avian savings institutions never need bailing out.

Birds may have developed agriculture before we did. As glaciers retreated ten thousand years ago, oaks moved north faster than other trees thanks to Blue Jays, who plant their forests skillfully—88 percent of the acorns they select are fertile, while only 10 percent of acorns on a given oak are fertile. Of course, the forests jays planted centuries ago can be chopped down by a human in minutes, but if that is proof of our superiority, then robbers and muggers must be the greatest of all.

Everyone knows that birds have bird brains while we humans are the most intelligent creatures on earth. Or are we? My family has a big cardboard windshield cover to keep our car shaded when it's parked. It carries a warning in bold letters for us supposedly intelligent people: "Warning. Do not drive with autoshade in place. Remove from windshield before starting ignition." Perhaps the human brain isn't all it's cracked up to be.

Notes

October

Palm Warblers nest on the ground in open tamarack–black spruce bogs, and can be found all summer in parts of northern Minnesota. They're abundant migrants in North Country, especially along the shorelines of Lake Michigan and Lake Superior. Fall migration begins in mid-August and lasts well into October.

9 Most warblers are gone from the Northland until spring, but a few yellowrumps and Palm Warblers remain, the small bits of yellow in their plumage gleaming like embers in a dying campfire.

A famous ornithologist and warbler authority once berated the Palm Warbler as dull and uninteresting, but I find watching this bird deeply satisfying. No other bird is as likely to hop up on the wall of the Lakewood Pumping Station and keep me company. Palm Warblers walk about on rooftops and grassy lawns, gracefully wagging their tails up and down to shyly draw attention to their lemon yellow undertail covert feathers.

As with most late migrants, Palm Warblers don't winter very far south of the border, and a great many vacation in Florida, where they greet homesick Northlanders with a wag of their tails. They're often called wagtail warblers or yellow tip-ups for this habit, and either nickname is more appropriate than their proper name, since few Palm Warblers spend any time at all in palms. The type specimen just happened to be shot from a palm tree in Hispaniola, and the name stuck.

Notes

10 October sends Golden Eagles our way. These birds of western wilderness are the same species as the European eagles that inspired legends and folklore. The Golden Eagle is a bird of open, hilly, or mountainous regions. Like the Bald Eagle, it sometimes scavenges, but unlike the bald, it doesn't eat fish. Ninety percent of its food is rabbits, squirrels, and prairie dogs.

Native Americans used Golden Eagle feathers in clothing and ritual, but reverence for what some called the Thunderbird protected eagles for millennia. It was Europeans who introduced eagle killing as a sport to America. More than twenty thousand Golden Eagles were killed just in western Texas and New Mexico between 1942 and 1961, when aerial shooting was finally prohibited by federal law, but they're still killed in shocking numbers in steel traps, at poisoned bait, and by electrocution at power lines. This avian symbol of excellence, which has inspired such phrases as "eagle eyes" and "legal eagle," is an essential part of our folklore and history, and my Joey's favorite bird. I pray that we bequeath him an earth where Golden Eagles flourish, and where Americans once again live in harmony with the world around us.

The Golden Eagle's scientific name, Aquila, is Latin for eagle. In contrast, the Bald Eagle is a sea eagle, as its scientific name, Haliaeetus, reflects. Bald Eagles average heavier than goldens—balds weigh up to fourteen pounds while goldens don't exceed twelve-and-a-half pounds—but both species may have wingspans to seven-and-a-half feet.

Notes

October

Adult Harris' Sparrows are easy to identify, with their bold black cap and bib—the only birds beginners are likely to confuse them with are Lapland Longspurs and male House Sparrows. Longspurs virtually never visit feeders, and have a short tail with white outer feathers. Young Harris' Sparrows are trickier but just as welcome.

11 All over the Northland, people are noticing sparrows. Juncoes, belonging to a genus of true sparrows, fly up from gravel roadsides with every passing car. Many are killed, but many more reach their wintering grounds, from tropical Minneapolis down to the central and southern United States.

If the junco is the most abundant sparrow in our region, the whitethroat is a close second. Few sing "Old Sam Peabody" in fall—males that attempt it produce a sickly melody, the notes trailing off pitifully at the end. Immature whitethroats are dully marked and spangled with fine breast streaking, but have the white bib that gave the species its name.

Fox Sparrows enthusiastically scratch the ground with both feet, throwing themselves into their work with gusto. Ours are mostly of the eastern race, rufous like foxes. Young White-crowned Sparrows, probably the most misidentified of all, have a buffy brown cap and are browner-backed than the gray adults. These huge sparrows with pink bills look like Field Sparrows on steroids.

Notes

12 Among the whitethroats crowding my feeder, we pick out a handful of White-crowned Sparrows. These handsome creatures are common year-round in the West, but merely pass through the Midwest between their eastern breeding grounds, in Hudson Bay, and their wintering range, from Texas and Kansas across to Virginia and Pennsylvania.

In October 1962, researchers captured and banded 574 whitecrowns near San Jose and shipped them to the Patuxent Wildlife Research Center in Maryland to see if they could find their way back, perhaps inspiring Bert Bacharach and Hal David's 1967 song "Do You Know the Way to San Jose?" The following autumn eight were captured back in San Jose. California researchers have studied the whitecrown's song, orientation, and navigation and the taxonomy of its subspecies. It's an excellent experimental subject because several subspecies are found together and they're easy to maintain in captivity, relatively abundant, and easy to catch. I watch them because they're beautiful, and because their brief passage through my world in spring and fall somehow brings my spirit closer to the wild Hudsonian world they call home.

White-crowned Sparrows have been studied in wind tunnels to see how fast they fly—their normal flight is about eleven and a half miles per hour in still air, and in order to hold their position relative to the ground in high wind, they've been clocked at thirty-nine miles per hour. They've actually managed to fly backwards in order to hold their position against a tail wind.

Notes

October

The Fox Sparrow seldom sings in autumn, but in spring we listen eagerly for its rich carol of clear, melodious notes, impossible to match with a human's mere larynx. It frequently sings during spring migration, but saves its longest, richest songs for its remote northern homeland. We can listen to Fox Sparrows year-round on recordings, but that doesn't compare with the perfection of hearing them on a spring morning.

13 Fox Sparrows visit Peabody Street every fall to fatten up before moving on south. They don't come to feeders in the huge numbers of White-throated Sparrows or juncoes, but some years I've had as many as thirty at a time, all exuberantly scratching the ground with both feet to expose weed seeds and insects under the fallen leaves. Named for their reddish foxlike coloring, these are among the largest, and hardiest, of sparrows. They're sturdy, weighing one and three-quarters ounces, and would require extra postage to be mailed. Banded birds have survived well over nine years.

Like most songbirds, Fox Sparrows migrate by night. Long ago, when the night sky was filled with stars, and the night earth was cloaked in darkness, celestial navigation was a simple matter. Now the artificial lights of cities, airports, and radio towers overwhelm the night darkness, and the starry map of the Fox Sparrow is more difficult to read. On foggy nights, some fly right into artificial lights. Every year Fox Sparrows are found dead beneath TV and radio towers during migration. One would think the earth big enough to hold both humans and sparrows.

Notes

14 A Northern Harrier floats on the wind above a Port Wing pasture, wings uplifted in a delicate V, white rump catching the sun. The marsh hawk reminds me of a Short-eared Owl, found in the same habitat, long wings flapping as buoyantly and delicately as butterfly wings, searching wetland vegetation with ears as much as eyes for mice, rats, frogs, snakes, and especially meadow voles to sustain its lovely flight. Harriers even look like owls, with enormous facial discs and forward-facing eyes. Once I watched a harrier follow a coyote through the marshy Aransas National Wildlife Refuge in Texas. The coyote flushed up rails and sparrows, which the harrier swooped at. I read that they sometimes hover ahead of prairie fires to catch escaping mice.

The harrier's dependence on marshes has reduced its numbers alarmingly. Everyone agrees that wetlands must be saved, but every city seems to have an urgent need for just one development project that will drain just one little wetland. Every discount department store built on a drained wetland represents another lost pair of harriers, ancient glacial treasures succumbing to the age of asphalt.

The harrier's name originated in sixteenth century England, from its European counterpart's habit of harrying poultry. The generic name *Circus* indicates that it's one of the circling hawks. Adult male harriers are silvery gray, females and immatures brown.

Notes

October

Nocturnal migrants sometimes get lost over open water, and often alight on boats or ships until they reach land. When Russ was in graduate school, he did some work on research vessels on Lake Michigan, and sometimes saw more warblers on board the ships than I was seeing at home in Madison.

15 Every now and then a bird does something so uniquely stupid as to justify the term "bird brain." Such was the case of the Blackburnian Warbler that set out for South America and crossed the Atlantic instead. This bird was apparently swept off course by westerly gales, becoming the first of its species to be found in Europe—on Fair Isle in Scotland.

Yes, even with the extraordinary instincts birds have for migration, they occasionally mess up. It's most likely that the blackburnian didn't cross the entire three-thousand-mile ocean on its own power—it probably hopped a freighter. Ocean travel puts birds in danger of drowning or starving over the open seas, and they're also in danger from gull marauders searching for a tasty snack. If, against all odds, a warbler does make it across, it needs tropical food—not easy to find in Scotland; and once spring comes, it can hardly return the way it came, bucking prevailing westerly winds. When a Bald Eagle accidentally flew to Ireland, it was flown back to America on a jet, but this poor little Blackburnian Warbler couldn't raise the airfare.

Notes

16 Many geese have figured out how to beat the hunting season. Since cities and towns usually prohibit the discharging of firearms, geese that stay in parks, arboretums, golf courses, and zoos have a better chance of surviving autumn than wilder geese. Geese are gregarious—one crippled or tame bird in a park attracts migrants flying overhead. As they discover that food is abundant and no one is shooting at them, they settle in, becoming an urban flock, often learning to take handouts from people. Some geese wintering in a Madison, Wisconsin, zoo were banded in the Canadian wilderness, where they return every spring. Canada Geese learn their migratory routes from their parents and grandparents, and, being true conservatives, when they find a system that works, they continue with it for generations.

One crippled goose may stay in a park year-round. If it attracts a mate during winter, the mate won't leave its side, and many of their babies will stay, too, attracting mates of their own during the next fall migration. From such small beginnings are urban goose problems born.

One fall, an injured Canada Goose hobbled along a road north of Duluth, its mate walking beside it. Every now and then the mate flew up, seemingly encouraging the other to fly, but after circling once or twice it always resumed walking. People watched the two make their way, mile after mile, for two days. Then the crippled bird was struck by a car. The mate stood by the body for a time, then flew off, alone.

Notes

October

If you ground up a blue feather from a jay, Indigo Bunting, or bluebird, you'd get a grayish brown powder. No feathers have blue pigment—blue is a structural color, coming from a unique cell layer overlying the feather. As light hits this layer, blue is reflected. Backlit, blue feathers appear grayish-brown, showing only the actual pigment.

17 The brilliant red flash of a hummingbird's throat feathers would change to dull black if we could see the feathers backlit or ground up. Turn an iridescent feather just slightly and the color vanishes.

Barbules, the tiny, hairlike parts of a feather, are flattened or twisted to produce iridescence. As the flat sides are turned to face the observer, the light they refract and reflect is of one specific wavelength—red in the ruby-throat—but from other angles the feather appears black. Feathers with these distorted barbules are missing some of the hooklets and flanges that normally zip the barbules together. This means iridescent feathers aren't as strong as other feathers, so birds never have fully iridescent flight feathers. Even the iridescent speculum feathers on a duck's wing are limited to an area of the wing that is least mechanically stressed by flight.

Feathers provide insulation against cold and heat, protection from rain and snow, strength to support birds in flight, and incomparable beauty—one of nature's finest inventions.

Notes

18 In Jack London's story, White Fang comes across a "moosebird"—a Gray Jay, which sometimes sits on moose, picking off ticks and deerflies or just hanging on for the ride. The bird gets food, the moose respite from pests. This kind of relationship, in which two species live in close association and in which one or both may benefit but neither is harmed, is called commensalism.

Many avian examples of commensalism can be found. Some songbirds, especially grackles, nest in the bottom sticks of eagle and Osprey nests. The grackles eat dropped food particles, giving the raptors help with nest sanitation in return for food and protection. African tickbirds groom buffalo, rhinoceroses, giraffes, and other mammals. The Ground Finch of the Galapagos Islands pulls ticks off marine iguanas and giant tortoises. The tortoises crane their necks and stretch high on their legs, remaining motionless for as long as five minutes while the finches pull out ticks from the crevices of their skin. Bird and reptile both come out ahead, though ticks strongly disapprove of the system. Gulls follow tractors for earthworms. The tractors aren't benefited, though—they apparently don't even harbor John Deere ticks.

One of the most satisfying of commensal relationships is between birds and humans. When birds come to our feeders, they get food, and we satisfy both our drive to nurture and our need to find aesthetic amusement.

Notes

October

Blue Jays seldom, if ever, sleep soundly during the daytime outside, and wake easily even at night. So many dangers threaten and unfamiliar things happen that they must remain alert at all times or risk death. Every time I've ever brought a baby jay in from outside, it has eaten and then fallen into a deep sleep. In the natural world, a good night's sleep may be harder to come by than a four-leaf clover.

19 One morning Jake the Blue Jay taps at the dining room window. We haven't seen him in weeks, and supposed he had migrated. We recognize him by three white spots on his blue nostril feathers and open the window to feed him a few peanuts—he flies right in. He wings through the house to his favorite stereo speaker, where he promptly falls asleep.

Is something wrong? Is he sick? We worry as he sleeps soundly, head tucked in behind, breathing steadily, for almost two hours.

When he awakens, I call, hoping he'll play like in the old days, but he's not the least bit interested in me. He flies to where Bunter's dish is supposed to be to steal some dog food, but we moved the dog dishes a couple of weeks before. I offer him grapes, but he refuses to take them out of my hand. When I set a dish of corn, grapes, and bird mix on the table, he pigs out, takes another short nap, and then flies to the door and pecks until we let him out. He apparently came to us simply because he needed a safe place to take a nice, long nap.

Notes

20   The first nights of below-zero temperatures in a season often occur before snow falls, which is hard on some birds. Snow Buntings and grouse prefer riding out the worst days and nights under a thick and literal blanket of snow. The air temperature may drop to 25 below, but under deep powdery snow it's often a balmy 25 above. Of course, snow also hides many birds' food sources. When weed seeds get covered, juncoes and native sparrows must retreat south. Snow also hides mice and voles in their burrows and tunnels, which makes the mice safe but leaves hawks, owls, and shrikes hungry.

Woodpeckers, chickadees, nuthatches, creepers, and other species roost in tree cavities, minimizing exposure to wind. As many as fifty titmice have been counted huddled in a single feather ball. In one laboratory study, 50 percent of House Sparrows roosted in contact with each other when the temperature was 14 degrees, while only 10 percent snuggled when the temperature rose to 32. Many July babies are produced under much the same circumstances.

How many sunflower seeds does a fifty-pound bag hold? When six-year-old Joey asked, we conducted a family experiment, counting five ounces of seeds one by one. There were almost exactly 3,000 in the ounce, amounting to 9,600 seeds per pound, or 480,000 per bag—almost half a million. During a normal winter, the Peabody Street birds used to eat about eight million sunflower seeds—now we're lucky if we get enough birds to take two million.

Notes

October

John Burroughs wrote in 1917, "If sound sleeping be a sign of a clear conscience, the Saw-whet Owl must have very few sins on its mind, for so deep is its slumber, huddled up in a spruce thicket or some other dense foliage, that frequently even clumsy man captures it alive."

21 The tiniest owl in eastern North America, the saw-whet, migrates along Hawk Ridge in enormous numbers. Dave Evans doesn't use bait to lure owls into his nets at night—the ones he catches just happen to be flying along where the nets are set out—yet he netted 850 in 1991, and 1,102 in 1989, mostly in October. Owls banded at Hawk Ridge have turned up in Wisconsin, Michigan, Missouri, Ontario, and even Maryland. One was recovered in Sawyer, Minnesota, over seven years later. Captive saw-whets have lived over seventeen years.

Most raptors are high-strung and nervous around humans. When netted, they're put in dark cylinders, wings held securely, to be processed and released as quickly as possible. But saw-whets are so tame that they're simply set on a shelf to wait their turn—they look about with placid yet observant eyes, calmly taking in the novel experience like fluffy little Miss Marples.

Outside, saw-whets sit tight all day, and are seldom noticed without the aid of chickadees' or other little birds' shouting tiny obscenities at them. Males call in early spring only until they've attracted a mate.

Notes

22 My Brownie Troop dissects a Great Horned Owl that was brought to me dead. I'm required by law to bring carcasses to the university, but the curator lets me use this one for teaching. I'm allergic to feathers—my sneezing shoots them everywhere. Before I pick up a scalpel, we look like we're in a bizarre pillow fight.

We talk about how sad we feel when birds die. If this owl had been left on the road, a scavenging raccoon or crow might also have been hit. We study talons, eyes, and pull back feathers to reveal enormous ears. Two girls draw back when I make the first cut, but most crowd in. We slice through huge pectoral muscles and saw away the keel. The liver is discolored from the car's impact. The heart looks like a chicken heart. We trace the digestive system. When the bird is a hollow shell, we finally see lungs, way in back, interspersed with ribs. I stick a straw down the trachea and blow, inflating air sacs like balloons, but the lungs stay flat. My Brownies know more about owls than they ever hoped to, and are pleased and proud of themselves—not one girl threw up.

Researchers must have permits to possess wild birds—even dead ones or their feathers. Pigeons from biological supply houses are safe and easy for children to work with, and teach the same lessons as wild birds. Intact chickens can be bought at some farms. It's legal to pick up dead House Sparrows, starlings, and pigeons, which were introduced and aren't protected by law, but I'd be nervous about exposing children to possible parasites or diseases.

Notes

October

Other than Lyme's disease and ultraviolet sun rays, the greatest dangers usually facing birders come from humans. In *Finding Birds in the National Capital Area*, Claudia Wilds warns birders "to carry with you nothing you cannot afford to lose, to leave nothing of value visible in a locked car, to keep your binoculars as inconspicuous as possible, and to stay alert for suspect behavior."

23 Bird-watching isn't as dangerous as, say, skydiving, but it has its risks. In 1982, Russ and I brought baby Joey to Arizona. Walking alone in Madera Canyon while Russ stayed with Joey, I suddenly heard an Ash-throated Flycatcher—a lifer! I searched the branches, all the time stepping backward to get a better vantage point, when suddenly the ground dropped out from under me. I'd literally backed off a cliff, but was caught by a tree that had fortuitously rooted itself in exactly the right place in the side of the canyon. I was so intent on that bird that I kept my binoculars focused the whole time, and the instant I landed, straddling a thick root two or three feet below the path, I saw it. I enjoyed the bird for at least a minute before I looked down and discovered just how far the canyon dropped right there. I clawed my way up, dislodging loose soil and rocks as I scrambled to get back on the trail. I made it back to our cabin shaken up, but having the presence of mind not to tell Russ. He has always considered me a sensible woman—I couldn't bear to disillusion him.

Notes

24 Ravens are migrating along the north shore and Hawk Ridge in big numbers now, but nobody seems to know where they're headed. No large concentrations of ravens are found in southern or central Minnesota or Wisconsin in winter, and states south of ours don't report many ravens period—we suspect that an organized group of ravens flies continually around the lake in a circular pattern just to confuse our counters. Quite a few winter in Duluth and Superior. They pretty much take charge of the dump on Wisconsin Point, and can sometimes be seen picking at garbage dumpsters behind restaurants, pinch-hitting for Ring-billed Gulls, which winter farther south.

Crows migrate, too, though, like ravens, many individuals remain in the Northland all winter. Ravens require wilderness more than crows do, especially during the nesting season. We seldom see ravens on Peabody Street in summer, where crows have nested right in our backyard, but ravens become regular city birds during some winters, often outnumbering crows on Duluth's Christmas Bird Count.

Ravens, which are believed to be even more intelligent than crows, may actually speak with intention to one another and, as it were, call one another by name. Ravens also definitely have a concept of number. In 1951, an ornithologist established that a raven could comprehend numbers well enough to count at least up to six.

Notes

October

Ornithologists have identified at least twenty-three different crow calls, each with a different meaning. The assembly call, given when a crow discovers an owl, attracts others to the scene. Recordings of American Crow assembly calls elicited the proper response from French crows, but French birds ignored American Crow alarm calls. The implications of this for French-American political relations are not known.

25 Field guides make it sound easy to distinguish crows from ravens, but it isn't really straightforward. Corvid calls are easy—crows caw while ravens croak—but unless we're trying to sleep with a window open, most of the corvids we encounter are silent.

Normally we identify big, black corvids in flight by their tails—crow tail feathers are all pretty much the same length, producing an evenly rounded appearance. A raven's central tail feathers are longer than the outer ones, giving the tail a wedge shape. Unfortunately, this rule doesn't work when tail feathers are molting, which often happens with both species in October.

Ravens are much larger than crows, but are similarly proportioned. They don't fly in mixed flocks, so size doesn't help unless we're watching a crow dive-bombing a raven. Ravens have a shaggy throat, which helps with sitting birds, and one odd field mark that is often helpful is the beak. Ravens often fly with their beaks hanging open like the jaw of a person who's fallen asleep in a car. Crows keep their mouths shut unless they have something to say.

Notes

26 The English language is richer for birds. The expression "silly goose" comes from domesticated geese, featured in children's stories and fables from Europe as well as America. Dictionaries don't take a gander at the origins of *goosing*, but it surely must come from geese attacking humans from the rear.

Quack, in the sense of a charlatan, is short for *quacksalver*, an archaic word taken from Dutch. *Salver* meant one who treated with salves, and *quack* came from the sound of the Mallard, common in Europe as well as America. Quacking has the connotation of blowing one's own horn, and quacksalver came to mean anyone who made loud, inaccurate claims to cure illness.

Jaywalking comes from the slang *jay*, referring to an ignorant, unsophisticated rustic. City people presumably crossed streets at corners while rural folk foolishly crossed anywhere. This expression was inspired by avian jays and reinforced by John Jay, the first Chief Justice of the Supreme Court, who fashioned an unpopular treaty with England—forever after, Americans thought him a naive and foolish old jay.

The word *turkey* used as an epithet did not come from Wild Turkeys, which are wary, intelligent birds. Domesticated turkeys—and unrelated Guinea fowl imported long ago from Turkish territory, called turkeys by some Europeans—are a bit lacking in native intelligence. The use of *turkey* in a derogatory sense dates at least to the 1920s, when it described plays that flopped.

Notes

October

The seabird blown in to the Ingalls' Dakota farmstead on an October blizzard was either a Dovekie or, more likely, an Ancient Murrelet. There are several records of both of these tiny ocean creatures in the inland United States, usually after storms. They eat tiny marine invertebrates, and quickly starve in freshwater lakes. The stomach of a Dovekie found dead under power lines in Wisconsin held nothing but a single piece of quartz.

27 Laura Ingalls Wilder mentioned birds often in her "Little House" books, but perhaps the most interesting account is in *The Long Winter*. After a fierce October blizzard that lasted many days, Pa found a little bird in a haystack:

They had never seen a bird like it. It was small, but it looked exactly like the picture of the great auk in Pa's big green book, *The Wonders of The Animal World*. It had the same white breast and black back and wings, the same short legs placed far back, and the same large, webbed feet. It stood straight up on its short legs, like a tiny man with black coat and trousers and white shirt front, and its little black wings were like arms . . . (It) would not eat. It did not utter a sound, but Carrie and Laura thought that it looked up at them desperately.

Finally they released it on Silver Lake.

Laura barely had time to see it, rising tiny in the great blue-sparkling sky . . . They never knew what became of that strange little bird that came in the dark with the storm from the far North and went southward in the sunshine. They never saw nor heard of another bird like it.

Notes

28 When Joey was in second grade, he started a penny collection, and I learned that collecting coins is like birding. The first is guaranteed to be new, whether it's a 1988-D or a starling. After that, finding the same penny or bird isn't exciting, but chances are the next one will also be new. The first twenty or thirty are easy, but each time we add one, we have one fewer to add again. Fortunately, our experience makes the next one easier to find. As the collection grows, the ones we need become more valuable and exciting.

American pennies have been completely documented. If Joey acquires every Lincoln cent minted since 1909, he can still add two or three newly minted ones every year. Birds aren't quite so simple—as soon as the American Ornithologists' Union declares that there are 702 species of birds on the continent, a new one from Asia slips into the Aleutians. After we've seen all the common birds, we still have uncommon, rare, and accidental species to list. When we've listed just about all of those, we can add to year, state, county, and backyard lists—acquisitive birders and coin collectors can keep busy for a lifetime.

Seeing a rare bird doesn't satisfy tactile senses as does holding a rare coin in one's hand, so I list birds that deposit tangible droppings on me. To be fair, I count only free birds, not ones I'm rehabbing, but my list includes Ruby-crowned Kinglet, Ruby-throated Hummingbird, and Pileated Woodpecker. Fastidious birders wishing a tangible reward from their hobby send list tallies to the American Birding Association—their totals are printed in an annual publication.

Notes

October

Blue Jays are quite good at remembering where they hide things. Whenever I let Sneakers out of her cage after she's been stuck in it for a few days, she immediately takes a Froot Loop from one of her hiding places. This has happened as long as two months after we've run out of them.

29 The motto of a Blue Jay might be "I came. I saw. I played with." Sneakers has several games. One is "Drop"—she drops things from high places just to watch them fall, and if something like a piece of paper or a maple seed falls slowly enough, she swoops and catches it before it hits the floor. She also plays "Peck it to Pieces" with crayons and pencils. Her favorite game is "Hide"—we find Lego people in our chairs, chandelier crystals in plant pots, pennies in drapery hems, and Froot Loops everywhere.

Peanuts have several features especially attractive to little jays. Like a birthday present, they're wrapped in a shell, which is fun to open. Once a hole is punched in the shell, it's fun to peek inside. After you've pulled out one nut, there's usually a second, and sometimes, joy of joys, a third. Nuts are exactly the right size for carrying around in a throat pouch, and just right for popping out unexpectedly to get a rise out of visitors unfamiliar with jays. Peanuts are fun to drop, fun to hide, fun to look at, and, when all that fun is finally over, fun to eat. Who could ask for anything more?

Notes

30 When presented with peanuts, Sneakers always carefully weighs each of them, carries the biggest to a high perch, and hacks into the shell. She's too excited to eat the first nut she pulls out—she's still itching to reach that other nut inside. So she pops the first in her throat pouch and hacks some more. Her pouch can't manage two peanuts, so when she gets the second out, she's faced with a dilemma—she can't swallow when her throat pouch is filled. So she spits out the first peanut to swallow the second. Now a Blue Jay can hold one peanut in her feet, but not two, so invariably one falls to the floor. Sometimes she flies down to get it, ending up with the same problem she started with, and sometimes she eats the one she has and then drops down for the other. But most of the time her mind wanders to the peanuts still sitting where I left them—like a child opening presents at a birthday party, she forgets about the peanuts she's already opened to grab another unopened one. Blue Jays get a lot more than nutrition from peanuts—they get fun and mental stimulation besides.

If I put five mealworms in Sneakers' dish, she grabs the biggest, and without taking the time to eat it grabs the next biggest, and the next, until they're all neatly stacked in her beak. As soon as she tries to eat one, they all fall out. Again she grabs the biggest and sometimes actually eats it, but as often as not she repeats the whole greedy procedure. You can't have your mealworm and eat it, too.

Notes

October

Snow Buntings are all about the pumphouse—flying above and gathering on the highway pavement below. They come from the tundra, and aren't accustomed to the hurried pace of urban society. Few drivers on Highway 61 moderate their speed to accommodate them, so migrating crow scavengers adjust their course to fly directly above the road, picking up a bunting breakfast as they move along.

31 While others pull out goblin costumes and pumpkins, I'm pulling out longjohns and binoculars, preparing for the last morning of Dawn Dickey Duty at the Lakewood Pumping Station. I shiver in the 13-degree dullness of dawn as Bunter licks frost off wilted clovers. We count ravens, Evening Grosbeaks, a scattering of goldfinches, Pine Grosbeaks, Bohemian Waxwings, and Boreal Chickadees. A few Lapland Longspurs rattle and whistle above, and the sweet notes of Horned Larks mingle with them. An adult Peregrine Falcon rushes past. I see it for only a few seconds, but seconds with peregrines are somehow better than hours with other birds.

One lone Yellow-rumped Warbler spends the morning near us. He and I chip back and forth, carrying on a conversation between my looking skyward and his searching the grass for one last insect. He doesn't fly off until I pack up my count sheet and head for my car—he chips farewell as Bunter and I climb in. I wish him a safe journey, wondering how he and the hundred thousand other birds I counted this fall will fare over the dangerous time ahead. Bunter gives me an impatient lick, and we head home for the winter.

Notes

November

November

One of the most delightful books for reading by a November fire is *Golden-crowned Kinglets* by Robert Galati, recounting the four years he and his wife spent perched in fifty- to sixty-foot rickety wood towers studying nesting kinglets.

1 I'm in a November funk. Two Fox Sparrows are the only migrants lingering at my feeders. The leaves are gone, the brown grass frozen. The days are short now, and getting even shorter. On a walk to Lester Park, the biting wind and leaden skies chill my heart. No birds sing, or even call, except a couple of crows. Even starlings are quiet. The Mallards at the mouth of the Lester River seem hunched down and somber.

Cedars in the park usually rouse my interest—maybe a Northern Saw-whet Owl lurks within their sheltering branches, but today I'm too pessimistic to even look. Suddenly a high-pitched "see-see-see" pierces my consciousness. Several Golden-crowned Kinglets, light as air, bright as fire, flit about the cedar branches, busy and gay, cheerful as a rising sun. One comes straight for me, pulling back as it realizes I'm no tree, but landing within an arm's reach. The crimson patch in the center of his golden yellow crown, which I see without binoculars, is more pleasing on this gray day than spring itself. These frolicsome little sprites facing the coming winter with light hearts are as bewitching as fairies, and the evil spell is broken.

Notes

2 My big brother once went hunting somewhere out beyond the Chicago suburbs and bagged two Mallards and a pheasant. I couldn't draw my eyes away as he pulled them out of his bag, so fascinated was I by the exotic colors and feather patterns. But those dead birds struck a dissonant note. I watched as he plucked and cleaned them—I even helped so he couldn't accuse me of being a girl—but I couldn't look into their lifeless eyes. A bird is so vital, so intensely alive, and then—in the flash of a shotgun blast, a speeding car, an unexpected picture window—it is transformed into something limp and diminished. An F-16 colliding with a flock of golden plovers can be rebuilt for twenty-seven million dollars. The entire national deficit isn't enough to rebuild a single four-ounce golden plover.

Everything takes its life's energy from other living things. Geese eat plants, foxes and hunters eat geese, and I've certainly eaten my share of Golden Plump chickens. We accept this and don't usually notice the sadness of individual avian death. But pity and compassion become us as human beings. If God Himself takes note of the fall of a sparrow, should we do less?

Dead birds are smaller than living ones. As a bird breathes, air passes through the lungs into bellowslike air sacs, which fill large spaces throughout its body. A sizable percentage of a bird's volume is insubstantial air—when the bird dies, much of its body literally collapses.

Notes

November

Of 3,400 ducks examined, 94.7 percent contained internal parasites—at least 1,600 tapeworms of six species have been found in a single duck. Seven kinds of roundworms attack Ruffed Grouse stomachs, intestines, gizzards, eyes, blood, and muscles—some can be transmitted to predators, including humans, if meat isn't thoroughly cooked. Eighty-one different parasites of fifty-one genera are known to attack starlings. When it comes to birds, it's a jungle in there.

Notes

3 Snarfy, a nighthawk with a broken wing, has tapeworms. I've had her since August, but I didn't notice the cestodes right away. They're disconcertingly attractive—five millimeters long, flat, glistening white. My veterinarian's lab technician cut off a segment, put it under a microscope, and showed me tiny tapeworm eggs with embryos wiggling around, complete with hooks.

Snarfy is healthy, and her wormy population will die out without intervention and without contaminating us—the eggs hatch in insects. She may have acquired them in something she ate, or via the mites and lice she had when she arrived. Tapeworms in nighthawks are unusual, so I sent samples to St. Paul for identification. Meanwhile, fifth-grader Joey brought one to school. He earned extra credit in the parasite unit of science class and made an important discovery in the lunch line: nobody likes to stand near a person with a tapeworm, even a very small one in a vial tucked away in a pocket. Joey found himself at the head of the line, smiling with the newfound knowledge that tapeworms are far more useful than most people realize.

4 In October 1988, a King Eider visited the Grand Marais harbor, and I almost went crazy thinking about that lifer swimming just 110 miles away. By the first week of November I couldn't stand it anymore, so one morning I told three-year-old Tommy and almost-five-year-old Katie to pack up a basket of toys so we could go for a nice ride in the car looking for a duck. An older child might have told me just what I could do with my duck, but Katie and Tommy were little enough to happily gather Triceratops, Tyrannosaurus Rex, Purple Psitticosaurus, and a basket of My Little Ponics together, anticipating a jolly good day.

A flock of Snow Buntings fluttered up from the roadside, and Katie added them to her list, imitating her mother precisely, as little children once imitated our mothers' vices by smoking candy cigarettes. An adult Bald Eagle flew above the car—Katie added that, too, and then turned to the dinosaurs. She and Tommy happily sang along with Raffi tapes, and stayed jolly for over half the ride. We only had to make one potty stop, and reached Grand Marais in less than three hours. What fun we were having.

Someday I want to make a movie about a bunch of college girls and a boy who looks like Jim Hutton piling into a car over spring break and, full of eager anticipation, heading up to Grand Marais as Connie Francis sings "Where the Boids Are." Grand Marais is the place for rare birds—in recent years, its avian visitors have included an Anna's Hummingbird, a Fork-tailed Flycatcher, a Fieldfare, and two different King Eiders.

Notes

November

I finally saw a King Eider in Grand Marais October 22, 1990, while all three of my children were happily in school. This lovely, and healthy, female had the prettiest penciling of any duck I've seen, and each time she dove she stayed under longer than any loon I've watched. I spent a satisfying morning sitting on the rocks in the bay watching this little visitor who somehow navigated wrong, missing an entire ocean.

5 When we finally reached Grand Marais in search of a King Eider, the temperature was in the low thirties and Tommy refused to leave the car—"too much windy." Katie took a polite but shivering glance at the ducks in the marina. She pretty much ignored the Black Ducks, wigeon, Bufflehead, goldeneyes, and even a Snow Goose, but expressed interest in Mr. and Mrs. Mallard before quickly joining Tommy in the car.

Meanwhile, I was getting more and more agitated that the eider was nowhere to be seen. A birder from Minneapolis had seen it minutes before we arrived, but it was gone now. I kept watch for two-and-a-half hours as the kids ate a picnic lunch in the car and played "My Little Ponies Meet the Dinosaurs." We found a bathroom and then checked the harbor one last time, but it was getting late. Tommy slept the long ride home, and we arrived after dark. Katie said it wasn't fair that she got so many new birds on her list when I didn't get a single one. She's far too generous to ever write a *Mommie Dearest* exposé about me, but one day she'll have plenty of stories to tell about her very own Mother Goose.

Notes

6 Why do Cedar Waxwings have red tips on their secondary wing feathers? These decorations are found on both males and females, on adults and occasionally even nestlings, year-round, yet many waxwings have none at all.

Thanks to two Canadian ornithologists, we now have a plausible explanation. Analyzing the number of red feather tips on birds of known age—museum specimens and living birds—they devised an elegant statistical method to show that even though individual young birds have them, overall the tips are larger and much more numerous in birds two years old and older. They concluded that waxwings breed assortatively—guided by the feather tips, older birds tend to choose older mates and young birds to choose young mates. Significantly more babies are successfully raised by parents with a high number of red tips—birds with experience. It's sometimes hard to see a connection between the beauty of birds and dry statistics, but when mathematics merges with ornithology, new and beautiful patterns emerge, renewing our faith in the order of nature, and giving us hope that age and experience really are more attractive than mere youth.

Individual waxwings are unlikely to return to the same nesting area from one year to the next. When an ornithologist bands a nestful, chances are they'll all be far away the next year, so following individual plumage development in the wild is difficult. Male American Redstarts also show delayed plumage maturation—they're dully colored until almost two years old—but waxwings are the only songbird known to have delayed maturation in both sexes.

Notes

November

The fiercest bird in the world is the Northern Goshawk, sometimes called "hell on wings" for its ferocity. This magnificent hunter of the northern forest takes mammals as big as snowshoe hares and birds from the size of ducks and pheasants to black-birds and jays, and even smaller ones when stressed by hunger. Goshawks are built for chasing birds in flight, but they also chase grouse and rabbits through the underbrush on foot.

7 Our family usually has waffles on Sunday mornings, but since normally one person finishes before the next one's waffle is done, breakfast isn't a sociable affair. One rare morning we kept the waffles in the oven so we could enjoy breakfast as a family. Sitting at the table, we spotted a Purple Finch coming right at us—or, rather, at our picture window. I jumped up and it must have seen me because it flipped up and away in the nick of time, its primary feathers brushing the glass. At that moment we realized a goshawk was chasing it at literally breakneck speed, headed straight for the window. At the sight, everyone jumped out of their chairs, which caught the bird's attention. It stuck out its legs and pulled back its wings, as if to brake, and we heard the click of its claws on the glass as it stalled and made a backward somersault in flight, landing ignominiously on the ground beneath the window. Hunched down below us, it looked as mortified as I've ever seen a bird, furtively glancing all around as if making sure nobody had seen it. Then it flapped off, unhurt in body if not in spirit.

Notes

8 A Northern Goshawk rushing along Hawk Ridge thrills visitors as much as an eagle. And when the naturalist brings an adult from the banding station to the main overlook, even the official counter sometimes takes a momentary break to peek at this exquisite lean, mean hunting machine. The delicate black, gray, and white etching on its underside, finer and more intricate than the streaking on any warbler or sparrow, and the fluffy white feathers beneath the tail are pleasing beyond compare. The black cap and eye line, accentuated by the white eyebrow stripe, give sharp relief to the ruby red eye, glaring at us all in untamable defiance. Young goshawks are also handsome, but their coarse brown streaks and yellow eye don't delight our human sensibilities quite as much.

Goshawks are counted and banded from Hawk Ridge every year, but their numbers rise and fall in a ten-year cycle, from 5,819 in 1982 to 106 in 1989, following the population cycle of grouse and snowshoe hares. An unbelievable 1,229 were counted on a single October day in 1982.

Our goshawk is also found in the northern forests of Europe and Asia, and takes its name from Anglo Saxon for a "goose hawk." Migrating goshawks tend to move generally southward to the mid-central states, though one banded at Hawk Ridge was recaptured at Yorktown, Saskatchewan, a month later. One thirteen-year-old goshawk originally banded at Hawk Ridge was recovered in northern Alberta. One falconer's goshawk lived in captivity almost nineteen years.

Notes

November

Pigeons usually mate for life, and are monogamous. We didn't know it at the time, but my brother's pigeon Rocky would never have contaminated those fancy bloodlines if only Jimmy had provided him with a mate.

9 When my big brother was ten, he developed a hankering to race pigeons, so he built a coop out of scrap lumber and set out on his bike to fetch himself a bird. At a nearby railroad yard, one dusty gray pigeon was so intent on eating spilled grain, or so stupid, that he allowed Jimmy to drop a paper bag over him. We named him Rocky, after the flying squirrel.

Rocky collected some ribbons in local pigeon races before Jimmy got interested in exotic breeds—tumblers, pouters, fantails, king pigeons, and such. Rocky's racing talents were eclipsed by his procreative prowess, and he spoiled Jimmy's breeding program, so after a tearful good-bye, he was dispatched to Florida with a vacationing buddy. Rocky beat the guy back to Chicago. Then he was sent to Manitoba on a fishing expedition. It took two weeks, but Rocky made it back again. Jimmy built a dividing wall in the coop to keep Rocky from his fancy-bred females, but, like Romeo, with love's light wings did Rocky o'er-perch those walls. Pigeon mongrels and purebreds abounded in our yard for years, but Jimmy had few birds that raced as well as Rocky, his common old railroad pigeon.

Notes

10 I usually don't worry much about getting older, but the day before my thirty-ninth birthday a Pileated Woodpecker cruising about my neighborhood stopped hitching up a telephone pole and turned to look at me, and it sure looked like it knew I was approaching the age when fungus starts growing in aspen trees. As the fungus grows, the tree develops heart rot, making its soft interior easy to excavate for a pileated nest chamber while the still-sturdy bark is tough enough to keep out squirrels and raccoons. Pileated Woodpeckers may prefer trees over forty years old, but few of them live longer than two or three years.

Birds show their ages more gracefully than we. If they get wrinkles or liver spots, they're hidden by feathers. The older waxwings get, the more attractive they appear to the opposite sex, but then again, the oldest Cedar Waxwings on record, living in captivity, survived only eight years, so I wouldn't swap places with one at this late date. I suppose there's nothing left to do but check myself for signs of fungus and heart rot and go to bed.

November lakes are dotted here and there with loons and diving ducks. Hawks, owls, and a few sparrows are still migrating, and a handful of robins pig out in mountain ash trees, but during deer season it's risky business to walk through the woods searching for them, even wearing blaze orange.

Notes

November

During the 1800s, many military officers who explored the American West or were assigned to military outposts collected and described the avifauna. Lewis's Woodpecker, Couch's Kingbird, Hammond's Flycatcher, Clark's Nutcracker, Bendire's Thrasher, Abert's Towhee, McCown's Longspur, McKay's Bunting, and Scott's Oriole were all named for veterans who are honored today.

11 The American military has a rich ornithological history, beginning in the 1700s and 1800s. During the world wars, many ornithologists served in the Army Signal Corps. Some worked with pigeons, and others acted as lookouts—discerning subtleties in the silhouettes and flight patterns of birds had prepared them to recognize enemy planes from a distance.

My closest tie to the military was my big brother Jim, who played Davy Crockett as a kid, teaching himself to shoot squirrels and birds. He and I were the only ones in our family who loved outdoor things, and as much as I hated killing any creatures, Jimmy was more a kindred spirit than the rest of my family. Over time, he and I worked out an unstated pact—I never made him feel like scum for shooting birds, and in turn, when I became a birder, he never made me feel like Miss Jane Hathaway for watching them. Jimmy went into the Vietnam War a skilled marksman, and came back alive. Too many others from our blue-collar Chicago suburb stayed boys in their tombs as the rest of us grew up—boys who never again would hear birdsong or see birds winging through the skies. We remember those gentle heroes today.

Notes

12   Unlike political hawks, real hawks don't aid humans in war except as mascots. Ironically, the birds most used in combat are Rock Doves, trained as homing pigeons. Their peaceful urge to return to home and mate has been exploited throughout much of history. Ancient Romans used pigeons to carry back to Rome news of Caesar's conquest of Gaul; word of Napoleon's defeat at Waterloo reached England by pigeon four days before it arrived by horse and ship; and during both world wars, pigeons carried messages in all theaters of action. During World War II, Allied forces dropped their agents with well-trained pigeons, a more secure means of communication than radio.

Modern telecommunications ended the U.S. Army Signal Corps Pigeon Service, but birds are still affected by humans' warring tendencies. Hundreds of thousands of birds died in the 1991 invasion of Iraq. Irish Republican Army car bombs have probably killed at least a few descendants of the heroic pigeons that helped the Allies win the war. It's a shame that people haven't evolved to the level of birds, defending our territories not with bullets, but with song.

Pigeons aren't the only birds that have served people during wartime. Large oceanic birds called frigatebirds carried the war messages of Polynesians, and cackling domestic geese are credited with saving Roman civilization in 338 B.C.—they alerted the sleeping city of an impending barbarian attack, changing the course of human history.

Notes

November

November sea ducks in Lake Superior include the elegant Oldsquaw, streamlined mergansers, and chunky scoters. A Harlequin Duck turns up every now and then. This exotic western species, named for the masked harlequins of the Italian stage, is a proficient diver, often seen swimming among jagged rocks in very rough waters.

13 November on Lake Superior can be a dismal time, with blustery winds and gray skies. But sea ducks bobbing on the choppy, frigid water dress up the lake as ornaments do a Christmas tree. And, encased in their thick down feathers and elegant feathered wet suits, they're perhaps as comfortable in the cold lake as a human would be in a heated indoor swimming pool.

The most common of our sea ducks are the Common Goldeneye and the Bufflehead, who are considered true sea ducks even though they spend much of their lives on fresh water. These two nest in cavities or wood duck houses on lakes and rivers, but many winter on the coasts or in lakes too large and deep for dabblers. The Bufflehead is nick-named the "butterball" by hunters, but since I plan to live out my years without ever eating one, I prefer its real name. *Bufflehead* comes from the large proportions of its puffy head, which reminded early ornithologists of buffalo. The generic name of both the goldeneye and Bufflehead, *Bucephala*, means "ox head" or "bull head" in Greek. The same word, in its masculine form, was the name of Alexander the Great's horse—Bucephalus.

Notes

14 A cat insinuates itself into our lives imperceptibly, and affection invades slowly but deeply, like an oak taking root in our hearts. I adopted a stray cat only to keep her from killing redpolls—Joey, Katie, and Bunter made friends with her before I could dispatch her to the shelter. Sasha was pathetically scrawny, but Joey and Katie fed her and roused her spirits playing peek and chase. I—the inveterate cat hater—brought her to the vet to be spayed and declawed, put awful, stinging drops in her ears, yelled whenever she even looked at a bird, and chased her from the door whenever the kids went out. So, naturally, I was her chosen human. For seven years, I couldn't write without her sleeping in my lap or plopping herself down and taking a bath on whatever I was reading. She nestled on or against me as I slept. I couldn't even go to the bathroom without a white paw reaching under the door.

Cats kill too many birds. They belong indoors—and not in a bird house like ours. But Sasha chased ambivalence away like a ball of yarn. Long before she collapsed with an embolism and died in my arms, she had playfully swept every feeling out of my heart except love.

People often asked how I kept a cat with so many birds. Sasha was banished to the bedroom whenever Sneakers or other song-birds were about, but the time Sneakers got loose and flew right over her head, Sasha crouched to pounce, but caught herself and ran from temptation to hide in my bedroom. Nighthawks just sit around, not enticing a cat like quick flutterers. I always trusted Sasha with them, and she never disappointed me.

Notes

November

Ravens seem to watch for eagles not only to locate thermals but also to have the fun of harassing them. In one kettle the eagles circled ever upward while ravens dashed in and out. Eagle wings are bigger and clumsier to maneuver than raven wings, so the eagles weren't in a position to fight back, but, just in case, the ravens always darted at them from above, keeping their distance from lethal talons and forbidding beaks.

15 Looking up one morning, we see scattered high clouds dotted with hawks. Three adult Bald Eagles, five Red-tailed Hawks, and a Rough-legged Hawk dance on the light northwest wind, and winter is in the air. All day the eagles pass over. I'm stuck indoors, finger painting with the kids, but every time I look out I see at least a couple of redtails or an eagle. One thermal carries a kettle of twelve redtails, two roughlegs, half a dozen ravens, and one immature and four adult Bald Eagles.

The world offers no more beautiful sight than eagles swirling in a blue sky over one's home, unless it's the shining eyes of little children watching them with wonder and delight. And the promise of snow that the eagles carry on their wings makes young eyes grow larger. Eagles tug the grim final days of autumn away on their glistening tails. They'll continue their migration along Lake Superior well into December, but when so many are afloat in a November sky, winter is never far behind.

Notes

16 Now and then in November, we run into a Yellow-rumped Warbler shivering in the cold. These sprites weigh about a third of an ounce—the same as a chickadee—but look smaller because the chickadee's down underwear is thicker and warmer. Warblers are essentially tropical insectivores that come north to raise their young. Yellowrumps occasionally winter in the northern states, but they always seem to regret the decision.

Yellow-rumped Warblers aren't hardier than their relatives so much as more versatile in food habits. They can forage near the trunks of trees, which keeps them protected from wind, snow, and rain—other warblers feed on the outermost branches, where they are exposed to the elements. Also, most warblers glean for insects on leaves, but both insects and leaves are gone now. Yellowrumps eat bayberries and the fruits of wax myrtles in winter, allowing some to stay as far north as the central states, though many retreat to Panama. Even the hardiest yellowrump will die if the weather gets too cold or food too hard to find, but apparently some yellowrumps prefer the cold to the hazards of migration.

Yellow-rumped Warblers remain in migratory condition well into the winter. While other species sleep through a January night, yellowrumps wake up after sleeping an hour or so. If the weather has been bad or food resources are dwindling, they move on. As northern weather improves at the end of February, yellowrumps grow restless again, and head north much earlier than other warblers.

Notes

November

The tongue of a Ruddy Duck

Many people live long, healthy, happy, productive lives without ever once thinking about the adaptive modifications and taxonomic value of the tongue in birds. I bought a 1925 monograph on exactly that topic at an American Ornithologists' Union convention—it bore the stamp of the University of British Columbia's Department of Zoology Library, where people apparently have interests other than bird tongues—most of the pages had never even been separated.

17 Leon L. Gardner of the United States Army Medical Corps was an authority on bird tongues. He wrote in 1925 that there are eight natural groups of bird tongues, none of which are used in sound production. Omnivores, including most songbirds, have a rather basic tongue with spines in back—when worked rapidly backward and forward it can force food down the throat. A fish-eater's tongue has sharp, stiff spines pointing backward, keeping slippery prey from sliding out again—the spines on a penguin tongue cover the whole surface, those on a loon cover only the base, and those on a merganser form a double row. Aquatic-food strainers, like most ducks, have a beautifully complex tongue with grooves, spines, and hairs. Predacious hawks and owls have a heavy, rasping tongue. Probing birds, like woodpeckers, have an extensible tongue with barbs on the tip to spear insects, though sapsuckers have more, and softer, barbs for lapping sap. Seed-and-nut-eaters, like parrots and finches, have a fleshy, strong tongue to work seeds out of the husk. Nectar-feeders have an extremely extensible, tubular tongue with a fringed tip. And food-bolters, like pelicans and nighthawks, have a tiny, rudimentary tongue that is pretty much worthless for anything.

Notes

18 How many feathers does a bird have? In 1933, obviously a slower-paced time than today, the Smithsonian Institution initiated a feather-counting project, and professional scientists actually counted, one by one, the feathers on selected species. Earlier ornithologists had also counted feathers—Ernest Thompson Seton counted 4,915 feathers on a Brewer's Blackbird in 1882, and Jonathan Dwight counted 3,235 on a Bobolink in 1900. Most songbirds have from 1,500 to 3,000.

The Tundra Swan (then called the Whistling Swan) had no competition for the most feathers of all, with 25,216, more than 15,000 on its neck alone. Waterfowl have dense feathering to keep their skin dry when swimming, and swans are the largest of waterfowl. One male Ruby-throated Hummingbird had the fewest feathers—only 940. A Ruby-crowned Kinglet had 1,119.

The number of feathers varies from season to season. House Sparrows collected in Michigan in January and February, when they needed heavy insulation, averaged 3,573; in July they averaged 3,167—11.5 percent fewer.

Except on ostriches, penguins, and a few other primitive birds, feathers don't sprout evenly over a bird's body, but grow in special areas called feather tracts. Overlapping feathers from adjoining tracts cover featherless spaces between feather tracts, making birds appear as if the feathers grew as evenly as a mammal's fur. The outer feathers that give the bird its characteristic shape and appearance are called contour feathers.

Notes

November

Sneakers enjoys the bustle of crowds, and relishes attention whenever people approach her cage. At the Rhinelander program, a thoughtful friend from Eagle River brought her Froot Loops, and toddlers held them near the cage bars— she reached through and took them from tiny fingers carefully and gently. She busily preened, ate meal-worms, and hid Froot Loops under the newspapers in her cage. Fred just sat quiet and still.

19 I get up at four in the morning to drive to Rhinelander for a presentation. Sneakers the Blue Jay looks sleepy but interested as I bring her cage to the car. Fred the Nighthawk gives me his "here we go again" look when I put him in the familiar cardboard travel box.

Fred is quiet and still on the ride, but Sneakers is frightened whenever oncoming headlights shine in. I pull over and cover her cage, but that makes her more scared, so I pull over again and take the cover off. The radio makes her really agitated—oddly, every station has sports scores at five in the morning. I try a Paul Simon tape, alarming her even more, so I switch to the soundtrack of the Broadway production of "You're a Good Man, Charlie Brown," which settles her right down. Our car has stereo speakers in front and back, and when I peek into the rearview mirror, she's sitting on her perch, intently craning her neck to study each corner of the car, apparently wondering where Snoopy is hiding. By the time the sun rises, she's whistling to the music, and has a jolly time on our four-hour ride. Fred just sits quiet and still.

Notes

20 Driving to Rhinelander, we hit unexpected snow in Iron River. It's "lake effect" snow—a dry high-pressure system dominates everywhere else within a hundred miles. Suddenly the snow is so thick I can't see beyond the headlights. I'm relieved to come to a truck ahead—we creep along at thirty miles per hour. A car comes up behind, and another, and another. They can't pass—there isn't enough visibility to try—and we make a little caravan moving through the white-out. We drive twenty or thirty miles together, me wondering whether they're as grateful for company, and taillights showing the way, as I. The truck turns off at Hurley, blinking brake lights in good-bye as he exits. I blink my headlights back. Now I'm the leader, going slower without the truck's lights to guide me. Still no one can pass. The car behind me turns off before Mercer—I'm surprised when that driver, too, blinks lights when turning off. The snow breaks just past Mercer, and we finally speed up to the limit. The cars behind don't rev up and pass—we stay in our little migratory flock until, one by one, we reach our destinations and blink farewell.

Flying in V formation, migrating geese conserve enough energy to give them 71 percent more flight distance than they'd achieve flying alone. Although Canada Geese often fly with blood relatives, no one really knows what impulse drives them or other migrating birds to join a particular flock. We wonder if they seek out birds they know and perhaps trust, or if it's random. Are they anonymous strangers brought together on flyways like automobiles meeting on a highway?

Notes

November

In December 1978, the Chicago birding hotline reported a Barn Owl and Saw-whet Owl in Lincoln Park. A guy with binoculars saw Russ and me blundering around and led us right to the birds—numbers 279 and 280 on my life list. Two years later, when I moved to Duluth, I recognized him—Kim Eckert, author of *A Birder's Guide to Minnesota*.

21 Hiking in the Morton Arboretum outside Chicago my first November of birding, I found some American Coots—number 111 on my life list. I was pleased with myself because I didn't mistake them for ducks—I found the right page in my field guide right off the bat—and excited and happy to have a lifer. A while later, I came upon two men with binoculars—my introduction to the birding community. We nodded as we passed on the trail, and one of them said there were crossbills up ahead. I was so proud to be taken into their confidence that I blurted out about the coots. Their look of disdain stung like a slap in the face.

The normal strategy when birding parties meet is to nod politely and move on—Party A speaks only if they've spotted something good, meaning uncommon. Party B thanks them for the information and moves on unless they can match or top the sighting. I was guilty of the shocking faux pas of assuming birders could be interested in coots. Mortified, I learned to hold my tongue—when I saw a Summer Tanager by the Red Cedar River on the Michigan State campus the following spring, I didn't dare mention it to anyone.

Notes

22 My favorite way to spend a frozen, sleety November day is to nestle indoors by a fire, Bunter's warm head resting on my lap, a cup of cocoa warming my tummy, and a good bird book warming my spirit.

There are so many books to choose from. The single one I couldn't live without is Terres's *The Audubon Society Encyclopedia of North American Birds*. Sometimes I want something more technical but still interesting—Campbell and Lack's *Dictionary of Birds*, Welty's *The Life of Birds*, or the ornithology textbooks by Gill or Van Tyne and Burger fit the bill. Robert's *The Birds of Minnesota* and Robbins's *Wisconsin Birdlife* are pleasingly local. Sometimes I want to read about a single species—McIntyre's *The Common Loon, Spirit of Northern Lakes*, Smith's *The Black-capped Chickadee*, Nero's *Redwings* and *The Great Gray Owl* (Nero's poetry is darned good, too), Nolan's treatise on Prairie Warblers, Nice's on Song Sparrows, and anything by Skutch, are wonderful. You can't beat a bird book and a good dog for company on a blustery day.

We learn delightful details about birds while browsing through Bent's life histories, the Department of Interior's *Birds in Our Lives*, National Geographic's *Water, Prey, and Game Birds* and *Song and Garden Birds*, and journals by Audubon, Lewis and Clark, and Thoreau. Children's books are just plain fun—Yolen's *Owl Moon*, McCloskey's *Make Way for Ducklings*, and Dr. Seuss's *Horton Hatches the Egg* are my favorites.

Notes

November

Every now and again I get a phone call about a Wild Turkey in someone's yard in the Northland. Most ornithologists presume these to be escaped from farms or zoos, but it's quite possible that some are the genuine article. Turkeys live their lives with unmatched vigor, and at least one has been recorded flying 55 miles per hour for a full mile.

23 No bird is so completely identified with a holiday as the turkey with Thanksgiving. The Wild Turkey, native only to North America, was originally found in mature chestnut, beech, and oak forests in what is now the southern United States and Mexico. It eats mast—the bulk of its diet used to be chestnuts, but since chestnut blight wiped out its food supplies, it now mainly eats beech nuts and acorns. A single turkey can eat a pound of acorns in a single meal—its powerful gizzard grinds the hard mast to a digestible paste.

The Wild Turkey was probably never found in Minnesota until settlers brought some in, and it wasn't very common in Wisconsin, either. The small population in southern Wisconsin was exterminated before the 1900s. Excessive hunting, habitat loss, diseases spread from domestic fowl, and chestnut blight reduced turkeys to dangerously low numbers throughout their natural range. Reintroduction programs have restored them to somewhat stable numbers, and it's now possible to find them in every one of the lower forty-eight states, though many are descended from domestic stock.

Notes

24 Domestic turkeys appear on tables in huge numbers this time of year. Russ and I have always defined our marriage as perfect because he eats the white meat and I the dark. Gallinaceous birds, including chickens, turkeys, and partridge, produce both kinds of meat because of their lifestyle—their wing and breast muscles are composed of white muscle fibers, which, compared to red fibers, are thicker in diameter, with few mitochondria, little fat but plenty of glycogen, and enzymes to break down the glycogen anaerobically. White fibers are fed by few blood capillaries, and contract rapidly but tire quickly. We seldom can flush a grouse twice, and virtually never three or four times—it's too exhausted.

Gallinaceous bird legs are moved by red muscle fibers, rich in enzymes for breaking down fat and protein aerobically. They require a rich oxygen supply, so are fed by abundant blood capillaries. These fibers contract more slowly than white fibers, but are capable of sustained activity. A partridge can keep on its toes all day long without ever grousing about how tired it is.

Geese and ducks, capable of sustained walking and paddling as well as sustained flights, need red muscle fibers in both their legs and wings—the meat of these birds is all dark. To fuel long migratory flights, wild duck and goose muscle is rich in fats, which can be broken down aerobically by enzymes to provide energy as the muscle works.

Notes

November

The Jackass Penguin, the only penguin of South Africa and Namibia, dives for fish but is too buoyant to stay underwater without help. It swallows stones into its gizzard to make itself heavier—an avian Pinocchio, who had to tie himself to a rock to stay underwater in his search for Monstro the whale.

25 Children are always fascinated with the little bag of innards stuffed into a store-bought turkey or chicken. In ancient Rome, trained experts called haruspices inspected the livers of sacrificial chickens, and from the shape and color they attempted to predict the future decreed by the gods. We find chicken livers more tasty than auspicious.

The gizzard, the muscular part of a bird's stomach, is strange and fascinating. The gizzards of Wood Ducks and Mallards can crush acorns and hard hickory nuts that the birds swallow whole. Turkey gizzards can pulverize glass beads, bend needles, and crush tubes made of tin plate that require eighty pounds of pressure to bend. The seeds of an endangered tree on the island of Mauritius possibly germinated only after passing through the digestive system of a Dodo, whose gizzard ground up the hard shell. The gizzards of some Nebraska ducks contained gold nuggets—when hunters found them in 1911, a small gold rush was started. A scaup killed in Louisiana had two gold nuggets in its gizzard. It's possible that the Burmese ruby mines were discovered after a ruby was found in the gizzard of a pheasant.

Notes

26 In this season of gluttony, we consider how much food birds pack away. A hummingbird daily consumes over twice its weight in nectar, or half its weight in pure sugar. To accomplish a similar feat, a big adult would have to scarf down 370 pounds of boiled potatoes or 130 pounds of bread instead of the two pounds of food most people eat each day.

A pair of loons and their two chicks consume over a ton of fish during the fifteen weeks of the breeding season. An eight-pound Brown Pelican eats four pounds of fish every day. The Black-footed Albatross is nicknamed the "feathered pig" because it can swallow half-pound chunks of shark meat in one gulp. Turkeys eat as much as a pound of nuts or acorns in a single meal. Robins eat about fourteen feet of earthworms every day. Condors and vultures sometimes eat so much they can't take flight. On a lucky night, an owl may swallow so many mice or rats that its stomach can't hold them all—the tail of the last one may hang out of its beak until some of the first have been digested. All in all, birds can make the biggest Thanksgiving pig-out look like pretty mild stuff.

Eating can be hazardous to a bird's health. A Red-tailed Hawk in South Dakota flew off with a weasel that got a death-grip on the hawk's throat in mid-air. Six Common Terns died on Long Island in 1962 after swallowing blowfish. And Golden Eagles have died pursuing porcupine meat. One rests, probably not in peace, in a display case in the University of Minnesota–Duluth Biology Department, quills still in place.

Notes

November

Beak tissue is similar to fingernails, with too small a blood supply to cause frostbite. A shunt in songbird legs sends circulating blood back up without entering cold toes. The small amount of blood in toes, and their hard tissue, keeps most bird feet safe. Songbird feet have too few nerve cells to feel cold or heat. One Gray Jay perched on a hot camp stove for minutes—something a barefoot Tommy would never attempt.

27 Tommy doesn't want to wear a hat—he tells me birds don't. We're in no hurry, so I put some celery in the freezer for a while. When we take it out, it's frozen solid but thaws to a sodden mess—freezing water inside the cells had expanded on freezing, bursting the cell walls. When frozen animal cells burst, we call it frostbite.

Tommy's blood carries warmth from deep inside him to his ears, but when it's very cold, his skin loses heat faster than blood can replace it. Except for dove feet, feathered birds seldom get frostbite—little boys don't have down covering every inch of their skin. Tommy remembers that baby birds have large patches of skin without any down feathers, called apteria—I don't tell him that most adults have these same patches, just covered up by outer, contour feathers.

Tommy insists that if birds don't need a hat, he shouldn't either. I remind him that Donald Duck wears one, but he retorts indignantly that Donald Duck isn't real. I put the hat on him with the only reason he'll accept—"Because Mommy said so."

Notes

28 Sometimes the gulf that separates birders from nonbirders is as wide as the Grand Canyon. Russ and I knew we'd have different interests when we set off for Arizona eleven years ago—I was far more interested in birds than in scenery—but he knew as sure as the sky is blue that I'd be impressed with the sheer magnitude of the Grand Canyon.

He obligingly accommodated birding stops all the way down from Minnesota, and we finally came to the first pull-off parking area where it was possible to see this wonder of the world, this spectacle he had seen long ago and was so eager to share with his beloved. As we hopped out of the car, a singing Western Bluebird caught my attention—a lifer! I got a quick glimpse at it before Russ turned me around to face the Grand Canyon in all its glory. I instantly turned back around to look at the bluebird—the only one I've ever seen to this day. Russ was shocked and disappointed that I preferred a bird to such magnificence. Actually, I thought the Grand Canyon was right pretty—I just figured it wasn't likely to take off and fly away anytime soon.

Joseph J. Hickey, whose *Guide to Bird Watching* gave me more knowledge and inspiration than any other single book I've ever read, describes how bewildered some people feel trying to figure out the point behind bird-watching. "By some, it is regarded as a mild paralysis of the central nervous system, which can be cured only by rising at dawn and sitting in a bog."

Notes

November

Sneakers pushes toy cars on our dining room table. She particularly enjoys Hot Wheels—they're small enough to handle in a Blue Jay beak and the wheels run fast and easy, even on carpet. She likes to push them and watch them go, taking particular delight when one runs off the table and crashes on the floor.

29 Sneakers the Blue Jay has become an important member of our family. She has rather good table manners for a jay, but occasionally steals corn or grapes right off our plates. Her favorite foods are ice cream and Froot Loops, and she's also partial to peanut-butter-and-jelly sandwiches. The only human food that she absolutely refuses is bananas. She used to play with sunflower seeds exactly like she played with Legos, but after I cracked a couple open for her to check out the food inside, she quickly learned that they're edible. Blue Jay survival in the wild apparently depends a great deal on young ones learning from adults and one another.

Sneakers loves to take baths, and I can't leave a sinkful of dishes without her hopping in. Once when five-year-old Tommy took his bath, Sneakers jumped right in the tub, opened her wings, and scooted along on top of the water. I fished her out thinking she probably wanted me to, but she hopped right back in, to Tommy's delight—he'd never been in a birdbath before. When Sneakers snatched a toilet paper tube from the wastebasket, she even mastered logrolling.

Notes

30 Mark Twain's favorite bird was the Blue Jay. He wrote:

There's more to a blue-jay than any other creature. He has got more moods and more different kinds of feelings than other creatures; and, mind you, whatever a blue-jay feels, he can put into language. And no mere commonplace language, either, but rattling, out-and-out book talk—and bristling with metaphor, too—just bristling! And as for command of language—why, you never see a blue-jay get stuck for a word. No man ever did. They just boil out of him!

You may call a jay a bird. Well, so he is, in a measure—because he's got feathers on him, and don't belong to no church, perhaps, but otherwise he is just as much a human as you be. And I'll tell you for why. A jay's gifts, and instincts, and feelings, and interests cover the whole ground. A jay hasn't got any more principle than a Congressman . . . A jay can cry, a jay can laugh, a jay can feel shame, a jay can reason and plan and discuss, a jay likes gossip and scandal, a jay has got a sense of humor, a jay knows when he is an ass just as well as you do—maybe better. If a jay ain't human, he better take in his sign, that's all.

Mark Twain was born on November 30, 1835, and died on April 21, 1910. "Baker's Blue-Jay Yarn," originally published in A Tramp Abroad, has been reprinted in many anthologies. Ironically, Twain, who was disillusioned with and felt bitter toward the human race, loved the Blue Jay not in spite of, but because of, its humanlike qualities.

Notes

December

December

When goldfinches are about, they usually turn up at feeders. They seem perfectly content with sunflower seeds, but their favorite feeder treat is niger seed, which tastes as good to them as real thistle seed but doesn't sprout on our soil.

1 December's opening can be a dismal time for children before skating rinks freeze up—it's usually too cold for biking, and there isn't enough snow for skiing yet. But a flock of goldfinches brightens the time considerably. The wild canary is handsome even in dull winter plumage. Its nickname is appropriate—canaries and goldfinches belong to closely related genera, and in captivity have successfully raised hybrid babies.

The goldfinch is pretty enough to be the state bird of Washington in the West, New Jersey in the East, and Iowa right in the middle. It was unofficially considered Minnesota's state bird until 1961.

Goldfinches wander in huge flocks in winter, and may be abundant in one location in a given year and completely absent the next. The Lake Superior region is usually too rugged for them—the winter of 1982–83 was the first on record that they were commonly reported throughout northern Minnesota all season. For Northlanders, winter goldfinches, like other forms of natural gold, will probably remain rare, a gift we long remember and treasure.

Notes

2 Fred the Nighthawk is a quiet bird. He makes a little "rit-rit-rit" when he spots a hawk, a tiny peep when he swallows too big a chunk of food, a hiss when alarmed, and for a time a foot-drumming in response to the toe-tapping of a female named Ginger. He's the only nighthawk I've ever had that made the "peent" call in captivity, but always in singlets—he'd call and I'd look, but he never repeats the trick—I could never observe how the sound was produced. He called often in spring and late winter, but month after month I couldn't catch him in the act. The problem was compounded when we started keeping Joey's starling Mortimer in the same room. Morty quickly learned to produce a perfect "peent," making me run to look dozens of times a day.

Finally, after twenty-one long months, I actually saw Fred peent. He looked excited—he moved his head back and forth and his throat quivered—so I kept patient watch and he suddenly puffed out his throat a wee bit, opened his mouth a little, and out came a "peent." Frankly, the anticipation far exceeded the actual event.

Nighthawks seem to me to be wonderfully expressive birds, with many facial feather postures to show mood. But I must admit that there's a certain amount of subtlety to nighthawk expressions—strange as it seems, Russ thinks they'd make excellent department store mannequins. In his eye they never seem to do much of anything at all.

Notes

December

More cars are named for horses than for birds, but we do have Ford Falcons, Buick Skylarks, and AMC Eagles. I'd like a sporty job for larking about free as a bird—I'd call it a Kinglet. A high-speed power machine might be named a Peregrine, and one for off-road travel a Cliff Swallow. Few consumers would feel secure in a car named a Turkey, and drivers would certainly worry about how a Least Tern handled curves.

3 When our Chevy Citation's odometer passed from 99,999 back to zero, I wished the rest of the car would instantly rejuvenate along with the mileage. But cars aren't built as strong, quite, as birds, and our ton of steel didn't have a prayer of lasting as long as a three-quarter-ounce Barn Swallow. In swooping back and forth to catch flying insects, a Barn Swallow's odometer clocks 100,000 miles every five and a half months. Barn Swallows fly round trip between North and South America every year, yet many of them last over eight years—longer than a lot of cars.

The all-time avian speed record was set in 1985—a Semipalmated Sandpiper banded at Plymouth Beach, Massachusetts, on August 12 was shot by a hunter in Guyana, 2,800 miles away, on August 15. The slowest flyer—the Poky Little Puppy of the bird world—was probably a young pigeon in the Bronx Zoo named 1708. She was sent to Washington, D.C., for a race in 1932. Her coopmates quickly returned, but it took her eight years to check in, covering an average of sixteen feet per hour—a speed my little Citation might envy on some frigid, blizzardy mornings in the Northland.

Notes

4 As I'm walking with Tommy to the school bus stop one morning, a whir of wings and a flash of orange catch my eye. Orange? A perfect adult male Northern Oriole lands in a bare birch tree.

Orioles don't belong in the Northland after October, and certainly not in December. This adult male in seemingly perfect health somehow prematurely lost his urge to migrate. I learned that he visited a yard a few blocks away for a few weeks, taking mostly grapes. In our neighborhood he's eating oranges set out in one yard, and visiting mountain ashes and crab apple trees, but a long winter without animal protein is hard on a bird that should be eating juicy tropical insects and spiders as well as fruit right now.

We enjoy this little piece of the tropics in the midst of the gray Northland winter, but a feeling of foreboding overshadows us. No orioles recorded in Minnesota or Wisconsin have ever survived through February. And our poor little neighborhood bird doesn't break the trend— the Peabody Street Merlin finally dispatches him for a colorful meal.

Unlike other migratory birds, individual orioles seem to have some flexibility in their migration habits. Since 1949, the number of overwintering orioles has been increasing in the Atlantic states. There are records of them overwintering in southern Wisconsin and even in southern Minnesota, but such a conspicuously bright orange bird in a bare black-and-white landscape is exceptionally vulnerable to predators. Without a balanced diet, it's also vulnerable to cold.

Notes

December

The sad song of turtle doves inspired two collective terms—a dole or a pitying of doves. Some collective terms conjure up more humorous images— a parliament of owls, a paddling of ducks, a gulp of cormorants, and an ostentation of peacocks. There's an unkindness of ravens and a murder of crows. Keeping injured and orphaned birds in my home, I mainly use just one collective term—a mess of birds.

5 Most people can distinguish a Snow Goose from a Canada Goose, but not many know the difference between a gaggle of geese and a skein of geese. It's logical— migrating geese form lines or Vs that reminded someone long ago of a skein of yarn. But when a flock of geese is on the ground, they mill around gregariously, forming a gaggle. Geese on golf courses join gaggles, but golfers often wish they'd form a skein and get the heck out of there.

Many collective nouns for birds are well known—a covey of partridge, a covey or a bevy of quail, a brood of chicks, a colony of gulls, and that most basic collective noun of all, a flock of birds. Some collective terms are more obscure—a congregation of plovers, a descent of woodpeckers, a watch of nightingales, and a fling of sandpipers. Sparrows form a host, pigeons a kit or loft, flamingos a stand, teal a spring, and peacocks a muster. Pheasants can form a bouquet, brace, covey, or nide. Mallards form sords or sutes. Gunners call groups of swans banks, games, or marks. The prettiest of all are an exaltation of larks, a murmuration of starlings, and a charm of finches.

Notes

6 As my first year of birding drew to a close and my life list approached 120, I led my husband through the Morton Arboretum. Suddenly, right next to our path on a thick oak branch, I spotted a Barred Owl watching us. I gazed at this heart-stopping lifer, then gave my binoculars to Russ. We walked within twenty feet of it, then fifteen, marveling at its tameness until it occurred to us that it hadn't moved a muscle or blinked since we spotted it. We walked to the oak and circled it twice before we realized that this was no owl—it was a misshapen branch with two knot holes where the eyes weren't.

At least we were looking at living tissue. Years later, in the Badlands of South Dakota, I scanned a prairie dog town for a Burrowing Owl, and finally found one atop a dirt mound. I walked toward it, getting more and more excited because it allowed me to come so close, when a sense of déjà vu came over me. I walked up and kicked it before I realized the truth. My Burrowing Owl was nothing more than a pile of dry buffalo dung.

On Christmas Bird Counts, we tally seven "Northern Shovelers" making their familiar scraping sounds in driveway habitats. There's the usual array of wooden, plastic, and metal birds— mostly cardinals, but also one flamingo, two loons, a strange hybrid between a crane and a heron, and one odd duck sticking out of the side of a chimney. In the Northland in winter, we'll take whatever birds we can find.

Notes

December

If we see a Red-bellied Woodpecker at exactly the right angle, we can sometimes discern a wash of pink on the underside. When I started birding, I never counted a bird until I had clearly seen every conceivable field mark. Fortunately, my first redbelly seemed to appreciate my high standards—she swung around a thin horizontal branch most courteously, showing off red tummy feathers to perfection, and sparking my lasting love for this species.

7 The first winter we lived in Duluth, a Red-bellied Woodpecker turned up at my feeder for two minutes—just long enough to stir up a powerful homesickness—and then it disappeared, never to return. This mast eater, characteristic of oak-hickory forests, usually ranges south of boreal forests, but does occasionally visit. One female stayed near my in-laws' feeding station in Port Wing for an entire winter, eating sunflower seed, suet, apples, and corn, and chasing Blue Jays away.

The redbelly eats three times more vegetal than insect matter, especially acorns, and often stores food in holes it has excavated. Its extraordinarily long, fleshy tongue, which Alexander Skutch called "a sort of lingual proboscis," can push food items deeper than chickadees, titmice, or even Blue Jays can reach. It spends a lot of time minding the store, apparently remembering where each morsel is hidden. A Red-bellied Woodpecker has between thirty-six and thirty-seven hundred feathers to insulate it. As long as it has a snug cavity to sleep in and enough fuel to stoke its metabolic furnace, it does just fine through the worst of a Northland winter.

Notes

8 My eyes are starting to mutiny. I've never needed strong eyeglasses, and I don't usually wear glasses at home except to watch TV. I never could see distant objects without them, but now I have to put them on to watch a chickadee ten feet from the dining room window.

Forty-one-year-old eyes don't adjust between near and far vision as they once did. I used to be able to read with my glasses on, but now it's impossible unless I hold the book at arm's length—without glasses, I still read just fine. I need glasses to see a blackboard, but have to take them off to read my notes. In organic chemistry lab, I have to take off my safety goggles and glasses and then put the goggles back on to pour chemicals and read the tiny lines on a graduated cylinder, and then I have to take off the goggles to put my glasses back on to find my lab table again.

Most frustrating, now I have trouble recognizing birds through the window unless I put on my glasses—but I have to take them off to consult a field guide or write in my field notebook. This looks like a job for—bifocals.

It's a good idea to select eyeglass frames that fit as close to the eyes as possible, to maximize the field of view when using binoculars. When I bought a new pair of glasses, which were set much closer to my eyes than my old pair, I suddenly had a much bigger picture through my binoculars—it was like getting brand-new higher-power binoculars for free.

Notes

December

Eyeglass wearers should select binoculars with long eye relief—at least fifteen millimeters if possible. Eye relief is the distance from the eye at which the binoculars provide the biggest picture. When we're wearing glasses, our binocular eyecups should be completely retracted to hold the lenses as close to the eyes as possible.

9 A thinning ozone layer affects people in subtle ways. I used to get headaches when I spent long days afield, but since I got ultraviolet protection on my eyeglasses, those headaches are gone. Glass lenses are more resistant to scratching than plastic—since birders are always pressing binoculars and spotting scopes against their eyeglasses, scratching can be a serious concern. Fortunately, plastic lenses can now be guaranteed against scratching, so we can finally can have UV and scratch protection in the same pair of glasses.

When you're spending long days outdoors, sunblock is a good idea. A wide-brim hat protects head and face from the sun while allowing sounds to reach our ears unimpeded. Long sleeves and slacks are important. To prevent our hands from getting sunburned, or to prevent an awkward tan on hands when wearing long sleeves, we wear lightweight, thin gloves in the field. Those with leather finger reinforcements are especially useful with binoculars. Gloves may seem old-fashioned, but they not only protect against sun, they keep mosquitoes away to boot.

Notes

10 The cardinal is indisputably one of the most popular birds in the United States—the state bird of seven states and the mascot of professional baseball and football teams and countless high-school teams throughout the country. The unparalleled popularity of the cardinal comes from its vivid plumage, loud, cheerful song, conspicuous habits, and abundance in even the largest cities.

Northern Cardinals used to be strictly southern birds. They feed primarily on the ground and in dense shrubbery, and could only survive where snow melted to expose bare ground in winter. As railroads started keeping long stretches of appropriate habitat open and spilling grain along tracks, cardinals started expanding their range northward. In the late 1800s, sighting a cardinal was news in Chicago. They started breeding around Madison, Wisconsin, around 1920 and in the Twin Cities in the mid-1930s, and are slowly wending their way toward Lake Superior—every year more individuals are reported in Duluth, and a few have even nested. Soon Northlanders may see as many real cardinals in winter as we see on our Christmas cards.

The word *cardinalis*, Latin for "principal," comes from the Latin *cardo* for "a hinge or pivot." Cardinal principles, cardinal sins, and Roman Catholic cardinals are all named for their pivotal or crucial importance. The bird is named for its color, which matches the robes of Catholic cardinals.

Notes

December

The gall bladder is a sac that collects bile from the liver and delivers it as needed into the small intestine to aid in the breakdown of fat. Bile doesn't actually digest fat—it emulsifies it like detergent acting on grease. When the gall bladder is removed or, in the case of many birds, when the gall bladder isn't there in the first place, bile drips continuously into the intestine.

11 Like people, most birds have a gall bladder. Penguins have enormous gall bladders. A male Emperor Penguin pigs out on fatty fish during part of his annual cycle, and then fasts for months while incubating his egg and chick. Bile produced during the fast is stored in the gall bladder to be used when the penguin needs it again.

Hummingbirds don't digest much fat and do their best never to go hungry—they have no need for a gall bladder. Pigeons glut out every morning and night, and often fast between, but they're digesting pretty much continuously—their crop releases food into the stomach a little at a time—so they also have no gall bladder. Cedar Waxwings may have one, though the Bohemian Waxwing's is missing. Ostriches and parakeets do just fine without one, and, oddly, so do Peregrine Falcons.

In a few species of mergansers, cuckoos, and cranes, some individuals have a gall bladder while others don't. This is probably due to natural variation, but I prefer to attribute it to a tiny, knife-wielding avian surgeon—maybe Dr. Killdeer himself.

Notes

12 Walking home from school, our little friend Erin spots a Barred Owl on a neighbor's rooftop and runs to tell me. My Peabody Street list includes Great Horned, Long-eared, and Saw-whet Owls, but this is the first barred I've had here—they prefer deeper woods than our neighborhood provides. Erin and I stare, and it returns our gaze with calm, soft brown eyes. After I recover from the unexpected pleasure of seeing it so close, I hurry home to get a vantage point where I can add it to my yard list. A house blocks the view, and I have no luck from our upstairs windows. I finally find a spot in the backyard where I can barely make out feathers rippling in the wind. My listing needs satisfied, I bring Tommy and Katie over to see it up close.

Barred Owls are heard more often than seen. They look large, but most weigh well under two pounds—like their close relative the Great Gray Owl, they carry most of their bulk in feathers and spirit. A captive Barred Owl lived twenty-three years, and banded ones have been recovered eight years later. Their greatest enemies are human beings and feathered tigers—that is, Great Horned Owls.

Barred Owls must be stressed from hunger to visit a well-settled residential neighborhood, but the Peabody Street visitor apparently figured out the system—it was found on and off throughout the winter sitting on bird feeders—apparently watching for shrews and voles that gathered on the spilled seed below.

Notes

December

For ages people believed that swallows burrowed into mud at the bottoms of ponds for the winter, but by the eighteenth and nineteenth centuries, the idea of avian hibernation had become so completely discredited that few ornithologists paid attention to the first studies about dormancy in swifts and hummingbirds, published in 1917 and 1933. Today, we realize that birds are more amazing than we'll ever fully understand.

13 On December 29, 1946, while hiking through the Chuckwalla Mountains of southeastern California, Edmund Jaeger discovered a Common Poorwill asleep in a small crevice in a rock wall. Jaeger picked it up and noted that its feet and eyelids were cold to the touch, and its respiration and heart rate were undetectable, but it was still alive. He shouted but couldn't rouse it, so he returned it to the crevice and left. Later he came back to band it, and took its temperature with a rectal thermometer—about 65 degrees, compared to a normal 106 degrees in active poorwills. He checked on it periodically all season, never detecting a heartbeat or respiration, and the bird slowly and continuously lost weight, exactly as mammalian hibernators do. It remained asleep for eighty-eight days, and took about a week to get back to normal when spring came.

Jaeger found the same poorwill hibernating in the same crevice for the next several winters. Ornithologists made a big fuss over him, though he was hardly the first person to notice the phenomenon—the Hopi Indians knew about it all along. Their word for the poorwill was *holchko*, which means "the sleeping one."

Notes

14 A Barred Owl dropped down some friends' chimney into a room they keep closed off in winter. Days later when they opened the door, whitewash streaked the walls and furniture, talons had sliced up furniture, and expensive treasures were smashed. When they gave their insurance company the bills, they got the biggest shock of all—standard homeowner's policies don't cover wildlife damage.

There are plenty of cases of House Sparrows incorporating lighted cigarette butts into their nests, setting whole buildings afire—that's covered. What if a Ruffed Grouse crashes through a window? According to insurance agents, that's not covered. Now if a kid throws a rock through a window, it's covered, so I asked the logical question, "What if a kid throws a Ruffed Grouse through a window?" The agents weren't sure, so they referred me to insurance adjustors. These are a suspicious and humorless lot, and not one would even speculate about whether a kid throwing a Ruffed Grouse through a window is covered on a homeowner's policy. So next time you see a grouse headed for your window, ask it to play with matches instead.

In 1987, a Bald Eagle carrying a fish came upon Alaska Airlines Flight 61 from Juneau to Yakutat. The startled eagle dropped the fish, which slammed into the fuselage. Eagle and passengers were fine, but the fish didn't survive. If an eagle dropped a fish onto a house, it's unclear whether a homeowner's policy would cover the damage.

Notes

December

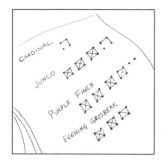

Christmas Bird Count data are compiled and published each year in *American Birds* magazine. That annual issue is a formidable volume—the 1991 copy is 1,058 pages long, citing 1,646 counts by 43,588 observers, recording millions of individuals of 628 species. Data from each year's count help keep track of population trends in various species, and although inaccuracies can always be expected in studies run by amateurs, overall the information is extremely valuable to researchers.

Notes

15 The Christmas Bird Count has been an annual tradition since Christmas Day 1900, when, to protest songbird hunting, Frank Chapman organized twenty-seven birdwatchers to count winter birds rather than shoot them. Now the event is sponsored by the National Audubon Society. More than 40,000 people, each paying five dollars for the privilege, take part in over 1,500 locations from Alaska to Central America and Hawaii. Every state and Canadian province is represented.

Groups set out at dawn, earlier if they're looking for owls, and hike, drive, or ski their area, searching for every wild bird they can find. If the weather's lousy, a distinct possibility in North Country, the experience loses a bit of its glamour—when the temperature drops below zero, binoculars frost up. A light snowfall melting to droplets on lenses causes many to concentrate less on birds than on imaginary designs for tiny windshield wipers. Blizzards are easier to deal with—binoculars stay snugly zipped under jackets all day since there aren't any birds to see. Worst-case scenario for a Christmas Bird Count is freezing rain. Birds and sensible birders hide out on those days.

16 Few birders who set out on a Christmas Bird Count are motivated by the research value of their work—they're concentrating on the hot competition. Birders thrill at finding more species than anyone else, and bird counts pit team against team, city against city, state against state in quests to see the most of all. In Minnesota, Duluth and Rochester usually vie for the annual championship as we shoot for, but rarely reach, sixty species. In Wisconsin, Madison and Milwaukee are arch rivals, aspiring to eighty species. Wisconsin always outdoes Minnesota because Wisconsin has more southeastern birds like Tufted Titmice and screech owls, and Madison and Milwaukee have more open water.

At the annual compilation dinner in Duluth, Kim Eckert tallies the numbers and species, holding everyone in suspense by saving the rarities until last. Each of us looks at the others and wonders if our Varied Thrush, Northern Hawk Owl, or wintering Merlin will be the bird of the day. Did anyone else see robins or cardinals? The outcome is as exciting as a basketball championship tournament, the statistics bandied about as earnestly as baseball stats by aficionados.

It isn't necessary to actually go outdoors to participate in a Christmas Bird Count—many people simply count feeder birds. Rarities that aren't found by official groups often turn up at feeders—these birds can be tallied, contributing to regional chauvinism, if the feeder owner reports them to the compiler. Those interested in joining a count group or reporting feeder birds should check their local newspaper for information about local counts.

Notes

December

A U.S. Air Force jet pilot developed a technique of shooting dead chickens from cannons to simulate high-speed collisions with waterfowl. His research proved that aircraft needed heavier windshields, and he developed new specifications. Ironically, he was copiloting a jet scheduled to be fitted with the newly designed windshield when it crashed into a Mallard hen, costing him an eye.

17 The Wright brothers took wing on December 17, 1903, providing the first opportunities in human history for midair collisions with birds. The first record of an airplane-bird collision was in 1910, in Long Beach, California. A gull got stuck between the plane's fin and rudder, and the pilot was killed. Now at least one out of every ten thousand aircraft flights intersects with the path of a bird. The result is always bad for the bird, whose carcass usually bounces off without harming the plane or its passengers, but if the bird is large enough, or if it collides with a critical part of the plane, the collision may result in human deaths as well.

Airports are often built on flat lowland areas where flocking birds are abundant—now some airports use falcons or other raptors to frighten birds away from runways. Bird-plane collisions usually happen at altitudes lower than 5,000 feet, but the highest on record took place at 37,000 feet over western Africa, when a Ruppell's Griffon, a kind of vulture, struck a commercial airliner. Perhaps Alfred the airsick eagle was right—it really is safer on the ground.

Notes

18 When I birded Texas in 1991, I left Dallas with a trip total of 199. Fortunately, we hit a storm halfway to Minneapolis—the plane went fifty miles off course to avoid the center. My seat, on the side facing the dramatic lightning bolts, was far enough back that I could watch the wing shudder in the turbulence. As we started our descent in Minneapolis, the pilot suddenly announced that we'd have to go up and circle again because a small aircraft on the runway was having trouble. The storm reached us, and we didn't have enough fuel left to keep circling, so we headed for Fargo. When the storm beat us there, we went on up to Grand Forks.

Waiting for another plane to return us to Minneapolis, I scanned out the window at the Grand Forks airport in hopes of a Snowy Owl. Suddenly a half-dozen business people were looking out, too—I felt like Dick Martin playing the old "Looking Up in the Air Gag." We didn't spot an owl, but I saw four Lapland Longspurs next to the runway, bringing my trip total to a nice even 200. Yes, a birding experience can be greatly enhanced thanks to the miracles of modern aviation.

Birds redeem many unpleasant situations. When Russ and I drove to Texas in 1978, as we were cruising somewhere around Laguna Atascosa, our gas gauge dipped below empty. Searching for a gas station in the barren Texas landscape, we became hopelessly lost. When I spotted two Crested Caracaras—lifers!—in a field, I felt a whole lot better. Inexplicably, it took a gas station to raise Russ's spirits—the only birds there were sparrows and grackles.

Notes

December

One November, I heard a baby crow calling. I ran outside to look—by fall young crows usually produce adult caws. All I found was a Blue Jay. Later I heard it again, and again there was the jay, as innocent as could be. I spied through the window to see it bowing and caw-cawing in perfect imitation of a baby crow. When it saw me peeking, it flew away, its practical joke a great success.

19 After our Christmas tree goes up, Sneakers is stuck in her cage until the new year. We try to pay attention to her, but it's not easy with kids home from school and rehab responsibilities and writing contracts. We have a game where Sneakers whistles and I answer, but one morning I was too busy. She whistled her hardest, knowing exactly where I was, and finally, in desperation, suddenly called out, clear as a bell, "Hi!" Her cage was in the front entry, and I thought somebody was at the door— when I came to check, she let out another "Hi!" ever so friendly and clear. I was so excited I brought her some of her favorite orange sherbet, and said "Hi!" over and over like a crazed parrot, but now that she had my attention, she didn't bother to repeat the trick.

There are several records of captive-reared Blue Jays learning to talk—they are, after all, close relatives of crows and ravens, with similar vocal apparatus. But Sneakers turns out to be rather taciturn. Three weeks later she said "Hi!" one last time, but that was the final speaking engagement for Sneakers, the amazing talking Blue Jay.

Notes

20 The winter solstice day lasts eight hours and thirty-two minutes on Peabody Street, and then it's dark for fifteen-and-a-half hours. Most birds sleep away this darkest evening of the year.

Little is known about avian sleeping habits except that active birds tend to sleep more soundly than sedentary ones. Circumstantial evidence indicates that swifts and Sooty Terns sleep on the wing, but many ornithologists doubt that it's possible. Warblers and chickadees I've cared for have slept very soundly, but not crows—every time I've approached a crow in the middle of the night, creeping in on soft carpet, the crow's eyes were watching me before I could see it. Blue Jays sleep more soundly, but rouse easily. Nighthawks seem not to sleep at all—day and night they sit around, calm and composed, eyes half-closed but opening wide if a hawk, or presumably an owl, flies by. Even the most active birds awaken at sounds of danger. Geese may have alerted the ancient Romans of a sneak attack in the fourth century B.C., and even today, thanks to their light sleeping habits, geese are used to guard a distillery in Scotland.

Northland chickadees sleep two-thirds of the time in winter, but come summer solstice, they'll be awake over sixteen hours every day. In the land of the midnight sun, birds may go days without sleep. The internal clock of most birds runs slightly fast. When they awaken and it's already light, their internal system is geared for increasing day length. If it's still dark when they wake up, they instinctively know days are getting shorter.

Notes

December

A sleeping bird's eyelids blink slowly. Ornithologists believe Barred Owls sleep when their eyelids are fully closed, but merely doze when the eyelids are partly open. Herring Gulls don't close their eyelids for more than sixty seconds at a time, but they seem to sleep more soundly when their bills are tucked under their shoulder feathers rather than facing forward. Birds also sleep more deeply when sitting than when standing.

21 A bird doesn't sleep in a bed, but does have a feather pillow—its back, wing, or breast—on which to rest its weary head. Songbirds sleep on branches—the flexor tendons of their feet shut tight when the leg is bent, locking the foot into the grip position for the night. Many shorebirds sleep on one foot. Ducks and geese sleep like this on land, or rock-a-bye in natural water beds. Many baby birds, and large flightless birds like the ostrich and rhea, sleep with head and neck extended vertically or along the nest or ground. Woodpeckers, chickadees, bluebirds, nuthatches, and some other birds sleep in cavities or birdhouses. A few birds sleep in old nests, but most land birds sleep in trees or dense weeds. The few roosting birds I've found outdoors were perched tightly against the trunks of trees, where they seemed unlikely to present a noticeable silhouette for owls and other night hunters.

On warm summer nights, birds sleep with smoothed feathers, but in winter they fluff out their down for warmth. A sleeping chickadee, head turned onto its back and down feathers erect, looks like a fuzzy golf ball with a spike tail.

Notes

22 This time of year, we long for loons. January 3 is the latest a Common Loon has ever been recorded in Wisconsin, and December 30 in Minnesota, but virtually all have vanished from North Country by November's end.

Exotic plumage and incomparable voice are the two features that people equate with the loon, and these are exactly the features a loon loses in winter. During its stay on the ocean, the loon is drab and quiet—casual beachgoers seldom notice it. Even its ruby eye becomes a duller shade—the color's importance in underwater vision is apparently exaggerated.

To survive in saltwater, loons have a gland above each eye that secretes excess salt, keeping blood salinity at about a third the level of ocean water. Baby loons that hatched this summer will remain on the ocean for three or four years, until they reach maturity. When we hear of loon carcasses washed ashore along the Florida coast in winter, we think of the chicks we've watched atop their mothers' backs, the babies we've watched learn to fish. These are our loons, and we mourn them.

Some loons do remain in North Country in winter—as Christmas presents. You can give—or receive—loon books and recordings, lamps, refrigerator magnets, napkins, napkin holders, jewelry, stationery, calendars, address books, aprons, sweatshirts, neckties, wind socks, bumper stickers, door knockers, mailboxes, beer mugs, and whiskey glasses. One company manufactures a loon bathroom sink and toilet, though these probably don't appear under many Christmas trees.

Notes

December

There once was a birder named Laura / Who sighted on fauna, not flora. / She searched hill and dale / For an elusive Black Rail, / But all she could find was a Sora.

Our old friend, the birder named Laura, / Went looking for Marsh Wrens and Sora. / What she thought was firm land / Was really quicksand, / Leaving no trace but her red fedora.

23 One way to survive a slow Northland Christmas Bird Count is to make up avian "hink pinks"—riddles with rhyming answers. What do you call a hungry bird? A hollow swallow. A thin bird? A narrow sparrow. A bird lawyer is a legal eagle. An avian airplane is an eider glider. A tennis-playing bird is a lobbin' robin, but when it loses it becomes a sobbin' robin. An eccentric bird is a quirky turkey. One without a tan is a pale quail. Who arrests illegal gamblers? The bunco junco.

Some hink pinks are geographical. A northern bird is a boreal oriole. Aegean finches are Dardanelles cardinals. Some are technical—a bird about to lay an egg is an oestral kestrel. There are sports hink pinks—a baseball-playing bird is a punting bunting. After four balls it takes a hawk walk. If it misses a pitch it gets a shrike strike. The best base stealer is the quicker flicker. Who would never dare steal a base? A slow crow. Who coaches? The tanager manager.

Which bird has the happier holiday? The merrier harrier. And here's hoping that you have a veery pheasant owl-iday, too.

Notes

24 A car gets stuck in the thick new snow covering Peabody Street. Russ heads out with a shovel, three other neighbors appear, and within minutes this stranger in our midst is on his way again. We know nothing about him—political party, nationality, sexual preference, whether he's a hunter or an animal rights activist, even his name. When you're caught in a snowstorm, none of that matters. Like Scout says in *To Kill a Mockingbird*, when it comes right down to it, there's just one kind of folks—folks.

Little acts of kindness—between family, friends, neighbors, strangers—strengthen the bonds of society and give meaning to human life. Generosity of spirit toward one another blossoms into generosity toward other living things, and into concern for the health and future of this small planet that we all share as neighbors. On this hushed and snowy silent night, as our family gathers at the window to watch the falling crystals, I think of the friends and neighbors I hold dear, of the wild birds that have touched and enriched my life, of the world of birds and friends I haven't yet met, and I think, "God bless us, every one."

Reading Christmas messages of friends and family, I'm inspired to start a list of Christmas card birds. There are penguins, puffins, cardinals, chickadees, jays, loons, titmice, nuthatches, kinglets, several ducks, and a tree sparrow. Plenty of jays on the ornaments, too, and also chickadees, two cardinals, loons, nuthatches, several improbably ornate doves, and a smattering of other unidentifiable species. A true lister can be happily engaged even indoors at midnight.

Notes

December

Birds can make wonderful gifts under the right circumstances. Parrots make fine pets, though it's illegal and seems immoral to buy birds kidnapped from the wild. Some large parrots and macaws are bred in captivity, but it's a long process, and they're expensive. Hand-raised cockatiels and parakeets make affectionate pets that learn to talk if given plenty of attention and love. Canaries and finches are happiest with some avian company.

Notes

25 After twelve days of gift giving by a certain true love, one would have a total of forty-two swans a-swimming, forty-two geese a-laying, thirty-six calling birds, thirty French hens, twenty-two turtle doves, twelve partridges in pear trees, and one heck of a messy house. The swans of this old English carol are most likely Mute Swans, which hold their necks in a graceful curve. Mute Swans were probably exterminated from Western Europe long ago, but were reintroduced from central Asia by the seventeenth century, and brought to America around 1900. Hans Christian Andersen's ugly duckling became a Mute Swan.

Geese a-laying were plain old farm geese, domesticated from Greylag Geese before the time of Homer. Calling birds were actually "colly birds," most likely European blackbirds related to our robin and kept as cage birds for their song, or baked in nursery rhyme pies. French hens are a dainty variety of Guinea fowl, and turtle doves smaller and paler than our Mourning Dove. The partridge? No Ruffed Grouse, but a smaller species—the Gray Partridge now introduced in America, or another quail-like bird. We're dealing with a true love who really knew how to give somebody the bird.

26 When a fierce blizzard struck Minnesota on December 26, 1988, a lost little Brambling found its way to East Grand Forks, Minnesota, and some friends and I drove across the state to see it. Bramblings are the most abundant birds on the highlands of Norway and Sweden—the Oles and Lenas of the bird world. Oddly, they occasionally turn up here and there in North America. The first one found in the lower forty-eight states was shot at a feeding station in Stanton, New Jersey, in December 1958—that bird now lies in state in the Princeton Museum, tail feathers missing. In 1984, Minnesota's first Brambling visited an Owatonna feeder. That same winter, Bramblings were also recorded in California, Utah, Colorado, Ontario, Nova Scotia, Manitoba, and British Columbia.

The Brambling that turned up at Angie Schneider's feeder was cooperative as hordes of birders from around the country descended upon East Grand Forks to add it to their life lists. While my friends and I were there, "Brambling Rose" flitted in a couple of times, but was apparently more at ease when only Angie was around—it must have heard about the Princeton Museum.

The Brambling takes its name from the brambles in its native home in northern Eurasia, though it's actually more commonly found in birch stands and mixed evergreen forests. The first Brambling ever recorded in North America was a male shot at a watch house on the Pribilofs on October 25, 1914. It's been found regularly in Alaska since then.

Notes

December

Deforestation is not simply a tropical issue. We're destroying the Pacific rainforest here in the U.S., and foresters manage the North Woods in the U.S. and Canada for shorter and shorter rotations to accommodate ever-expanding paper and wood fiber industries. Birches are dying everywhere—perhaps acid rain makes them more vulnerable to disease. The inexorable decline of mature northern forest habitat has surely contributed to the dwindling numbers of finches and other winter birds.

27 Christmas riches—toys and other presents under the tree, my jolly family, neighborhood children filling the house—all this wealth infuses me with a sense of well-being, until I look out at my empty feeders. When we moved to Peabody Street in 1981, our feeders overflowed with birds—this time of year we had scores of grosbeaks, hundreds of siskins or redpolls, several chickadee flocks. Twelve years later, squirrels outnumber birds, we've only two chickadee flocks, and the last two winters we've had no finches at all. Three robin pairs always vied for space in our summer bird bath, now only one. And Tree Swallows have vanished.

The oldest houses on Peabody Street, like ours, were built in the 1910s, the newest in the 1950s. Well-settled neighborhoods provide marginal habitat for birds, but when avian populations were healthy, good habitat teemed with birds and marginal habitat held the surplus. Finches still crowd some country feeders, encouraging complacency among those who would believe that no matter what we inflict on our environment, everything will be hunky dory. But "extra" birds are gone now, and Peabody Street will never be the same.

Notes

28 So many things destroy songbirds that we will never identify a single primary cause for their decline, or a single solution. Habitat destruction on breeding, wintering, and migratory grounds can be obvious or subtle. The destruction of the rainforest is tragically obvious, but fragmentation of northern breeding habitats may be equally disastrous—with so much edge, we've skewed the balance between predator and prey, and crow and domestic cat numbers are especially inflated to dangerous levels. Cowbirds parasitize nests where deep forests once kept them out, where Neotropical migrants haven't had time to evolve strategies for withstanding their parasitism. Scores of species decline as cowbird numbers reach ever-higher peaks.

Pesticides destroy land birds and their food. Water contaminants, from pesticides to PCBs and heavy metals, take a toll on water birds, and on land birds that eat emergent insects. Lighted TV and radio antenna towers and skyscrapers kill millions of migrants. Then there are picture windows, highways—the list goes on and on. Avian survival against nature is hard enough—will survival on our altered planet prove impossible?

When five-year-old Katie saw Passenger Pigeons at the Bell Museum of Natural History, tears of outrage and loss filled her eyes as she learned she could never see one alive. We've lost the Dusky Seaside Sparrow since her 1983 birth, and she'll never see Ivory-billed Woodpeckers or Bachman's Warblers. We'll have to hurry to see condors before they're gone, too. To squander our own gifts is foolish—to squander our children's legacy unconscionable.

Notes

December

The hatred crows feel for the Great Horned Owl is fueled by instinctive memories of the deaths of crows of thousands of generations. The owl keeps silent watch by day, and under cover of darkness, its soft feathers muffling its approach, it flies in and kills crows as they sit helplessly. Owls raiding some roosts have been recorded eating nothing but crows' brains. Mobbing crow screams rise into a literal roar of rage.

29 The soft hush of winter envelops us as the barometer falls. Thick snow muffles our footsteps, and airborne flakes swallow every other sound. The sky is muted—soft and gray, snowfall obscuring the horizon, blending earth and clouds together. Birds, fluffed against the cold, take on a softer aspect—their plumped-up bodies seem to muffle even their own calls. The soft warbles of Pine Grosbeaks grow even softer, and siskin and redpoll chatter is muted like children's talking through thick wool scarves.

On such a day, a Great Horned Owl flies in from the Far North. It's of the Arctic race, its plumage the soft grayish brown of aspen bark. It rests in the sheltering boughs of a spruce, its unforgiving eyes staring not at me, right beneath it, but at the crows all about. I count twenty-five of them flying at it in dead earnest. As a raven symbolizes death to a superstitious person, so an owl symbolizes death to a crow, on more substantial evidence. On this snow-silenced morning, the crows are ghostly shadows enveloped in falling snow, their screams muted to ineffective shouts.

Notes

30 In the falling snow, I stand beneath an owl and a pack of crows. Three perch just above it, one jabbing from behind—the owl's head spins around to glare, its steady gaze seeming to memorize the crow's features. Two crows goad each other on to dart at it. Their speed and agility keep them safe even as bravado carries them millimeters from the owl's face. When five crows attack at once, the owl's head spins from side to side, trying to keep them all in view at once. It looks at me, seemingly asking my sympathy for all it endures.

Great Horned Owls are perfect birds—their feather markings perfect camouflage, their silent flight perfect for sneaking up on prey, their talons perfect for fulfilling a murderous function. Crows, too, are perfect, their black feathers absorbing sun rays to warm them in even the coldest northern winter, long, powerful beaks precisely right for probing into ears of corn or the nests of other birds, intelligence and curiosity making them the world's finest opportunists. This hushed snowy morning, with perfect crows, a perfect owl, and I all watching one another in the winter stillness, may be the start of a perfect day.

Crows seldom, if ever, cause serious damage to Great Horned Owls, though I once saw a crow draw blood, stabbing the back of an owl's head. When they first discover an owl, crows keep their distance, but as more and more gather, attracted by the others' assembly calls, the flock becomes bolder. Each crow stays at eye level or above the owl, never down where the owl could suddenly drop and snatch it.

Notes

December

When Russ and I put our family photographs in order, we couldn't recall dates—like one excursion to the Morton Arboretum. Joey was missing a front tooth so it must have been—no, Katie's hair had grown out from her experiment with bunny scissors so it couldn't have been before . . . I remembered three Hooded Mergansers in the pond, checked my bird lists, and had the exact date. No one should go through life listlessly.

31

As the year draws to a close, many people look through photographs of their past. I pull out bird lists and field notebooks. I seldom record more than date, place, weather, and species, but even that conjures vivid memories—four Buff-breasted Sandpipers running in the grassy park where I walked in solitude after my father's funeral, an adult Bald Eagle flying over the hospital as I held my newborn Tommy to the window, the time Russ photographed nodding trillium as I waited impatiently, antsy to see birds, not flowers. Even as I sighed audibly to hurry him along, my lifer Pileated Woodpecker flew in so close that I felt the rush of air as he landed. I remember a Herring Gull cruising over Hawk Ridge while Katie, one and a half, sat in her stroller. She couldn't pronounce the "s" sound yet, so she pointed up and said "eagull!" A dozen birders automatically pulled their binoculars up—and then gave her disparaging looks for misleading them.

Leafing through my notebooks, I remember other times, other birds. Lists unlock memories of auld acquaintance both avian and human—a lasting record of years of jolly times and friendships and birds and love.

Notes

Index